The United States in the Indo-Pacific

Manchester University Press

The United States in the Indo-Pacific

Obama's legacy and the Trump transition

Edited by

Oliver Turner and Inderjeet Parmar

Manchester University Press

Published by Manchester University Press
Altrincham Street, Manchester M1 7JA
www.manchesteruniversitypress.co.uk

British Library Cataloguing-in-Publication Data
A catalogue record for this book is available from the British Library

ISBN   978 1 5261 3501 8   hardback
ISBN   978 1 5261 3503 2   paperback
ISBN   978 1 5261 3502 5   open access

First published 2020

The publisher has no responsibility for the persistence or accuracy of URLs for any external or third-party internet websites referred to in this book, and does not guarantee that any content on such websites is, or will remain, accurate or appropriate.

Typeset by Newgen Publishing UK

Contents

Figures

Contributors

Atul Bhardwaj is a former Indian naval officer and an Honorary Research Fellow at City, University of London. He is also an Adjunct Fellow at the Institute of Chinese Studies, Delhi. He holds a PhD in History from Ambedkar University, Delhi. He is the author of *India-America Relations (1942–62): Rooted in the Liberal International Order* (Routledge, 2019).

Nick Bisley is the Head of Humanities and Social Sciences and Professor of International Relations at La Trobe University, Australia.

Christopher K. Colley is an Assistant Professor at the National Defense College of the United Arab Emirates. His research focuses on the international relations and security of the Indo-Pacific with a particular focus on China and India. He holds a PhD in Political Science from Indiana University Bloomington and an MA in Chinese studies from Renmin University of China in Beijing.

Malcolm Cook is a Senior Fellow at the ISEAS-Yusof Ishak Institute in Singapore. Malcolm has worked in Japan, South Korea, the Philippines, Australia and Singapore with a focus on regional security in East Asia.

Bruce Cumings is Gustavus F. and Ann M. Swift Distinguished Service Professor in History, at the University of Chicago. He is the author of numerable books and articles, including *The Origins of the Korean War*, volumes one and two (Princeton University Press, 1981 and 1990) and *Dominion from Sea to Sea: Pacific Ascendancy and American Power* (Yale University Press, 2009).

Matteo Dian is an Assistant Professor at the University of Bologna, Italy. His work on US foreign policy in East Asia and Japanese and Chinese foreign policies appears in *Pacific Review*, *International Relations* and *International Politics*, among others. His most recent monograph is *New Regional Initiatives in Chinese Foreign Policy: The Incoming Pluralism of Global Governance* (Palgrave Macmillan, 2018, with Silvia Menegazzi).

Sumit Ganguly is a Distinguished Professor of Political Science and holds the Tagore Chair in Indian Cultures and Civilizations at Indiana University, Bloomington. Professor Ganguly is also a Senior Fellow at the Foreign Policy Research Institute in Philadelphia, a Fellow of the American Academy of Arts and Sciences, and a member of the Council on Foreign Relations.

Peter Gries is the Lee Kai Hung Chair and founding Director of the Manchester China Institute, and Professor of Chinese politics at the University of Manchester. He is author of *The Politics of American Foreign Policy: How Ideology Divides Liberals and Conservatives over Foreign Affairs* (Stanford University Press, 2014) and *China's New Nationalism: Pride, Politics, and Diplomacy* (University of California Press, 2004). He is also co-editor of *State and Society in 21st Century China* (Routledge, 2004) and *Chinese Politics: State, Society and the Market* (Routledge, 2010).

Christian Hansmeyer is one of the founding members of Greater Pacific Capital and a senior investment manager based in Shanghai. Previously, he worked in the investment banking division of Goldman Sachs.

Maryanne Kelton is Senior Lecturer in International Relations at the Jeff Bleich Centre for the US Alliance in Digital Technology, Security, and Governance at Flinders University of South Australia.

Börje Ljunggren is former Swedish Ambassador to China and Vietnam, and former Head of the Asia Department of the Swedish Ministry for Foreign Affairs and the Swedish International Development Agency. He is an Associate of the Asia Center at Harvard University and the Swedish Institute of International Affairs, and author of *Den Kinesiska Drömmen – Xi, Makten Och Utmaningarna (The Chinese Dream – Xi, Power and Challenges*, Hjalmarson & Högberg, 2017).

Michael Mastanduno is Nelson Rockefeller Professor of Government at Dartmouth College. His recent work on international relations theory and US foreign policy has appeared in *Security Studies* and *British Journal of Politics and International Relations*.

Prashanth Parameswaran is a Fellow at the Wilson Center's Asia Program and senior editor at *The Diplomat* magazine based in Washington, DC. His work on Southeast Asia, Asian security issues, and US foreign policy in the Asia Pacific has appeared in a range of publications in the United States and in Asia.

Inderjeet Parmar is Professor of International Politics and Head of the Department of International Politics at City, University of London. He is a Fellow of the Academy of Social Sciences (FAcSS) and a former president of the British International Studies Association. His latest book is *Foundations of the American Century: Ford, Carnegie, and Rockefeller Foundations in the Rise of American Power* (Columbia University Press, 2012).

Ketan Patel is the founder and Chief Executive Officer of Greater Pacific Capital and was previously a Managing Director at Goldman Sachs. His career spans industry, consulting and investment banking. He is the author of *The Master Strategist* (Arrow Books, 2011).

Zac Rogers is Research Lead at the Jeff Bleich Centre for the US Alliance in Digital Technology, Security, and Governance at Flinders University of South Australia. His research combines a traditional grounding in national security, intelligence, and defence with emerging fields of social cyber security, digital anthropology and democratic resilience.

Robert Sutter is Professor of Practice of International Affairs at the Elliott School of George Washington University. He has published 22 books, over 300 articles and several hundred government reports dealing with contemporary East Asia and relations with the United States.

Oliver Turner is a Lecturer of International Relations at the University of Edinburgh, UK. His work on US and wider Western power and policies in Asia appears in his monograph, *American Images of China: Identity, Power, Policy* (Routledge, 2014), and peer-reviewed journals including *European Journal of International Relations, Review of International Studies, Third World Quarterly* and *Geopolitics*.

Abbreviations

ADF	Australian Defence Force
ADMM	ASEAN Defence Ministers Meeting
ADMM+	ASEAN Defence Ministers Meeting Plus
AIIB	Asian Infrastructure Investment Bank
APEC	Asia Pacific Economic Cooperation
ARF	ASEAN Regional Forum
ASD	Australian Signals Directorate
ASEAN	Association of South East Asian Nations
BRI	Belt and Road Initiative
CCP	Chinese Communist Party
CPTPP	Comprehensive and Progressive Agreement for Trans-Pacific Partnership
DMZ	Demilitarised Zone
DPJ	Democratic Party of Japan
DPRK	Democratic People's Republic of Korea
EAS	East Asia Summit
EDCA	Enhanced Defense Cooperation Agreement
FDI	Foreign Direct Investment
FNO	Freedom of Navigation Operation
ICBM	Intercontinental Ballistic Missile
IOR	Indian Ocean Region
IPR	Intellectual Property Rights
ISIL	Islamic State of Iraq and the Levant
JSDF	Japanese Self Defense Forces
LDP	Liberal Democratic Party of Japan
LMI	Lower Mekong Initiative
NAFTA	North American Free Trade Agreement
NATO	North Atlantic Treaty Organization
NDS	National Defense Strategy
NRO	National Reconnaissance Office
NSA	National Security Agency
NSS	National Security Strategy
OCR	Out-of-Cycle-Review
PACOM	Pacific Command
PLA	People's Liberation Army
PLAN	People's Liberation Army Navy

PRC	People's Republic of China
RAAF	Royal Australian Air Force
RCEP	Regional Comprehensive Economic Partnership
RIMPAC	Rim of the Pacific Exercise
ROC	Republic of China
RTRG	Real Time Regional Gateway
SIGINT	Signals Intelligence
SIPRI	Stockholm International Peace Research Institute
SLOC	Sea Lines of Communication
THAAD	Terminal High Altitude Area Defense
TPP	Trans-Pacific Partnership
TTIP	Transatlantic Trade and Investment Partnership
UN	United Nations
UNCLOS	UN Convention on the Law of the Sea
USMCA	US–Mexico–Canada Free Trade Agreement
WTO	World Trade Organization
YSEALI	Young Southeast Asian Leaders Initiative

Introduction: The United States in the Asia and Indo-Pacifics

Inderjeet Parmar

After eight years in office in January 2017, Barack Obama's time as president of the United States drew to a close. Obama made history as the first non-white president and the first to have been born outside the continental United States. Yet his leadership is being judged by far more than race and upbringing alone.[1] From an election promise of "Change" and the restoration of America's global standing after George W. Bush's disastrous wars on Iraq and terrorism, Obama embarked upon a host of political projects at home, and leaves a significant footprint abroad. Obama began by negotiating the new START nuclear weapons deal with Russia before restoring diplomatic relations with Cuba, and signing the Paris Climate Agreement as well as a UN Security Council-backed agreement with Iran to halt its nuclear programmes. Equally, the Obama administration failed to close the Guantanamo Bay detention and torture facility; oversaw a dramatic rise in civilian casualties from intensified military drone strikes (including targeted assassinations); backed a virtually unrestrained Saudi war on Yemen; and curtailed Bush-era rises in development aid to sub-Saharan Africa. This is just a hint of the variations and complexities in the set of global legacies Obama's presidency leaves behind.

Obama's international legacy of 2009–17 will be assessed and debated for years, and perhaps nowhere more so than in his engagements with the actors and institutions of the Indo-Pacific – a region which has only recently become more vivid within American political imaginations in the time since Obama left office, and which is now typically imagined to encompass the actors and maritime boundaries traditionally seen to make up the vast Asia Pacific region, from the western coasts of the United States and South America to the territories of East and Southeast Asia and Oceania, and then further west to include the Indian Ocean and its main constituent state actors such as India, Pakistan and Sri Lanka. It was the more narrowly defined Asia Pacific which quickly became a key foreign policy priority for Obama as he set about trying to escape the imperial quagmires of Iraq and Afghanistan to which so many US resources had been devoted during the post-9/11 era. Obama's "Pivot" (or "Rebalance") to Asia, formally announced in late 2011, was arguably his administration's key foreign policy programme across two terms in office.[2] The United States, to quote his Secretary of State Hillary Clinton, was entering a 'Pacific Century'. This is where the 'future of politics' would be decided, she argued, and the United States was to be 'right at the centre of the action'.[3]

What, then, are President Obama's chief achievements, failures and legacies in the Indo-Pacific? Was there a distinctive underlying philosophy and strategy for the region that guided Obama's thinking and policies, for example a "pragmatic realism", hegemonic ordering/liberal internationalism, or hawkish humanitarianism? And, in its first two years, between early 2017 and early 2019, what has President Donald Trump's "principled realism" meant in practice? How far has the Trump administration progressed in challenging or disrupting Obama's Pivot to Asia? What differences can we discern in the declared or effective US strategy towards Asia and to what extent has it radically shifted or displaced Obama-era legacies? Finally, what might be the longer-term consequences for American power and for Asia more generally of the strategies pursued by the Trump administration and its predecessors?[4] Though we appear to be at a key historical moment, this is hardly the first time American elites have faced uncertainty over grand strategy – either in general or in relation to specific regions.[5] Yet, the stakes now seem a lot higher, as the spectre of economic and military conflict hangs over the region.

In Asia, Kenneth Lieberthal argues, 'Obama moved boldly to shift the center of gravity among the key multilateral organizations in Asia, favoring those that include the United States and leading them to take approaches favored by Washington but are neuralgic for Beijing.'[6] Obama ordered bolder US military moves in the Yellow and South China seas, pressed Beijing to push North Korea to curb its nuclear programmes (to little avail), and advanced US leadership in numerous multilateral organisations, especially ASEAN and the East Asia Summit. Obama also promoted the Trans-Pacific Partnership (TPP) (which excluded China) as a strategy of "hegemonic ordering" in the tradition of post-1945 US-led liberal internationalist theory and practice.[7]

This was designed as a system of rules that claimed to bind both hegemon and junior partners in a mutually beneficial regime of transparency, protection of intellectual property rights, labour protections and market-promoting trade rules. Sometimes referred to as the WTO-plus system, the TPP was in practice the adaptation to the Asia Pacific of the hegemonic ordering strategy established in Western Europe during the early Cold War. Enhanced economic, diplomatic and security agreements with numerous Asian states and institutions were illustrative of Obama's efforts to promote a more networked and self-reliant international order, in a region where the United States had traditionally sustained a "hub-and-spokes" system of bilateral relations with Washington at the centre.[8] Its intent was also partly to force domestic reforms in China, to encourage a weakening of its state-capitalist model and the perceived basis of its economic challenge to US hegemony.[9]

Several of the authors in this book argue that Obama had begun to stiffen Washington's positions on North Korea and China, and that neither ASEAN nor the East Asia Summit lived up to their potential during his time in office. To this extent, change had already begun in ways which came to steer Trump's more aggressive posture after his inauguration in 2017. Obama's "strategic patience" to North Korea was accompanied by additional sanctions and enhanced US weapon sales to the region, much to China's chagrin.

In place of Obama came President Donald Trump in 2017, whose character, personal and business background, and broad approach to global affairs are in stark contrast to those of his predecessor and, indeed, to perhaps every other US president of the recent past.[10] Despite this, the broad importance of great powers in world politics was recognised by the George W. Bush administration, and the shift away from the Middle East towards Asia had to some extent already begun before 2009. This suggests that stark departures are highly unlikely in grand strategy, however heated may be the rhetoric of "Change" from the ineffectiveness, failures and weaknesses of previous administrations.[11] It is in the context of already heightened bipartisan worries about China's role in Asia and the world – from rule taker to rule maker – that the Obama administration's sense of urgency, and the Trump administration's radical and undiplomatic rhetoric, may at least in part be understood.

Yet, their understandings of how US power should work to mitigate upcoming threats (especially from "rising" China armed with a bigger military arsenal, including nuclear weapons, new China-centred international institutions such as the AIIB, and the world-spanning Belt and Road Initiative), require careful study, analysis and interpretation. For instance, after two years in office since 2017, President Trump appears to have had greater success than Obama in leveraging US market access power over China and other trading partners.[12] Hence, there remains broad support for an American policy of "congagement" with China – a mix of containment with engagement.[13] Trump's tariffs policy has raised the temperature of Sino-US relations and undermined Chinese elites' confidence that the United States will step back from the brink of an all-out trade war, while also generating criticism of Xi in China for being too robust in promoting Chinese leadership ambitions.[14] In this regard, Trump's "America First" principled realism, with its greater focus on 'bilateral transactionalism',[15] may represent an important shift, at least of emphasis, and possibly a return to the hub-and-spokes system in Asia. Only time will tell, but the consequences are likely to be globally significant in character. The overall goal remains a shared one regardless of the specific strategy: to maintain America's global power superiority by subordinating "rivals" like China and "foes" like the EU.

Aims of the volume

The primary aim of this book is to analyse Obama's two-term record in what is now increasingly referred to as the Indo-Pacific region, between 2009 and 2017, and the legacies he leaves behind. In addition, it is to examine the continuities of, and divergences from, that legacy evidenced under the leadership of Donald Trump in his first two years in office between 2017 and early 2019. The authors of this volume speak to these legacies in the context of both the Asia and Indo-Pacifics, to reflect the shifting rhetoric and policy priorities of the two administrations to 2019; inevitably, and because the term "Indo-Pacific" was routinely absent from the lexicon of most scholars and policy makers (both in the United States and the Asian region) during Obama's time in office, the authors individually explore the record of Obama in particular within the Asia Pacific region his administration identified as the most crucial to American interests.

A key focus of this volume, then, is the examination of transition. Within this transition of US foreign policy from Obama to Trump there lie continuities and changes, durabilities and disruptions. To interrogate and make sense of these complex dynamics, the volume draws together the expertise of leading academics in the field and practitioners of international affairs. It identifies and explores US engagements with the key actors and issues of the Indo-Pacific – its nation states, organisations and institutions, as well as the events and developments which have defined America and the region since 2009.

It is significant that no other volume to date exists which explores in detail Obama's presidential record and/or legacy across Asia and the Pacific. The relevant literature includes many fine volumes on Obama's policy approach towards Asia with a particular focus on the Rebalance/Pivot strategy, but not on the entire record.[16] Our volume, therefore, is unique, and offers readers something entirely new. In particular, this volume stands out in three main ways.

First, it offers readers a comprehensive analysis of Obama's policy approach to the region across his full eight-year term as US president, along with the legacies he leaves behind. It does so with attention to Washington's relations with key regional state actors such as China, India, North Korea and Japan, as well as its most significant international institutions such as ASEAN and the East Asia Summit.

Second, it revisits those relations as they evolved throughout approximately the opening two years of the presidency of Donald Trump, to examine the continuities and divergences which appeared, and the extent to which Obama's legacy seems set to endure or dissipate in the region.

Third, it reaches beyond academia to incorporate the views of relevant practitioners – former diplomats, a former naval officer, and leading scholars – who offer their professional views on US policy and presence in Asia and the

Pacific since Obama's inauguration in 2009, including the direction in which they see Washington's regional relationships heading in the future.

Structure of the volume

The book is organised into three main sections, the first assessing Obama's regional policies and legacies (eight chapters); the second considering Trump's initial forays into the Indo-Pacific across his first two years in the White House (three chapters); and the third providing selected practitioners' views of developments and challenges in the region (three chapters). Of course, reality is hardly so neat. This means that there are critical overlaps and points of connection between the issues and themes pursued in each section, helping make more comprehensible the identified continuities and change in strategy. In the round, then, the volume provides a detailed, systematic study of the United States under Presidents Obama and Trump in the decade between 2009 and early 2019 in its policies, approaches and effects in the Indo-Pacific. It is, we believe, the most informative, detailed empirical analysis in one volume of this globally strategic region's institutions' and states' relations with the world's sole superpower.

In Chapter 1, Turner emphasises that just as the Trump administration emerged from deep roots and developments of US domestic politics, culture and society, let alone America's global hegemony, so the country's relationship with Asia is steeped in its history and culture. This is especially true given the frequent and often violent intrusions of Western colonial empires – British, French, Dutch, Spanish, Portuguese, German and American – in Asia. Unequal treaties, extra-territorialism, treaty ports won through "opium wars", orientalist attitudes and assumptions underpinning Western worldviews, all play a role, more or less subtly, in framing relations between the West and the rest, including Asia. This is underlined by, for example, candidate Trump's appeals to 'socio-racial conservatives (white nativists)' in his references to 'Yellow Hordes' imagery about the Chinese threat (Gries, Chapter 2). It is further evidenced by Obama's Secretary of Defense Leon Panetta's complaint about 'inscrutable' North Koreans who do not care to provide the United States with the information it wants (Cumings, Chapter 5). Turner provides an analysis of this historical encounter and how it shaped narratives, outlooks and policies. Turner argues that 'the United States has consistently pursued a position of imperial hegemony throughout the Asia Pacific', considering itself a local actor but one whose reach creates local resistance requiring a powerful military presence. The significance of race in US foreign affairs in general, and towards Asia in particular, requires serious analysis, especially given the importance of such narratives among policy makers, both historically and today.[17]

The book then moves to study the United States' relations with numerous selected countries: China (Gries), India (Colley and Ganguly, Chapter 3), Japan (Dian, Chapter 4), North/South Korea (Cumings, Chapter 5), and Australia (Kelton and Rogers, Chapter 6); the regional institutions of ASEAN (Parameswaran, Chapter 7) and the East Asia Summit (Cook, Chapter 8); in its regional political/diplomatic, security, and economic strategies (Sutter, Chapter 9; Bisley, Chapter 10; and Mastanduno, Chapter 11); and the perspectives of practitioners with regional experience and expertise (Ljunggren, Chapter 12; Patel and Hansmeyer, Chapter 13; and Bhardwaj, Chapter 14). The aim here is to inject rich empirical detail into the discussion of Obama's Pivot to Asia in practical terms, its legacies, and the platform which that established for the Trump administration which followed.

The contributions individually and collectively paint a portrait of anxiety amid changing power balances and great power strategies that are difficult to read and predict, driven by increased attention to the region by increasingly assertive Chinese and American leaders. That anxiety is driven by the real-world meaning of potentially clashing "Firstisms" – of both America and China. The dilemma is palpable for the United States as well as for its principal allies. The big question is how to manage increased (and largely welcome) economic opportunities created by China's economy, and its several international institutions that are potential future rivals to those of the US-led liberal order, while at the same time handling its undoubted increased naval and military assertiveness. That dilemma became increasingly obvious during Obama's second term of 2009–13, leading to more robust attitudes towards China's military moves and trade rules violations via the offices of the WTO. But it was not China alone that generated anxiety among the region's powers and peoples. Asian states, including India (Colley and Ganguly, Chapter 3) also worried about the sovereignty effects of the Asia Pivot and the hegemonic ordering strategy built in to the TPP. Similar concerns clearly apply to the recently developed US Indo-Pacific naval strategy that Bhardwaj sees as a wrong-headed response to the land-based Eurasia strategy implicit in the Belt and Road Initiative. A land route that connects eastern China to Western Europe via the Middle East, if practicable, would be a significant threat to the sea power based American strategy (Bhardwaj, Chapter 14).

Trump's presidential election campaign and his subsequent administration are seen by our authors to have added unpredictability and even greater anxiety over the future, especially the potentially devastating levels of conflict that may ensue should Trump's aggressive style and trade tariff strategy be followed through with military confrontations (Mastanduno; Sutter; Ljunggren). Obama's policy of "strategic patience" over North Korea did not change with the Asia Pivot, although continued nuclear testing and development by that country led to greater Sino-US cooperation over sanctions (Cumings). From threats of 'fire and fury' to militarily devastate North Korea, Trump's volte-face leading to two historic summits with Kim Jong-un in June 2018 reduced tensions in East Asia, at least in the short term.

Yet, the February 2019 Trump–Kim summit collapsed, which probably indicates how insurmountable are the contradictory aims of the two states, contradictions no leader could resolve, however skilled a deal maker they claimed to be. The twilight of Obama's more measured, clear, multilateral and hegemonic leadership strategy is lamented either overtly or subtextually by several authors (Sutter; Patel and Hansmeyer; Gries). The resulting 'vacuum', it is broadly agreed, is being filled by greater Chinese self-confidence and US allies' moves to increase cooperation among themselves and explore a rapprochement with China (Dian; Ljunggren; Gries; Mastanduno; Patel and Hansmeyer).

Nevertheless, the picture remains opaque to some authors (Bisley; Bhardwaj). The latter claims that despite rhetoric, Trump has strengthened alliances and retained the One China policy; rhetorical change has not been followed up with radical action or ruptures with the past. Still, it is noted that even the shift of rhetoric and political and diplomatic style has changed the mood music. Seeing the region through bilateral lenses, leaving key ambassadorial posts unfilled, means policy inertia or neglect has recently strengthened China's positions (Bisley; Gries).

While the United States under Trump is generating anxiety, uncertainty and greater inter-allied cooperation, and though the process began before Trump emerged on the political scene, China is currently seen as the biggest winner in the region. China reaped the benefits of US-led globalisation, including via admission to the WTO in 2001 (Ljunggren), when the United States hoped for China's transformation into a (junior) global stakeholder (Mastanduno).

Most ominously, it is the responsibility of the Trump administration to manage the dilemma brought about by an undoubted success of the US-led liberal international order. As such, regional consequences will be profound if US–Chinese relations continue to become more confrontational in security, economics, or both. The Asia/Indo-Pacific, it would appear, is not big enough to accommodate two dominant powers (Mastanduno).

The stakes could hardly be higher or articulated more baldly: the future of the region's societies and peoples is, at least in part, being determined by a "great game" played between Washington and Beijing. Equally, we cannot underestimate the roles of Japan, India, Australia, ASEAN and others as they each seek to steer and influence the contours of arguably the early twenty-first century's most dynamic and rapidly evolving region.

Notes

1   I. Parmar, L. B. Miller and M. Ledwidge (eds.), *Obama and the World* (London: Routledge, 2014).
2   O. Turner, 'The US "pivot" to the Asia Pacific', in Parmar *et al.*, *Obama and the World*, pp. 210–30.

3   H. Clinton, 'America's Pacific Century', *Foreign Policy* (11 October 2011), http://foreignpolicy.com/2011/10/11/americas-pacific-century/, accessed 6 March 2019.

4   For an examination of the impacts on allies of Trump's rhetoric and policies, see 'Trump and the Allies' article series, *Foreign Affairs*, 96:5 (2017).

5   For an analysis of four major grand strategies discernible in US foreign policy from George Washington to George W. Bush (neo-isolationism, selective engagement, cooperative security, and primacy), see J. J. Hentz (ed.), *The Obligation of Empire: United States' Grand Strategy for a New Century* (Lexington, KY: University Press of Kansas, 2004).

6   K. J. Lieberthal, 'The American Pivot to Asia', The Brookings Institution (21 December 2011), www.brookings.edu/articles/the-american-pivot-to-asia/, accessed 13 March 2019.

7   D. Nexon and I. Neumann, 'Hegemonic-order theory: A field theoretic account', *European Journal of International Relations*, 24:3 (2018), pp. 662–86.

8   C. Hemmer and P. Katzenstein, 'Why is there no NATO in Asia? Collective identity, regionalism and the origins of multilateralism', *International Organization*, 56:3 (2002), pp. 575–607.

9   White House, 'Statement on Steps to Protect Domestic Technology and Intellectual Property from China's Discriminatory and Burdensome Trade Practices' (29 May 2018), www.whitehouse.gov/briefings-statements/statement-steps-protect-domestic-technology-intellectual-property-chinas-discriminatory-burdensome-trade-practices/, accessed 13 March 2019.

10 C. Laderman and B. Simms, *Donald Trump: The Making of a World View* (London: I. B. Tauris, 2017).

11 B. van Apeldoorn and N. DeGraaff, *American Grand Strategy and Corporate Elite Networks* (London: Routledge, 2016).

12 T. Mitchell, 'Trade Wars: China Fears an Emerging United Front', *Financial Times* (11 September 2018), www.ft.com/content/ee361e2e-b283-11e8-8d14-6f049d06439c, accessed 13 March 2019.

13 Z. Khalilzad, 'The Case for Congagement with China', *National Interest* (19 June 2017), http://nationalinterest.org/feature/the-case-congagement-china-21232, accessed 12 March 2019. Congagement refers to a policy of containment and engagement with China. Arguably, that is what most US administrations have been doing, with differences of emphasis depending on specific circumstances. Even with the shifted balance towards containment and active tariff increases and threats, the 'balance of financial terror' in Sino-US affairs is a major indicator of the interdependence between the two powers. See also A. Friedberg, 'A new economic strategy toward China?', *Washington Quarterly*, 40:4 (2017), pp. 97–114.

14 Kissinger Institute on China and the United States, 'A Decade of US-China Relations: From Engagement to Rivalry' (13 September 2018), www.wilsoncenter.org/event/decade-us-china-relations-engagement-to-rivalry, accessed 13 March 2019.

15   I. Parmar, 'Behind the Paeans to McCain, A Lament Over New Tactics of Hegemony', *The Wire* (5 September 2018), https://thewire.in/world/john-mccain-donald-trump-united-states, accessed 13 March 2019.

16   See for example: K. Campbell, *The Pivot: The Future of American Statecraft in Asia* (New York: Twelve, 2016); C. Wang, *Obama's Challenge to China: The Pivot to Asia* (London: Routledge, 2016); H. Meijer, *Origins and Evolution of the US Rebalance Toward Asia* (London: Palgrave Macmillan, 2015); CPPR – Centre for Strategic Studies, *The US Rebalance and the Asia Pacific Region* (Kochi, India: CPPR, 2015). On Asian security see for example S. M. Ali, *Asia Pacific Security Dynamics in the Obama Era: A New World Emerging* (London: Routledge: 2012). On China see for example J. A. Bader, *Obama and China's Rise: An Insider's Account* (Washington, DC: Brookings Institution Press, 2013).

17   I. Parmar, 'Racial and imperial thinking in international theory and politics: Truman, Attlee, and the Korean War', *British Journal of Politics and International Relations*, 18:2 (2016), pp. 351–69.

Part I

Obama's legacy in Asia and the Pacific

1

US imperial hegemony in the American Pacific

Oliver Turner

Introduction

The question of this volume, as important as it is, is not simply of what legacy Barack Obama leaves in the Indo-Pacific after eight years in office, or, indeed, of how Donald Trump has engaged with that legacy during his first two years in charge. It is of the historical legacies of American power in the twenty-first-century Indo-Pacific of which both Obama and Trump themselves are constituted, which frame and steer their ideas and actions, and which they challenge or reinforce. Individuals and their administrations matter, but so do underlying knowledges and truths about the world which endure, sometimes for centuries, to be inherited by new presidents and their advisors because they defy party politics and the whims and cycles of popular opinion. These are the legacies about which this chapter is concerned.

The argument is not that Obama, Trump or any other occupant of the White House is somehow irrelevant – that there exist timeless and all-powerful understandings about the United States and the Indo-Pacific which render any given president and their administration a helpless conduit of deterministic discourses or wisdoms. It is that in any discussion of presidential legacy, it is useful in the first instance to step back to assess the historical conditions which explain how they could come to be, and what the past tells us about their likely future direction.

This chapter begins by speaking to debates around whether US internationalism represents empire or hegemony, and their applicability to the United States' place in Asia and the Pacific. To make sense of that place and its varied manifestations across space and time, it is argued that the United States has consistently pursued a position of imperial hegemony throughout the Asia Pacific (rather than the wider Indo-Pacific, about which this volume *in toto* is concerned). The next section argues that, in this pursuit, the United States has sought to construct an American

Pacific framed by the perceived civilisational values and physical authority of the American self. The formations of this American Pacific are traced from the earliest periods of US expansionism, showing how it has always been seen as an extension of US territory and identity. The chapter then turns to the 2009–17 presidency of Barack Obama and how his policies and worldviews were informed by centuries of historical logics about the United States and its role in the Asia Pacific. It also assesses what the first two years of the Donald Trump presidency reveal about the deep-rooted legacies of the American Pacific in the post-Obama era, not least with regard the re-imagining of the region into a larger "Indo-Pacific". The chapter concludes by arguing that key legacies of the American Pacific for twenty-first-century US administrations are of largely unquestioned truths about the United States as a local actor throughout a region imagined to extend from the Western United States to the furthest reaches of Asia, and that an ever-expanding reach of influence and authority has meant an ever-expanding responsibility to sustain and defend itself there.

On American empire and hegemony

Debates over whether the United States constitutes an empire are long-running and recently oxygenised by the aggressive unilateralism of the George W. Bush administration of 2001–09; Michael Mann criticised the post-9/11 'American bid for Empire',[1] while Bush-era imperialism also had its proponents.[2] In 2000 Bush himself argued that 'America has never been an empire. In fact, we may be the only great power in history that had the chance, and refused.'[3] Jack Snyder agrees, arguing that the United States 'has no formal colonial empire and seeks none'.[4] On the contrary, following its creation in 1776 the United States quickly acquired a colonial empire and never lost it. The United States, indeed, is perhaps the most efficient and "successful" colonial power in history; efficient in the speed and vigour by which it occupied and seized the central North American continent, and successful in how that occupation was legitimised in the name of civilisation, never to face retreat from the lands it claimed.

Beyond the settler colonialism of North America, it is claimed that any international US empire today is qualitatively different to those of the past. The United States, it is argued, has built an informal empire with institutional, rather than state-centric, formations. John Ikenberry argues that the American-led global system is organised by consent-based networks of rules, institutions and partnerships, with the term hegemony more appropriate than 'misleading' assertions of empire or imperialism.[5] Andrew Hurrell concurs, but suggests that notions of an institutional American empire often neglect the centrality of force and coercion to US foreign policy, and its intrusions into others' domestic affairs.[6]

As suggested by Ikenberry who sees a deeply rooted 'neo-imperial logic' in US political culture,[7] hegemony and empire are not mutually exclusive. Charles Maier, indeed, laments the polarising nature of the word empire and resists its application to the United States which, he says, 'reveals many, but not all … of the traits that have distinguished empires' of the past.[8] For Maier, empire is not only the accumulation of foreign lands, but the processes by which 'the social elements that rule in the dominant state … create a network of allied elites in regions abroad who accept subordination … in return for the security of their position in their own administrative unit (the "colony" or, in spatial terms, the "periphery")'.[9] Robert Young similarly sees imperialism as 'the exercise of power either through direct conquest or (latterly) through political and economic influence'. Imperialism, in this view, is 'the deliberate product of a political machine that rules from the centre, and extends its control to the furthest reaches of the peripheries'.[10]

Following these debates, it is understood here that the historical and contemporary American presence throughout the Asia Pacific is not easily termed either empire or hegemony. Difficulties emerge primarily from radical variations in the spatio-temporal contours of that presence across the region; stark differences in the interactions with US power and influence experienced by China, the Philippines and Australia, to name just three – including at various points throughout their own histories – make single, uniform designations such as empire or hegemony analytically problematic. With its devastating defeat and occupation by the United States in 1945 and the subsequent rewriting of its constitution by American officials, for example, Japan has been more exposed to violently imperialistic dimensions of American military and political power than almost anywhere else. Yet Japan formally retained its sovereignty. With US support it also experienced rapid economic growth for much of the Cold War and entered a close security alliance with Washington in which it remains a willing participant today. Elsewhere, of course, US authority has been comparatively absent, more typically within continental than maritime Asia.

What more meaningfully binds the encounters of the multitudinous actors of Asia and the Pacific with the regional American presence is the United States' centuries-long project of what is termed here imperial hegemony. As will be shown, this project has always been designed to realise a hegemonic region-wide influence of American identity and its core values and practices. US imperial hegemony in the Asia Pacific has, particularly in the post-1945 era, utilised Ikenberry's consent and rules-based networks of institutions and partnerships. Yet the establishment and maintenance of those networks has always been enabled by the availability, and sometimes direct use of, superior material power. Arguments of informal US empire or hegemony can thus be overly myopic, with "willing" partners such as Japan and the Philippines the previously unwilling recipients of overt, imperialistic US political expansion and military power from at least the mid-to-late nineteenth century, as the long-term conditions for core American values were aggressively moulded.

To speak of US imperial hegemony, then, is to look to the institutionalised and even consensual formations of American power where they are found, while affording serious concern to their fundamental reliance upon varyingly intensive impositions of political and economic systems and administrative rule – and even physical conquest – alongside the critical role of the American military, in enabling the exertion of sometimes violent control from the centre to the peripheries. The aim is to make sense of the complex and uneven landscape of the American presence across Asia and the Pacific; the United States may not have achieved a ubiquitous dominance or hegemony of material and ideational power, but its efforts at imperial hegemony have, as explored below, been sustained and ubiquitous in scope. The argument, it should also be noted, is not that these efforts have been uniformly unwelcome and/or harmful. Like in Europe, post-war US involvement in Asia and the Pacific has, at least for some, constituted something akin to an 'empire by invitation'.[11]

The formations of an American Pacific

The region we know today as the Asia Pacific is not a natural entity. Beliefs that an Asia Pacific exists, indeed, are traced only to the 1970s and an emphasis on increasing interconnections between North America and East Asia and ongoing regional US security concerns.[12] As an imaginative geography, the Asia Pacific along with its constituent actors are socially and politically spatialised, or geographed.[13] Their physical realities are made up of powerful ideas, so that regional US activities have always been at least partly determined by understandings about the American self and its Enlightenment-inspired, democratic-capitalist values.

In its pursuit of imperial hegemony throughout the Asia Pacific, the United States has sought to establish and maintain an American Pacific. This is a geography of the imagination as much as the physical Earth, where civilisational ideas and values perceived to represent the core of the American self – democracy, freedom and liberty, and its capitalist economic system[14] – as well as material dominance, are seen to be required. As a space defined by the operations of US power and values, as we will see, the American Pacific has been conceived in Washington not just as a site of material competition, but more fundamentally an extension both of US territory and identity, to legitimise its defence against those who seek to threaten and/or rework it.

Early US presidents like Thomas Jefferson declared a need to avoid 'entangling alliances' abroad.[15] John Quincy Adams argued that Washington should refrain from searching the world for 'monsters to destroy'.[16] Yet the nascent United States set out to discipline and civilise Native Americans of the then-foreign lands of North America. With "monsters" in its near-neighbourhood and "empty" spaces to occupy, the United States had no cause for risky internationalism overseas. Instead, it engaged in an internationalist project to seize the continent. The appellation Expansion Era – used to describe the United States' rapid territorial and economic growth during the nineteenth century – subtly glorifies intensive and violent colonialism.

Frederick Jackson Turner observed that territorial US expansion towards Asia was a 'logical outcome' of this westward march to the Pacific.[17] What mattered was not just physical geography, but the mythical frontier which has always been an opportunity for the United States to inflate what Jefferson envisioned as an Empire for Liberty. With American self-identity forged not around an ethnic group or religion but powerful principles of freedom, liberty, modernity, and so on, the United States is 'peculiarly dependent upon representational practices for its being'.[18] As such, a frontier to be conquered has always been necessary to the United States, for without it the nation would stagnate and risk losing its purpose, or Manifest Destiny, of advancing the global good.[19] 'American democracy', argued Turner, 'gained new strength each time it touched a new frontier'.[20] Ultimately, the American frontier has always been conceived as 'the outer edge of the wave – the meeting point between savagery and civilization'.[21]

The United States began laying the foundations of a hegemonic presence in Asia and the Pacific and expanding its frontiers there in parallel with its colonial North American empire, with the gains of each simultaneously fuelling and rationalising the other. In 1844 for example when the Union consisted of just twenty-six states, Americans took advantage of imperial China's weakness after its defeat in the first Opium War with the British. Washington drew up the ("unequal") Treaty of Wanghia, which a shell-shocked Beijing promptly signed. The treaty was designed to help the United States exploit opportunities through China's forced abandon-ment of practices Washington and others considered anachronistic and unciv-ilised, such as quotas on foreign trade and prohibitions on foreigners in most Chinese ports. But the treaty was about more than economic gain. With the inten-tion to Westernise China, it granted the United States privileges in diplomacy and law and gave Americans the previously forbidden right to learn the Chinese lan-guage. It worked to turn China into an overseas site not just of American profit but of the American self.[22]

Via the gunboat diplomacy of Matthew Perry's Black Ships, Washington signed the Treaty of Kanagawa with Edo (Tokyo) in 1854 which similarly required Japan to open its ports to American trade and refuelling vessels, and accept a resident US consul. Japan became another site of American political, economic and military power as its Pacific frontier further expanded; like China, Japan was geographed as backward and uncivilised to be forcibly aligned with Western norms of diplo-macy and commerce, becoming a strategic layover for an increasingly ambitious

American navy. Claims were made to, among others, Baker Island, Howland Island and Jarvis Island, and after its purchase in 1867 Alaska was transformed from a disconnected, largely ungoverned, majority Native American region, to a district, then a territory, and finally a state in 1959. By then its white population was three times larger than its Native population, and a new constitution remodelled its political structures in line with the bicameral legislatures of US states, with the creation of a Senate and House of Representatives.

The year 1898 was a landmark in the formation of the American Pacific when the United States claimed possession of Hawaii, Guam, and the Philippines from Spain. As in Alaska, Hawaii's legal and political institutions were restructured to conform to those of the United States, eventually transitioning to statehood in 1959. Military bases including Pearl Harbor were established on what was seen as a strategically valuable settlement. 'We need Hawaii just as much and a good deal more than we did California', asserted William McKinley in 1898. 'It is Manifest Destiny.'[23] The acquisition of Guam and its people meant that the island became another de facto US colony, under the jurisdiction of the Department of Defense and headed by a succession of US Navy-appointed governors. These governors had near absolute authority, with supreme legislative, executive and judicial oversight. Guamanians had no say in the choice of their governor or head of state, and with the island principally for use by the American armed forces, it was in effect an American-administered military dictatorship.

During the Pacific war with Japan in the 1940s, the island societies of Hawaii[24] and Guam[25] were stripped to their essential elements in the US imagination, with President Franklin Roosevelt grouping them with the uninhabited islands of Wake and Midway as strategic 'outposts' of military-security concern. The 1950 Guam Organic Act passed jurisdiction of the island and its people to the Department of the Interior. Guam's reclassification as an unincorporated organised territory enabled partial self-governance and democracy for Guamanians, but restricted their representation in American politics and codified their location at the political and societal periphery. Washington exerted colonial authority over the Philippines until 1946. From the beginning, the aim of the United States (in the words of former US Secretary of the Philippine Commission) was to transplant 'the ideas and improvements of one civilization upon another'.[26] Even after granting the Philippines independence, the United States continued to intervene in its affairs and the Military Bases Agreement of 1947, which gifted Washington rent-free control of Clark airbase and Subic Bay naval base, was signed by a Filipino elite with personal motivations.[27] Both served as key Cold War US military hubs.

The Cold War saw the foundations of the American Pacific considerably widened and reinforced, with permanent military presences established in Japan following the close of the Second World War, and on the Korean Peninsula from the outbreak of the Korean War. More than 550,000 US troops were stationed in East Asia in 1953, with numbers peaking in the late 1960s at nearly 800,000.[28]

President Dwight D. Eisenhower invoked the myth of the American frontier when he argued that the Korean War was being fought on the 'frontier of freedom',[29] and that South Vietnam, South Korea and Taiwan were 'frontier nations' in the struggle against communism.[30] President John F. Kennedy later spoke of reinforcing the 'frontiers of freedom' in Vietnam, to counter the non-democratic north.[31] East and Southeast Asia were spatialised in a way that brought faraway conflicts closer to home, to within the boundaries of an American Pacific whose "domestic" political cultures, economic and trade norms, military-security outposts, and even white populations had to be defended. Distant South Vietnam, South Korea and others were seen as vulnerable extensions of US territory and identity, at the outer edge of the wave between the civilised and non-civilised.

From the 1970s, US troop numbers in Asia decreased through to the end of the Cold War in 1989.[32] Yet to a significant extent the Cold War in East Asia, not least for Washington's security establishment, endured in a zombie-like form. The war on the Korean Peninsula went unresolved, while communism (or more accurately, authoritarianism), unlike in Europe, survived in Laos, North Korea, Vietnam and elsewhere. A rising China filled the communist threat void left in American imaginations by the collapsed Soviet Union, and the United States retained heavy military presences in Japan, South Korea and Guam, as well as its extensive hub and spokes system of regional security alliances and treaties.

Twenty-first-century legacies of the American Pacific

The Obama presidency, 2009–17

As an imaginative geography, the material realities of the Asia Pacific and its actors remain constitutive of particular ideas which give them meaning, and it is here that we find powerful legacies of the American Pacific throughout Obama's two-term approach to the region. In particular, the so-called Pivot or Rebalance to Asia formally announced in late 2011, was the flagship international policy of the Obama presidency. The Pivot was envisioned as a grand strategic shift of US attention and resources from the post-9/11 theatres of Iraq and Afghanistan to a region deemed of foremost long-term significance. Most typically, it has been interpreted by observers as a response to the physical "rise" of China.[33] However, the decision to Pivot to Asia was grounded not simply on understandings of a new material competitor and its physical impacts on regional dynamics.

During the Obama era (as before and since) large, rapidly rising India failed to generate significant security concerns in Washington. The Obama administration repeatedly emphasised India's democratic credentials and shared values, seeking closer and more cooperative ties. India was a rising power, but importantly too a particular rising identity which reaffirmed the liberal-democratic identity of the United States. Non-democratic rising China, meanwhile, was seen to contradict the American self. It was routinely described as fundamentally different, requiring guidance and discipline and presenting a challenge to regional order. While China's physical capabilities expanded more rapidly than India's, this alone fails to explain Obama-era contrasts in US policy and perception.[34]

As we have seen, China, alongside regional others, has throughout history been understood to lack such essential standards of civilisation as Western-style democracy, liberty and capitalism. The 1844 Treaty of Wanghia was designed to export these values to China and advance the frontiers of the American Pacific. In a 2015 statement on the main economic pillar of the Pivot, the Trans-Pacific Partnership (TPP), Obama argued that 'we can't let countries like China write the rules of the global economy. We should write those rules.'[35] Whatever the normative arguments around the merits or dangers of a Chinese-led global economy, 'countries like China' was code for those who still lack a full display of civilised values. The planned inclusion in the TPP of non-democratic Vietnam and Brunei demonstrates that China's physical contours were not irrelevant. However, the Pivot was no mere realpolitik response to the challenges and/or threats posed by the capabilities of a material competitor. Obama's Secretary of State John Kerry remarked that 'The United States and China ... have different political systems, different histories, different cultures, and ... different views on certain significant issues.'[36] By most measures this applies equally to the United States and India. Yet there the focus was on naturally closer ties, 'rooted in common values and interests.'[37] In sum, 'India's rise is not simply less dramatic and quantitatively different to China's; in American imaginations it is qualitatively so.'[38]

Modern political leaders, rarely, if ever, speak of Empires for Liberty or the savagery or barbarism of others. In 2014, however, Obama explicitly echoed Eisenhower, Kennedy and others when he identified the boundary between South and North Korea as 'freedom's frontier'. South Korea is 'a country like ours', he asserted, and '[t]he 38th Parallel now exists as much as a contrast between worlds as it does a border between nations.'[39] Countries 'like ours' were (and remain) embodied by the American Pacific, where a traditional US hegemony of ideas and the authority to enforce them had to endure. As Secretary of State Hillary Clinton explained, the Pivot was formulated to 'sustain our leadership, secure our interests, and advance our values.'[40] Guam could also be seamlessly reduced to Roosevelt's strategic 'outpost'; for Obama the island was a 'strategic hub', to which he decided he could transfer thousands of US troops from Japan without significant controversy.[41] As it has since the late nineteenth century, the US military remained in effective control of Guam, occupying almost 30 per cent of the island and keeping the society and its people reliant upon its economic presence.

As will be shown throughout the remainder of this volume, Obama distinguished himself in important ways from presidential predecessors in

Asia, leaving legacies of his own making. Equally, however, Obama came late to ingrained understandings of the region and the United States' place within it. His policies and worldviews were to some extent themselves the legacies of centuries of US imperial hegemony in a fantasised American Pacific he inherited and subscribed to. The Obama administration mantra, for instance, was of the United States as a Pacific power or nation. It was a term historically driven to situate the United States as an organic resident of the Pacific *in toto*, perpetuating the essentially unquestioned necessity of a Pacific-wide reach of US activity and influence. The term "Pacific power/nation" was 'an inherently performative call to action, turning foreign problems into domestic problems by helping to ensure that the United States acts in distant Asia as naturally as Vietnam, the Philippines, and, most importantly, China'.[42]

For the Obama administration, then, China was not rising in a distant Asia Pacific, but into a geographed American Pacific defined by American values, where long-standing US imperial hegemony was now increasingly questioned. It remained an extension of US territory and of the American self, justifying, as Obama explained, 'a larger and long-term role in shaping this region and its future'.[43] To this end, Obama pledged to increase the proportion of the US naval fleet in the Pacific to 60 per cent by 2020, and from 2012 a new contingent of US marines was stationed in Australia. Washington strengthened security ties with the Philippines, Singapore, Vietnam and others, and regional US arms sales increased. As an imaginative geography it could also still be reconstructed at will; Clinton argued that it stretched 'from the Indian subcontinent to the western shores of the Americas',[44] inflating its traditionally accepted boundaries.

When Obama came to office in early 2009 the United States had approximately 79,000 military personnel stationed throughout the Asia Pacific. By the end of his second term in 2016 there remained approximately 68,000,[45] a decline of around 15 per cent, but in line with post-Cold War trends. A fuller retreat from the imaginary frontier (the existence of which, as we have seen, Obama explicitly acknowledged), still conveniently reified in such places as the Korean border and US military bases in Japan and Guam, could conceivably have been achieved; at the time of Obama's election victory in 2008, nearly half of Americans believed the United States spent too much on its military, the highest proportion since the early 1990s.[46] Significant proportions of Americans (just as now) also believed that the United States should abandon its military bases in Japan.[47]

To withdraw, however, would have been to implicitly validate the other, less civilised world of which Obama spoke at a time when his administration was actively promoting a regional Pivot designed, at least in part, to contain its influence in the form of a rising anti-democratic China and ongoing threats from a nuclear-arming North Korea. Fundamentally, it would have challenged ingrained and traditionally unquestioned truths of the United States as a resident actor, even in the furthest reaches of the region. In Hawaii and Guam the United States boasted territorial sovereignty and in Japan, South Korea and elsewhere its political and economic systems had been exported, remaining vulnerable to threatening influences from the peripheries. Centuries of US political discourse to this effect had been deployed to legitimise wide-ranging internationalist projects in the Asia Pacific, often at great cost, and they could not be overturned by one administration, even had the will existed.

The early Trump presidency, 2017–19

Donald Trump is an aberration within the roll call of American presidents. He is the least formally qualified, having never previously occupied political office, and the only one to have seriously questioned Washington's post-war commitments to the so-called US-dominated world order. In the Asia Pacific, President-elect Trump's conversation in late 2016 with Taiwanese leader Tsai Ing-wen broke decades of carefully maintained protocol with China; his praise for controversial Philippine President Rodrigo Duterte was a characteristically Trumpian departure from diplomatic norms; and his rhetoric towards North Korea and willingness to engage directly with Kim Jong-un has been a radical shift from the strategic patience of his predecessors. While the means by which the Trump administration seeks to advance American interests might diverge significantly from those of Obama and his predecessors, however, we find in its regional strategies long-spoken truths and historical legacies of US imperial hegemony, and powerful underlying continuities of policy and worldview.

Trump's first US National Security Strategy (NSS), for example, pledged to 'rebuild our military, defend our borders, protect our sovereignty, and advance our values'.[48] It argues not simply that China (alongside Russia) is a material competitor, but a 'revisionist' nation looking 'to shape a world antithetical to US values and interests'. With China promoting authoritarianism and expanding its state-centric economic model, it explains, 'a geopolitical competition between free and repressive visions of world order is taking place in the Indo-Pacific region'. Just like the Asia Pacific during the Obama era, the Indo-Pacific – a term increasingly normalised under Trump, for example with the US Navy's Pacific Command renamed the US Indo-Pacific Command – is imagined to stretch 'from the west coast of India to the western shores of the United States'.[49]

Regular references not simply to an Indo-Pacific, but to a 'free and open Indo-Pacific', confirm its endurance as a fantasised extension of American territory and identity. A Trilateral Dialogue with India and Japan established in 2011 (alongside a Trilateral Strategic Dialogue with Japan and Australia) continued under Trump, intensifying in mid-2018 with a collaborative infrastructure plan.[50] Democratic India, whose economy is projected to overtake that of the United States before 2050, remains conceived as a strategic partner central to 'a rules-based order'.[51] The option of withdrawing from the frontier in Asia stays beyond mainstream debate, even for this most unorthodox of administrations, with Secretary of State Mike Pompeo explaining that 'the United States is committed to growing our presence in the region'.[52] The 2017 NSS echoes Eisenhower, Kennedy and Obama by pointing to the importance of America's frontier nations of Japan, South Korea and Taiwan in regard to North Korean aggression and in defence of the One China policy. The Trump administration, indeed, is firmly committed to the United States' 'forward military presence' in the Asia Pacific[53] and, to a significant extent, like those of Obama, Bush and Clinton before it, continues to act out the Cold War in the region. The long-term decline in the regional US troop presence will likely persist at least in the short term, but essential Cold War structures remain intact, most notably in its regional military bases and hub and spokes network of alliances which, with exceptions such as Vietnam, prioritises non-authoritarian allies.

The Asia Pacific and, increasingly, the Indo-Pacific, under Trump, then, has remained an American Pacific, as an imaginative geography of the American self defined by the twin requirement for its core values of Western-style democracy/freedom and capitalism, and its physical authority, to endure. Under Trump, the United States continues to pursue imperial hegemony in the region through institutionalised and consensual, or Ikenberry's 'informal', networks of power; Secretaries of State Rex Tillerson and Mike Pompeo attended the ASEAN Regional Forums of 2017 and 2018 respectively and the United States seems willing to remain an active participant of the multilateral landscape. The maintenance of those networks, however, continues to be enabled by the explicit availability and impositions of political/economic and military power, with some more exposed than others.

The Trump White House, for example, has so far avoided such staples of postwar US foreign policy discourse as democracy promotion and the protection of human rights, while continually restating its seemingly hard power foreign policy doctrine of "America First", including in Asia, with its focus on revising trade and other economic agreements in favour of US interests and strengthening the American military. Yet as we have seen, the basis for American engagement adheres to historically familiar, value-driven logics of the American self. Washington still assesses regional partnerships, not least its "great power relations" with India and China, on the presence or absence of shared political values.[54] In early 2018 the Trump administration withdrew financial assistance to Cambodia over 'setbacks to democracy' there.[55] Typically now in the absence of physical conquest, the United States still manipulates the long-term conditions for American values to exert control from the centre to the peripheries; '[T]he US Government doesn't tell American companies what to do', explained Secretary of State Pompeo at the Indo-Pacific Business Forum. 'But we help build environments that foster good, productive capitalism. We help American firms succeed so that local communities can flourish, and bilateral partnerships can grow.'[56]

In the military-security realm, the Trump administration actioned the Enhanced Defense Cooperation Agreement (EDCA) with the Philippines, formulated under Obama, to help reassert regional US authority from one of its traditional military hubs. Like the Military Bases Agreement of 1947, controversy followed the EDCA after being approved only by the Philippine Executive, bypassing scrutiny from the Senate.[57] Obama-era plans to relocate troops from Okinawa to Guam also remain in place, so that the island under Trump, still denied full democratic representation, stays conceived first and foremost as a strategically valuable outpost for use by, and deployment of, the US military. As noted by Secretary of Defense James Mattis: '[H]aving these forces on US territory, whether it be Guam or Hawaii … allows us certain freedoms of actions and sustainment out there.'[58]

Conclusion

Washington's policy makers ascribe to long ingrained truths of the United States as a local Pacific Power, in an American Pacific imagined to extend from the Western United States into the furthest reaches of Asia. Like Obama, the Trump administration uses history to sustain the normality of an American presence many thousands of kilometres from the US mainland: '[t]he US interest in a free and open Indo-Pacific extends back to the earliest days of our republic',[59] notes the 2017 NSS, reasserting Washington's timeless project to secure its Enlightenment-inspired, democratic-capitalist values. As ever, this project primes Washington to see threats in those whose values contradict the American self. With the reach of American power and identity throughout the Asia, and now Indo-, Pacific expanding over time in the forms of domestic political cultures, economic and trade norms, military bases and outposts, and, in places, its dominant linguistic and racial foundations, perceived responsibility over their maintenance and defence has expanded with them. These are key legacies of the American Pacific for twenty-first-century American presidents.

These physical and ideational legacies have been centuries in the making and play a key role in the contemporary operations of US foreign policy. Having steadily, if unevenly, transformed the landscape of the region from at least the middle of the nineteenth century, from Alaska to Guam to the Philippines to Japan and beyond, the United States maintains its pursuit of regional imperial hegemony today. It does so through institutionalised and consensual networks of partners and allies, enabled by the availability and application of political/economic and military power to extend control from the centre out to vulnerable frontiers. Washington's Cold War security frameworks, in Japan and Korea and in its hub and spokes network of bilateral alliances, are maintained in a region seen as one of rising challenges as much as economic development. But the United States keeps a Cold War on life support which, for most, ended thirty years ago.

Authoritarian China is now the largest trade partner and among the largest investment partners of almost every Asian economy. Most regional governments also strongly favour a plurality of regional power where no single actor dominates; a rising China generates uncertainties and tensions, but from a position of preponderance the United States has a long history of forceful and destructive impositions. In historically familiar ("civilised vs. uncivilised") terms, the Obama and Trump administrations have identified the existence of two distinct worlds: one defined by the operations of American values and the other by their problematic absence. Yet even where democracy and capitalism thrive in Asia, the region has commonly conformed to Western models only in Western imaginations.[60] In today's less polarised post-Cold War world, moreover, regimes which have long resisted US democratisation efforts now feel emboldened and tacitly supported by China's state-centric rise.

Diplomatic and security allegiances in the Indo-Pacific, then, are evolving and its geopolitical contours are increasingly fluid. The United States must also adapt, but questions remain over the extent to which it is willing to do so and how it will make sense of the first long-term diminishments in its regional grip on ideas and physical power in at least 150 years. Historical legacies of the American Pacific haunt twenty-first-century Washington administrations, handing down the responsibility to sustain US authority throughout an ever-inflating imaginative geography now reconstructed from an "Asia" to an "Indo" Pacific. Yet established truths can be challenged and cycles of policy can be broken. Today more than ever, radical thinking towards Asia and the Pacific in Washington's foreign policy circles is required.

Notes

1   M. Mann, *Incoherent Empire* (London: Verso, 2003), p. 16.

2   For example, S. Mallaby, 'The reluctant imperialist: Terrorism, failed states, and the case for American empire', *Foreign Affairs*, 81:2 (2002), pp. 2–7.

3   G. H. W. Bush quoted in K. Raustiala, 'America Abroad: US May Not Be Imperial, But It Does Have an Empire', *New York Times* (2 July 2003), www.nytimes.com/2003/07/02/opinion/IHT-america-abroad-us-may-not-be-imperial-but-it-does-have-an-empire.html, accessed 5 March 2019.

4   J. Snyder, 'Imperial temptations', *The National Interest*, 71 (2003), p. 29.

5   J. Ikenberry, 'Power and liberal order: America's postwar world order in transition', *International Relations of the Asia Pacific*, 5:2 (2005), p. 149.

6   A. Hurrell, 'Pax Americana or the empire of insecurity?', *International Relations of the Asia Pacific*, 5:2 (2005), pp. 153–76. The US-led liberal international order is argued elsewhere to be a class-based hegemony underpinned by colonial/imperial (as well as racial) thinking. See I. Parmar, 'The US-led liberal order: Imperialism by another name?', *International Affairs*, 94:1 (2018), pp. 151–72.

7   Ikenberry, 'Power and liberal order', p. 136.

8   C. Maier, *Among Empires: American Ascendancy and its Predecessors* (Cambridge, MA: Harvard University Press, 2006), p. 7.

9   *Ibid.*, p. 3.

10 R. Young, *Postcolonialism: An Historical Introduction* (Oxford: Oxford University Press, 2016), p. 27.

11 G. Lundestad, 'Empire by invitation? The United States and Western Europe, 1945–1952', *Journal of Peace Research*, 23:3 (1986), pp. 263–77.

12 N. Bisley and A. Phillips, 'A rebalance to where? US strategic geography in Asia', *Survival: Global Politics and Strategy*, 55:5 (2013), p. 98.

13 E. Said, *Orientalism* (New York: Pantheon Books, 1978); G. Ó Tuathail, *Critical Geopolitics* (Minneapolis: University of Minnesota Press, 1996), p. 2.

14 F. Cameron, *US Foreign Policy after the Cold War: Global Hegemon or Reluctant Sheriff?*, 2nd edition (London: Routledge, 2002), p. 2.

15 T. Jefferson, 'First inaugural address', in B. Oberg (ed.), *The Papers of Thomas Jefferson*, Vol. 33 (Princeton, NJ: Princeton University Press, 2006), pp. 134–52.

16 Quoted in W. H. Seward, *Life and Public Services of John Quincy Adams* (New York: Miller, Orton and Mulligan, 1856), p. 132.

17 F. J. Turner, *The Significance of the Frontier in American History* (New York: Henry Holt and Company, 1921), p. 315.

18 D. Campbell, *Writing Security: United States Foreign Policy and the Politics of Identity* (Minneapolis: University of Minnesota Press, 1992), p. 105.

19 D. Madsen, *American Exceptionalism* (Edinburgh: Edinburgh University Press, 1998), pp. 1–2.

20 Turner, *The Significance of the Frontier*, p. 293.

21 *Ibid.*, p. 3.

22 O. Turner, *American Images of China: Identity, Power, Policy* (London: Routledge, 2014), pp. 48–9.

23 Quoted in H. W. Morgan, *William McKinley and His America*, revised edition (London: The Kent State University Press, 2003), p. 225.

24 F. D. Roosevelt, 'Address to the Congress on the State of the Union. January 6, 1942', in *Public Papers of the Presidents of the United States: Franklin D. Roosevelt, 1942*, Vol. 11 (New York: Macmillan, 1942), p. 32.

25 F. D. Roosevelt, '127. "We are going to win the war and we are going to win the peace that follows" – Fireside chat to the nation following the declaration of war with Japan. December 9, 1941', in *Public Papers of the Presidents of the United States: Franklin D. Roosevelt, 1941*, Vol. 10 (New York: Macmillan, 1941), p. 525.

26 Quoted in J. Go, 'Introduction', in J. Go and A. Foster (eds.), *The American Colonial State in the Philippines: Global Perspectives* (London: Duke University Press, 2003), p. 1.

27 See A. Yeo, *Activists, Alliances, and Anti-US Base Protests* (Cambridge: Cambridge University Press, 2011), pp. 37–43.

28 T. Kane, 'Global US Troop Deployment, 1950–2005', The Heritage Foundation (24 May 2006), www.heritage.org/defense/report/global-us-troop-deployment-1950-2005, accessed 6 March 2019, p. 7.

29 D. D. Eisenhower, 'Remarks at the headquarters of the Korean Army's Sixth Corps. June 20, 1960', in *Public Papers of the Presidents of the United States: Dwight D. Eisenhower, January 1, 1960 to January 20, 1961* (Washington, DC: Government Printing Office, 1961), p. 520.

30 D. D. Eisenhower, 'Special message to the Congress on the Mutual Security Program. February 16, 1960', in *ibid.*, p. 183.

31 J. F. Kennedy, 'Special Message by the President on Urgent National Needs' (25 May 1961), www.jfklibrary.org/Asset-Viewer/Archives/JFKPOF-034-030.aspx, accessed 6 March 2019.

32 Kane, 'Global US Troop Deployment'.

33 For example, E. Ratner, 'Rebalancing to Asia with an insecure China', *The Washington Quarterly*, 36:2 (2013), pp. 21–38; C. Le Mière, 'Rebalancing the burden in East Asia', *Survival: Global Politics and Strategy*, 55:2 (2013), pp. 31–41. On the connotations of the term 'rising' see Turner, *American Images of China*, pp. 152–3.

34 See O. Turner, 'China, India and the US rebalance to the Asia Pacific: The geopolitics of rising identities', *Geopolitics*, 21:4 (2016), pp. 922–44.

35 White House, 'Statement by the President on the Trans-Pacific Partnership' (5 October 2015), https://obamawhitehouse.archives.gov/the-press-office/2015/10/05/statement-president-trans-pacific-partnership, accessed 6 March 2019.

36 US Department of State, 'Remarks on US-China Relations' (4 November 2014), https://2009-2017.state.gov/secretary/remarks/2014/11/233705.htm, accessed 6 March 2019.

37 H. Clinton, 'America's Pacific Century', *Foreign Policy* (11 October 2011), http://foreignpolicy.com/2011/10/11/americas-pacific-century/, accessed 6 March 2019.

38 Turner, 'China, India and the US rebalance', p. 934.

39 White House, 'Remarks by President Obama to US Troops and Personnel at US Army Garrison Yongsan' (26 April 2014), https://obamawhitehouse.archives.gov/the-press-office/2014/04/26/remarks-president-obama-us-troops-and-personnel-us-army-garrison-yongsan, accessed 6 March 2019.

40 Clinton, 'America's Pacific Century'.

41 Ministry of Foreign Affairs of Japan, 'US-Japan Joint Statement: The United States and Japan: Shaping the Future of the Asia Pacific and Beyond' (25 April 2014), www.mofa.go.jp/na/na1/us/page24e_000045.html, accessed 6 March 2019; B. Kovach and C. Carter, 'US-Japan Deal Withdraws 9,000 Marines from Okinawa' (27 April 2012), https://edition.cnn.com/2012/04/27/world/asia/japan-us-okinawa/index.html, accessed 6 March 2019.

42 Turner, 'China, India and the US rebalance', p. 933.

43 White House, 'Remarks by President Obama to the Australian Parliament' (17 November 2011), https://obamawhitehouse.archives.gov/the-press-office/2011/11/17/remarks-president-obama-australian-parliament, accessed 6 March 2019.

44 Clinton, 'America's Pacific Century'.

45 Defense Manpower Data Center, 'DoD Personnel, Workforce Reports, & Publications' (2018), www.dmdc.osd.mil/appj/dwp/dwp_reports.jsp, accessed 6 March 2019.

46 Gallup, 'Americans Not Convinced US Needs to Spend More on Defense' (21 February 2018), https://news.gallup.com/poll/228137/americans-not-convinced-needs-spend-defense.aspx, accessed 6 March 2019.

47 The Chicago Council on Global Affairs, 'Public Opinion and the US-Japan Alliance at the Outset of the Trump Administration' (17 February 2017), www.thechicagocouncil.org/publication/public-opinion-and-us-japan-alliance-outset-trump-administration, accessed 7 March 2019.

48 White House, 'National Security Strategy of the United States of America' (December 2017), p. I.

49 *Ibid.*, pp. 45–6.

50 US Department of State, 'Remarks on "America's Indo-Pacific Economic Vision"' (30 July 2018), www.state.gov/secretary/remarks/2018/07/284722.htm, accessed 7 March 2019.

51 US Department of Defense, 'Mattis: Meeting With Indian Defense Minister Comes at Time of Strategic Convergence' (26 September 2017), www.defense.gov/News/Article/Article/1325107/mattis-meeting-with-indian-defense-minister-comes-at-time-of-strategic-converge/, accessed 7 March 2019.

52 US Department of State, 'Remarks on "America's Indo-Pacific Economic Vision"'.

53 White House, 'National Security Strategy', p. 47.

54 US Department of State, 'Remarks on "America's Indo-Pacific Economic Vision"'.

55 White House, 'Statement from the Press Secretary on Reduction in Assistance to the Government of Cambodia' (27 February 2018), www.whitehouse.gov/briefings-statements/statement-press-secretary-reduction-assistance-government-cambodia/, accessed 7 March 2019.

56 US Department of State, 'Remarks on "America's Indo-Pacific Economic Vision"'.

57 P. Parameswaran, 'Philippine Court Upholds New US Defense Pact', *The Diplomat* (12 January 2018), https://thediplomat.com/2016/01/philippine-court-upholds-new-us-defense-pact/, accessed 7 March 2019.

58 S. Limtiaco, 'Defense Secretary Weighs in on Guam Role in Region', *Pacific Daily News* (21 June 2018), https://eu.guampdn.com/story/news/2017/06/21/defense-secretary-weighs-guam-role-region/414576001/, accessed 8 March 2019.

59 White House, 'National Security Strategy', p. 46.

60 See Turner, *American Images of China.*

2

Humanitarian hawk meets rising dragon: Obama's legacy in US China policy

Peter Gries

Introduction

After seven years of a George W. Bush foreign policy focused on the "war on terror", Barack Obama came into office in 2009 seeking to "pivot" US foreign policy towards a growing Asia. Together with his Secretary of State Hillary Clinton, he was particularly keen to reset a US relationship with China that had withered under a Bush administration engrossed in the Middle East. Working with China, Obama and Clinton hoped, would help resolve a growing list of bilateral, regional and global security challenges.

Instead, the eight years of the Obama administration witnessed an unmistakable deterioration in US–China relations.[1] A variety of academic, policy and media reports all suggest that Obama was repeatedly rebuffed both personally and in his China policy. For instance, at the 2009 UN Climate Change Conference in Copenhagen, Chinese premier Wen Jiabao sent a second-tier official to sit in his place opposite Obama. This was widely seen as a snub.[2] Similarly, Obama's 2009 speech to students in Shanghai, in which he spoke of the importance of political expression and participation, was censored in the Chinese media after a negotiated agreement to not do so. In 2016, Obama was denied a red-carpet reception at Hangzhou Airport and forced to unceremoniously disembark from Air Force One through the belly of the plane.[3]

By contrast, on his first state visit to China in November 2017, Donald Trump was treated to an 'unprecedented' grand red-carpet welcome.[4] Does that make Obama's China policy a failure and Trump's a success? Two years into the Trump administration, what can we say about Obama's China policy legacy?

Appraising the legacy of an individual or group is relatively straightforward. For instance, The Beatles' legacy can be assessed through the music they left behind. Assessing a bilateral policy legacy is more complex. At the interpersonal level, if a relationship deteriorates then who is to blame? Did one or both parties do the wrong things, or not try hard enough? One side can do all the right things, but if the other side does not reciprocate the relationship can deteriorate nonetheless. Alternatively, both sides can make an effort and do the right things but circumstances can conspire against them. Inter-nation relations are no different; it takes two, and the right international conditions, to make a successful bilateral relationship.

This chapter will argue that circumstances conspired to undermine Obama's China policy, and that the deterioration of US–China relations during his administration was largely beyond his control. Obama's Pivot to Asia suffered from an inability to extract the United States from the wars in the Middle East he inherited from Bush, and the rise of Chinese nationalism stymied his hopes of resetting US–China relations. Obama's Pivot to Asia did, however, leave both the Trump administration and US allies in a position of relative strength in 2017 Asia.

The chapter further argues that despite an ego-gratifying red-carpet welcome to Beijing in 2017, bilateral relations deteriorated much more during the first two years of the Trump administration. Halfway through his term in office mutual trust is at a new low, talk of a "Thucydides Trap" is increasing, and the spectre of another US–China conflict looms. Meanwhile, an "America First" Trump has turned his back on Asia, not least by rejecting the Trans-Pacific Partnership (TPP). Trump has undermined the regional position of the United States and its Asian allies, and initiated a damaging trade war with China. Together with Chinese President Xi Jinping, Trump is also undermining stability in the Taiwan Strait.

To make this argument, the chapter begins with Obama and his administration's broader foreign policy orientation. It then examines his Pivot to Asia, and his plans for a reset of US–China relations. It next explores the events of 2008 that conspired to undermine the prospects for improving US–China relations even before the Obama administration began. Trump's volatile China policy and the further deterioration of US–China relations is then interrogated. The chapter concludes with thoughts on the future of Obama's legacy in US China policy.

Obama: Humanitarian hawk

To understand Obama's China policy, one must first understand his broader foreign policy orientation. Obama was no dove. George McGovern and the anti-war activism of Vietnam-era liberals has created the widespread impression that post-Vietnam Democrats are doves and Republicans, hawks. Like many stereotypes, there is some truth to this view: *on average*, Republicans are more nationalistic and militaristic than Democrats.

Averages can hide important differences within groups, however. A plurality of Democrats today are actually 'forceful idealists' or 'humanitarian hawks', willing to deploy military force to achieve idealistic foreign policy goals.[5] They want to defend religious liberty, combat hunger and disease, and promote democracy and human rights around the world, and are willing to use force to do so.

Obama was one such humanitarian hawk. When the Nobel Committee selected him as their 2009 Peace Prize laureate, they likely mistook him for a dovish counterpoint to George Bush's hawkishness. His words and deeds soon proved them wrong. 'Within America, there has long been a tension between those who describe themselves as realists or idealists – a tension that suggests a stark choice between the narrow pursuit of interests or an endless campaign to impose our values around the world', Obama declared during his Nobel lecture in Oslo. 'I reject these choices.'[6]

Instead, like Reinhold Niebuhr and other progressive Christians before him, Obama did not abandon the Social Gospel but adapted it to a hostile world. Following Martin Luther King, he believed that 'love without power is mere sentimentality. Power without love is dangerous. Love plus power equals justice.'[7] 'Clear-eyed', he concluded his 2009 Nobel lecture, 'we can understand that there will be war, and still strive for peace.'[8]

Obama chose a fellow forceful idealist – Hillary Clinton – to lead his foreign policy team. 'I've never understood the division between so-called realists and so-called idealists', Clinton said in a 2011 interview with the *Atlantic*.

> I don't know how you get up in the world every day … if you don't have some sense of idealism, because you have to believe that as hard as it is, you're going to prevent the dictator from oppressing his people, you're going to help to stop the war, you're going to figure out a way to get clean water to thirsty people and cure kids of disease. And at the same time, I don't know how you go through the day and expect to be successful without being very hard-headed and realistic.[9]

Obama and Clinton did not just talk the talk about a hard-headed idealism, they walked the walk. For instance, in March 2011 Obama ordered a military attack on the Libyan army that prevented a massacre in Benghazi. Less than two months later, Obama overrode the objections of Republican Defense Secretary Robert Gates to authorise Operation Neptune Spear, in which US Navy SEALs assassinated Osama bin Laden in Abbottabad, Pakistan. But neither Obama nor Clinton saw force as the solution to every global problem. They were both philosophical pragmatists,[10] and that hard-headedness informed their China policy.

China featured prominently in the United States' foreign policy Pivot to Asia. Obama and Clinton sought mutual cooperation, but China was 'one of the most challenging and consequential bilateral relationships the United States has ever had to manage'.[11] A long-standing critic of China's human rights record, in 2011 Clinton declared, 'we live in the real world … [and] we don't walk away from dealing with China because we think they have a deplorable human rights record'.[12]

Obama felt similarly on China policy: tough when needed on humanitarian issues, but pragmatic. His previous life experiences as an African American and a lawyer likely contributed to his focus on human rights issues in China.[13] Yet Obama's pragmatism and anti-militarism led him to embrace working with China to resolve bilateral, regional and global security challenges. Like his predecessors, Obama talked tough on China during his election campaign, only to soften his stance once in office.[14] As president, Obama repeatedly claimed that the United States welcomed the rise of China; against many Chinese critics, I believe he truly meant it. Obama viewed China as a potential partner.

Many Chinese, for their part, initially judged the new president as easier to work with than his predecessor. But timing was against the new administration. While the Middle East preoccupied the White House, many Chinese – proud and confident after decades of rapid growth – advocated a more assertive foreign policy as China sought to take its historical place as the leading power in East Asia. Washington's alleged containment policy was seen to stand in the way.

A Pacific president: Obama's Pivot

US–China relations, former Secretary of State Colin Powell declared in 2004, were 'the best they have been since President Richard Nixon first visited Beijing more than 30 years ago'.[15] That is decidedly *not* how Chinese at the time viewed the relationship.[16] Bush had come into office in January 2001 with a team of neoconservatives who were hawkish on China, and the April 2001 Hainan spy plane collision sent bilateral relations to lows not seen since the Tiananmen Massacre of 1989. Then-Defense Secretary Donald Rumsfeld, muzzled during the delicate negotiations over the release of the plane's US crew, held a press conference immediately upon their release to lambast China and blame the dead Chinese pilot Wang Wei for both the crash and his own death. The Chinese government continued to place full blame for Wang Wei's death on the United States.

Five months later, the US terrorist attacks of 11 September 2001 changed everything. The Chinese government sent its condolences, and the Bush administration and its neocons turned their gaze towards Afghanistan and Iraq. Powell is correct that *on the surface* US–China relations seemed to improve, but most Chinese security analysts viewed 9/11 merely as a reprieve from the wrath of the neocons. America, in their view, was 霸道 (hegemonic/ bullying) by nature, and only temporarily directing its innate aggression elsewhere.[17] After seven years of the war on terror and a Bush Doctrine that emphasised unilateralism and a provocative policy of preventative war, Obama ran for president on a platform of extricating the United States from the Middle East. Where Bush was willing to go it alone in Iraq with or without UN support, and even that of US allies, Obama was far more of an internationalist, believing that global problems required diplomatic and multilateral solutions.

Obama billed himself "the first Pacific President" in November 2009, and first announced his Pivot to Asia in November 2011. Michael Green argues that Barack Obama was not actually the first Pacific president, but the first to pursue a genuinely Asia-first strategy.[18] Regardless, it is no coincidence that Obama's first foreign visitor was Japanese Prime Minister Tarō Aso. South Korean President Myung-Bak Lee received the Obama administration's first formal state visit, and his Secretary of State Hillary Clinton's first trip abroad was to Asia.

Having grown up in Indonesia and Hawaii, Obama may have been better placed than many East Coast American statesmen and women to recognise the growing geopolitical importance of a rising Asia, and he and Clinton set about Pivoting to Asia. Kurt Campbell, Obama's Assistant Secretary of State for East Asian and Pacific Affairs, and the Pivot's primary architect, has argued at length that Obama's Pivot to Asia was a 'necessary course correction' after a decade focusing on terrorism and the Middle East.[19] Campbell further argues that as Asia grows the US role in Asia must evolve as well, from a 'gardener' dutifully tending to the region, to an 'orchestra conductor' coordinating the increasingly independent efforts of Asian states and their multilateral institutions, such as the Association of Southeast Asian Nations (ASEAN).[20]

Socialised into an anti-imperialist nationalism,[21] many Chinese feared the Pivot was an effort to block their country's rise, and yet another effort to humiliate China and deny its rightful place atop the East Asian order. Pointing to Obama's 2011 announcement of rotations of increasingly larger groups of US Marines through Darwin in northern Australia, these Chinese analysts argued that the Pivot was a policy of balancing against China's rise, both through a US military build-up and reinforcing US alliances in Asia. Many Chinese considered the economic pillar of the Pivot, the TPP, to have been designed to exclude China and its state-centric economy, while drawing up an American-designed blueprint for regional trade. Many Chinese saw the TPP as a long-term threat to its interests and sought to create alternative economic arrangements like the Regional Comprehensive Economic Partnership (RCEP).[22] The Pivot, they claimed, was containment with a new name.

The Pivot was about 'increasing ties to Asia', Campbell responded to such critics, 'not containing China'.[23] It sought to embed China policy within a broader regional framework, not to obstruct China's rise. Campbell would not convince Chinese nationalists, and China's overreaction to the Pivot only confirmed the worst fears of American nationalists, contributing to a hardening of many US China policies, from cyber security to the South China Sea.[24] Indeed, Campbell concludes his book, *The Pivot: The Future of American Statecraft in Asia*, with a metaphor: the United States must bolster its Asian partnerships by adding a 'tire' to the traditional hub and spokes alliance structure, joining each and every allied spoke.[25]

For instance, the Obama administration worked hard to reconcile Japan and South Korea, America's two closest allies in Northeast Asia. Though not particularly successful at overcoming their misgivings about each other, US efforts to bring Japan and South Korea together do suggest that external balancing against China was one driver of Obama's Pivot to Asia. Indeed, the administration's plans to install the Terminal High Altitude Area Defense (THAAD) missile system in South Korea drew criticism from China. The Obama administration claimed that it was needed to counter the threat of increasing missile launches from North Korea, but Beijing argued that it was actually directed against them. The Chinese government was consistent and systematic in its repeated criticisms of THAAD, extending formal diplomatic protests immediately after its announcement.[26] Beijing also allowed major Chinese nationalist protests and boycotts against South Korean companies, and put restrictions on tourism to South Korea, and the import of K-pop. The Obama administration further fuelled Beijing's discontent when it approved arms sales to Taiwan, Singapore and other Chinese neighbours concerned about Beijing's future ambitions. For instance, the Obama administration lifted a half-century embargo on lethal weapons sales to Vietnam.

Ultimately, the Pivot failed to live up to its full potential because Obama could not extricate the United States from the Middle Eastern challenges it had inherited from the Bush administration. Obama, and China's new President Xi Jinping, appeared to strike an early friendship, manifest in the broadly positive messages which emanated from the 2013 Sunnylands Summit in California between the two. Their joint statement described a relationship which had the potential to become more cooperative and mutually beneficial, rather than antagonistic.[27] While Iraq, Syria and Afghanistan would continue to occupy Washington's attention, however, China would begin rolling out its Asian Infrastructure Investment Bank (AIIB), Belt and Road, and other megaprojects, to take the initiative in East Asia.

The 2008 Beijing Olympics

With hindsight, it becomes apparent that two events in 2008, before Obama was even elected, powerfully shaped the prospects for his China policy. The Beijing Olympics and the global financial crisis of 2007/8 were successfully utilised by the Chinese Communist Party (CCP) to boost Chinese nationalism and solidify its legitimacy. They also contributed to a more aggressive turn in Chinese foreign policy in general, and China's US policy in particular.

The CCP used preparations for the Olympics to hammer home the core nationalist message of its post-Tiananmen Patriotic Education Campaign (爱国教育运动): that the CCP had rescued China from Western and Japanese imperialism in the past, and would restore China to its proper place atop the world stage in the future. A Herculean propaganda campaign portrayed the Beijing Olympics as the culmination of a 'century-long Olympic dream' (百年奥运梦) of the Chinese people, restoring their 'dignity', and wiping away the 'Century of

Humiliation' (百年国耻) at the hands of European and Japanese imperialism.[28] The placement of countdown clocks in public squares in cities all across China in the years leading up to the Games manufactured an intense personal desire for redemption and recognition among ordinary Chinese. The Games themselves were virtually flawless. The Opening Ceremony, directed by filmmaker Zhang Yimou, was on an awe-inspiring scale, featuring 2008 People's Liberation Army (PLA) performers and spectacular visual effects. The performance highlighted China's five millennia old "Brilliant Civilisation" and its "Glorious New Era" under the CCP. Like a debutante at its ball, China was stepping out into international society to be admired by all, and demanding recognition.

Confronting China's rise from the intimacy of their own homes, Americans appear to have become warier towards China.[29] US media coverage of scandals surrounding an underage Chinese gymnast who denied an American a medal, and a lip-syncing girl during the opening events, contributed to an American view of the Chinese as cheats. To add insult to injury, China won the most gold medals at its Olympics, beating out its nearest rival, the United States.

Ultimately, the Beijing Olympics put pressure on US–China relations from both sides. The CCP became a victim of their own success, facing increasing domestic pressure from a nationalist public opinion of its own making and which increasingly demanded that a newly modernised China must be respected. Meanwhile, the Obama administration confronted an American public that increasingly viewed China as a cheat which competed unfairly, threatening US global dominance.

The global financial crisis and a newly assertive China

Later in 2008, the global financial crisis provided yet another opportunity for the CCP to boost its nationalist legitimacy. It was also good for Obama's presidential election campaign as he and his running mate Joe Biden benefited, while their rivals John McCain and Sarah Palin suffered. For Obama, a national economic crisis was good electoral fortune; inheriting Republican George W. Bush's economy, McCain declared in September 2008 that 'the fundamentals of our economy are strong'. That very day Lehman Brothers collapsed, just seven weeks prior to the election.[30]

The financial crisis was bad news, however, for Obama's subsequent China policy. Like the Beijing Olympics it fundamentally transformed Chinese expectations about their place in Asia and the world. 'China emerged from the global financial crisis cocky on the international stage but insecure at home,' Tom Christensen notes, 'a toxic combination that has made managing relations with it even more difficult than usual.'[31] Prior to 2008, China had pursued a largely cautious policy of reassurance towards the United States and its East Asian neighbours. In large part this was because when "China threat" discourse first emerged in Japan and Southeast Asia in the 1990s, Chinese analysts awoke to the dangers of the security dilemma.[32] Military policies in the East and South China Seas which China viewed as benign and defensive were viewed with alarm by its Asian neighbours, bringing the possibility of counterbalancing, military build-ups and strengthened alliances, with the potential to undermine China's security environment.

Reassurance quickly became a guiding principle of Chinese foreign policy. China's neighbours would be made to understand China's peaceful intentions, to help ensure they resisted the temptation of working together to obstruct China's rise. Multilateralism was one way in which China sought to reassure its Pacific neighbours. Having fought against a US-led United Nations force in Korea, Cold War China had long been hostile to international organisations. In the 1990s, however, China began a dramatic reversal, actively engaging ASEAN and other regional and international organisations.

Were China's neighbours reassured? Some were not, arguing that Deng Xiaoping's famous dictum of 韬光养晦 or 'quietly hiding one's talents and biding one's time' suggested that the Chinese policy of reassurance was actually a wolf in sheep's clothing; once China was strong, its aggressive nature would reveal itself. For the most part, however, the United States and China's East and Southeast Asian neighbours were reassured, and spent most of the first two post-Cold War decades benefiting from trade and investment relations with China. At first, there was a bipartisan consensus in the United States on engaging China.[33]

The financial crisis of 2008 changed all that. Contrasting China's speedy implementation of a stimulus package and rapid economic recovery to the West's slower response and more difficult recovery, the CCP engaged in a sustained media campaign to argue to its people that China had emerged on top; the crisis was said to have proven that the "Chinese model", or "Beijing consensus", of state-led economic development was superior to the neoliberal "Washington consensus" on the centrality of market-based economic solutions.

The success of this triumphalist CCP propaganda campaign (reminiscent of Liberal triumphalism and the 'End of History'[34] following the demise of the Soviet bloc) was a mixed blessing for Chinese elites. Many Chinese began to brim with self-confidence. Former US Treasury Secretary Hank Paulson relates how as early as 2008 Vice Premier Wang Qishan, China's anti-corruption tsar, lectured him at length about US economic failings, posing China's economic model as a superior alternative.[35]

This was more than just talk. Chinese elites were soon acting on their post-financial crisis confidence. In 2009, PRC Ambassador to the UK Fu Ying threatened the oil company BP over a planned development project with Vietnam, implying that BP's much larger China business was at stake. At a 2010 ASEAN meeting, then PRC Foreign Minister Yang Jiechi bluntly declared to China's neighbours that 'China is a big country, and other countries are small countries, and that's just a fact'. He had listened to Southeast Asian diplomats express concerns about PRC military activities in the South China Sea, but was in no mood to respond calmly.[36] In Chinese foreign policy after the financial crisis, gentle reassurance was out, and blunt power displays were in.

But the Chinese elite were arguably also the victims of their own propaganda's success. The Chinese people largely appear to have bought into the CCP's post-2008 message that the Chinese economy was now the world's strongest, and they began expecting that their government demand the respect a newly dominant China deserved. For instance, when the Senkaku/Diaoyu Islands dispute flared up again between China and Japan in 2012, Beijing's elite foreign policy makers appear to have been forced to toughen their policy towards Tokyo to placate nationalist public opinion. Circumstantial evidence strongly suggests nationalist opinion was a powerful driver of a toughening China Japan policy in 2012–13. Spikes in anti-Japanese sentiment online in Chinese cyberspace, and anti-Japanese protests on the streets of most major Chinese cities, preceded each sequential hardening of China's foreign policies towards its East Asian neighbour. Chinese popular nationalists, furthermore, directed their ire not just at Japan but also the CCP for "weak" responses to perceived Japanese provocations.[37] These nationalists, in other words, were directing the party-state's own language of nationalist legit-imation back towards it.[38]

In short, the 2008 Beijing Olympics and global financial crisis appear to have doomed Obama's attempted reset of US–China relations before he even took office. Washington's conciliatory gestures towards Beijing, Richard McGregor argues, went unreciprocated.[39] Following the crisis, Chinese nationalism transformed confidence and influence into hubris and assertiveness.[40] China recalibrated its foreign policy from Deng Xiaoping's tactic of maintaining a low profile to a new policy of speaking and acting loudly. History is likely to judge the Obama years as the period when China regained its position as the major power in Asia. Towards the end of the Obama administration, a fundamental rethinking of US engage-ment policy of China was well underway.[41]

A China policy under Trump?

During his presidential campaign, Donald Trump blamed China for a variety of American woes, from its trade deficit to unemployment. This was a winning strategy in the Republican Party primaries, as cultural (Christian right), economic (business) and political (libertarian) conservatives are more anti-communist than their liberal counterparts, and as socio-racial conservatives (white nativists) are more prejudiced than civil rights liberals.[42] Trump thus found a receptive audience in the most conservative Republicans when he floated the old spectres of "Red China" and the "Yellow Hordes" at his campaign rallies.[43]

In the first two years of Trump's presidency however, his narcissism got the better of him and his China policy has been incoherent, swaying back and forth towards whomever at hand could best satisfy his insatiable need for flattery. As E. J. Dionne and others have noted, Trump's policies from immigration to gun control shift according to whoever is in the room with him.[44] His China policy is no different.

Taiwan got to Trump's ego first. In December 2016, ROC President Tsai Ying-wen called Trump directly to congratulate him on his election victory. The conversation broke decades of established diplomatic protocol between Washington and Beijing and talk emerged of the Trump administration revisiting the One China policy which China insists upon, and which many Taiwanese from Tsai's Democratic Progressive Party now oppose. In a February 2017 conversation with PRC President Xi Jinping, however, Trump abruptly reversed course, affirming that the United States would continue to support the "1992 Consensus" on One China. 'Trump lost his first fight with Xi, and he will be looked at as a paper tiger', Shi Yinhong boasted to the *New York Times*.[45]

In November that year, the CCP rewarded Trump with a lavish state visit to Beijing. Playing to Trump's vanity, the visit was 'unprecedented' in its pomp.[46] Trump basked in the spectacle, and rewarded Xi by avoiding sensitive issues like human rights, press freedom, and even the American jobs he had promised to defend during his election campaign. Many Chinese lauded Xi's triumph. 'The leader of the world's number one power has just made a pilgrimage to him', Shanghai pundit Chen Daoyin gloated, 'this is naturally how all Chinese people will see it'.[47] Just a month later, however, Trump's first National Security Strategy (NSS) described China as 'challenging American power, influence, and interests, attempting to erode American security and prosperity'. The NSS argued that decades of US engagement with China had not worked, and emphasised US–China competition and possible confrontation.[48]

The January 2018 National Defense Strategy (NDS) was even more alarmist. Secretary of Defense Jim Mattis claimed that China 'seeks Indo-Pacific regional hegemony … and displacement of the United States to achieve global pre-eminence'.[49] Nationalism was now becoming the predominant framework for understanding US–China relations on both sides of the Pacific. The next month, the US Senate unanimously passed the Taiwan Travel Act which Trump promptly signed, encouraging visits between US and Taiwanese officials at all levels. Although non-binding, China's Ministry of Foreign Affairs warned that the Act 'severely violates the one-China principle and the three joint communiques between China and the US'.[50]

The Taiwan issue, largely dormant during the Obama and Ma Ying-jeou administrations, is re-emerging under Trump and Xi as a flashpoint in US–China relations.[51] Seen as a double "window of opportunity", 2019 is shaping up to be a dangerous year in the Taiwan Strait. While President Xi and Chinese nationalists desperately desire reunification, Trump's isolationist "America First" rhetoric only emboldens such reckless thoughts, while Taiwanese remain passive and unable to confront the threat.

Tensions in the South China Sea continue to mount as well. In January and March 2018, the USS *Hopper* and USS *Mustin* carried out freedom of navigation operations within 12 nautical miles of Scarborough Shoal and Mischief Reef respectively. While the US side claimed they were innocent passages well within international law, the Chinese side responded through the lens of anti-imperialist nationalism.[52] The United States 'seriously harmed Chinese sovereignty and security', claimed a Chinese Defence Ministry spokesman.[53] Angry words were also paired with action. The People's Liberation Army Navy (PLAN) paraded its aircraft carrier *Liaoning* and over forty other ships and submarines through the South China Sea in April 2018.[54] Aboard the PLAN destroyer *Changsha*, Xi Jinping, donning a military uniform, instructed the PLAN to be on 'full alert'.[55] It is hard to overemphasise how negatively China's aggressive actions in the South China Sea have impacted American public opinion towards China.

Trump pulled out of the TPP at the beginning of his presidency, and in March 2018 he imposed tariffs on steel and aluminium imports. Most of these imports came from US partners like Canada, and Trump's trade policy created as much opposition from close allies as it did from China. On the same day in Chile, eleven Pacific Rim countries signed a revised TPP, the Comprehensive and Progressive Agreement for Trans-Pacific Partnership (CPTPP), affirming Obama's vision of regional free trade, and rebuffing Trump's embrace of protectionism. As of early 2019, Trump's narcissism and pugnaciousness has contributed to a new nadir in US–China relations. An 'enormously destructive dynamic' has developed across the Pacific, in which worst-case thinking threatens to become a self-fulfilling prophecy.[56]

Obama's China legacy revisited

This chapter has argued that circumstances conspired to thwart Obama's China policy, and that the unmistakable deterioration of US–China relations during his eight years in office was largely out of his control. First and foremost, the Middle East demanded continued US attention, inhibiting a full Pivot to Asia and China. Second, the 2008 Beijing Olympics and global financial crisis were successfully utilised by the CCP to boost popular Chinese nationalism, contributing to a toughening of Chinese foreign policy in general, and to its US policy in particular. An American counter-reaction was predictable. The widespread perception of an aggressive turn in Chinese foreign policy, moreover, did not just set US–China relations back. Many of China's neighbours started rethinking their relations with Beijing and sought to strengthen their ties with the United States.

So Obama's China legacy must be understood within the broader context of his Pivot to Asia, which had mixed results. Obama was not able to fully extract the United States from the "forever wars" he inherited, so the Pivot did not live up to its full potential. However, the Obama administration's efforts to put tires on the hub and spoke system of US alliances in Asia, to borrow Bader's metaphor, paid dividends. From Japan to Vietnam, Asian states were driven by their growing fears of China into an embrace of closer relations with both the United States and each other. As a result, Trump was handed a robust network of relationships in Asia within which to engage China.

From the vantage point of early 2019, has Trump squandered this Obama legacy? Yes. The TPP is an illuminating case. Trump withdrew from a partnership Obama had promoted since 2009. The Obama administration viewed the TPP as more than just a trade agreement – it was to be the political cement that kept the United States engaged in Asia. From a political and security perspective, Trump's withdrawal was a major error, ceding leadership in East Asia to China. It was also a blow to one of Obama's China policy successes. Like a zombie, the TPP has also risen from the dead, though without American participation. The signing in March 2018 of the CPTPP by eleven of Washington's important regional partners not only affirms Obama's economic vision of free trade and spurns Trump's protectionism, but supports the Pivot's political vision of an Asia Pacific tied together through open networks and multilateral agreements.

Trump's bellicose threats over trade towards both China and some of Washington's closest and most long-standing allies, to fulfil his narcissistic need for affirmation from his protectionist supporters, threatens to further undermine Sino-American relations and the liberal international order so central to the postwar peace. It is also misplaced; the Trump administration has prioritised balance of trade issues, at the expense of more important problems including Chinese intellectual property theft, non-tariff barriers to free trade, and the probation of foreign investment in selective sectors of its economy.

Trump may be squandering Obama's legacy in Asia, but China also currently appears to be wasting the opportunity Trump presents to take a positive leadership role in East Asia, as Xi's assertiveness alienates a number of China's Asian neighbours. Trump's successor will therefore likely confront an Asia eager to support American re-engagement, and Obama's Pivot to Asia may well re-emerge in a new form.

Notes

1   For example, H. Harding, 'Has the US China policy failed?', *The Washington Quarterly*, 38:3 (2015), pp. 95–122; T. Christensen, 'Obama and Asia: Confronting the China challenge', *Foreign Affairs*, 94:5 (2015), pp. 28–36.

2   B. Glaser and C. Norkiewicz, 'State visit-plus summit buys time, but friction
      mounts', *Comparative Connections*, 19:3 (2018), pp. 19–32; M. Lynas, 'How Do
      I Know China Wrecked the Copenhagen Deal? I was in the Room', *The Guardian*
      (22 December 2009), www.theguardian.com/environment/2009/dec/22/
      copenhagen-climate-change-mark-lynas, accessed 9 March 2019.

3   B. Glaser and A. Viers, 'US-China relations: China prepares for rocky relations in
      2017', *Comparative Connections*, 18:3 (2017), pp. 17–25.

4   Glaser and Norkiewicz, 'State visit-plus summit buys time'.

5   P. Gries, *The Politics of American Foreign Policy: How Ideology Divides Americans
      and Conservatives over Foreign Affairs* (Stanford: Stanford University Press, 2014).

6   B. Obama, 'Nobel Lecture: A Just and Lasting Peace', The Nobel Prize (10
      December 2009), www.nobelprize.org/prizes/peace/2009/obama/26183-nobel-
      lecture-2009/, accessed 9 March 2019.

7   J. Kloppenberg, *Reading Obama: Dreams, Hope, and the American Political
      Tradition* (Princeton, NJ: Princeton University Press, 2011), p. 26.

8   Obama, 'Nobel Lecture'.

9   See J. Goldberg, 'Hillary Clinton: Chinese System is Doomed, Leaders on a "Fool's
      Errand"', *The Atlantic* (10 May 2011), www.theatlantic.com/international/archive/
      2011/05/hillary-clinton-chinese-system-is-doomed-leaders-on-a-fools-errand/
      238591/, accessed 9 March 2019.

10   Kloppenberg, *Reading Obama*.

11   H. Clinton, 'America's Pacific Century', *Foreign Policy* (11 October 2011), https://
      foreignpolicy.com/2011/10/11/americas-pacific-century/, accessed 9 March 2019.

12   See Goldberg, 'Hillary Clinton'.

13   C. Li, 'Assessing US-China Relations Under the Obama Administration', The
      Brookings Institution (30 August 2016), www.brookings.edu/opinions/assessing-u-
      s-china-relations-under-the-obama-administration/, accessed 8 March 2019.

14   O. Turner, 'China and the 2016 US Presidential Debates: Curiosities and
      Contradictions', Swedish Institute of International Affairs, Brief no. 3 (2015),
      www.ui.se/globalassets/butiken/ui-brief/2015/china-and-the-2016-us-presidential-
      debates-curiosities-and-contradictions.pdf, accessed 9 March 2019.

15   C. Powell, 'A strategy of partnerships', *Foreign Affairs*, 84:1 (2004), pp. 22–34.

16   P. Gries, 'China eyes the hegemon', *Orbis: A Journal of World Affairs*, 49:3 (2005),
      pp. 401–12.

17   *Ibid.*

18   M. Green, *More Than Providence: Grand Strategy and American Power in the Asia
      Pacific since 1783* (New York: Columbia University Press, 2017), p. 519 and p. 539.

19   K. Campbell, *The Pivot: The Future of American Statecraft in Asia* (New York:
      Twelve, 2016), p. 2.

20   *Ibid.*, p. 346.

21   P. Gries, *China's New Nationalism: Pride, Politics, and Diplomacy* (Berkeley: University
      of California Press, 2004).

22   M. Du, 'Explaining China's tripartite strategy toward the Trans-Pacific Partnership
      Agreement', *Journal of International Economic Law*, 18:2 (2015), pp. 407–32.

23   Campbell, *The Pivot*, p. 22.

24   Li, 'Assessing US-China Relations'.

25   Campbell, *The Pivot*, p. 347.

26   See E. Meick and N. Salidjanova, 'China's Response to US-South Korean Missile Defense System Deployment and its Implications', US-China Economic and Security Review Commission (26 July 2017), www.uscc.gov/Research/china's-response-us-south-korean-missile-defense-system-deployment-and-its-implications, accessed 8 March 2019.

27   R. Bush, 'Obama and Xi at Sunnylands: A Good Start', The Brookings Institution (10 June 2013), www.brookings.edu/blog/up-front/2013/06/10/obama-and-xi-at-sunnylands-a-good-start/, accessed 8 March 2019.

28   Gries, *China's New Nationalism*.

29   P. Gries, M. Crowson and T. Sandel. 'The Olympic effect on American attitudes towards China: Beyond personality, ideology, and media exposure', *Journal of Contemporary China*, 19:64 (2010), pp. 213–31.

30   H. Hertzberg, 'Recession Election', *The New Yorker* (1 November 2010), www.newyorker.com/magazine/2010/11/01/recession-election, accessed 8 March 2019.

31   Christensen, 'Obama and Asia', p. 28.

32   S. Tang and P. Hays Gries, 'China's Security Strategy: From Offensive to Defensive Realism and Beyond', National University of Singapore East Asian Institute, Working Paper no. 97 (2002).

33   Harding, 'Has the US China policy failed?'.

34   F. Fukuyama, *The End of History and the Last Man* (New York: Free Press, 1992).

35   H. M. Paulson, *Dealing with China: An Insider Unmasks the New Economic Superpower* (New York: Twelve, 2015).

36   R. McGregor, *Asia's Reckoning: The Struggle for Global Dominance* (London: Penguin, 2017), p. 248 and p. 250.

37   P. Gries, D. Steiger and T. Wang, 'Popular nationalism and China's Japan policy: The Diaoyu Islands protests, 2012–2013', *Journal of Contemporary China*, 25:98 (2015), pp. 264–76.

38   Gries, *China's New Nationalism*.

39   McGregor, *Asia's Reckoning*, p. 255.

40   M. D. Swaine, 'Perceptions of an assertive China', *China Leadership Monitor*, 32:2 (2010), pp. 1–19.

41   Harding, 'Has the US China policy failed?'.

42   Gries, *Politics of American Foreign Policy*, ch. 9; P. Gries, ' "Red China" and the "yellow peril": How ideology divides Americans over China', *Journal of East Asian Studies*, 14:3 (2014), pp. 317–46.

43   For an exploration of these and other powerful perceptions throughout history, see O. Turner, *American Images of China: Identity, Power, Policy* (London: Routledge, 2014).

44   E. J. Dionne, 'The Needy Salesman in Chief', *Washington Post* (11 March 2018), www.washingtonpost.com/opinions/the-needy-salesman-in-chief/2018/03/11/e6034cb2-23cd-11e8-94da-ebf9d112159c_story.html, accessed 9 March 2019.

45 See J. Perlez, 'Trump, Changing Course on Taiwan, Gives China an Upper Hand', *New York Times* (10 February 2017), www.nytimes.com/2017/02/10/world/asia/trump-one-china-taiwan.html, accessed 7 March 2019.

46 Glaser and Norkiewicz, 'State visit-plus summit buys time'.

47 Quoted in T. Phillips, 'Chinese Media Hails Success of Trump's "Pilgrimage" to Beijing', *The Guardian*, www.theguardian.com/us-news/2017/nov/10/chinese-media-hails-success-of-trumps-pilgrimage-to-beijing, accessed 14 March 2019.

48 White House, 'National Security Strategy of the United States of America' (December 2017), p. I.

49 J. Mattis, 'Summary of the National Defense Strategy of The United States of America: Sharpening the American Military's Competitive Edge', US Department of Defense (2018), www.defense.gov/Portals/1/Documents/pubs/2018-National-Defense-Strategy-Summary.pdf, p. 2, accessed 7 March 2019.

50 B. Glaser and K. Flaherty, 'Hurtling toward a trade war', *Comparative Connections*, 20:1 (2018), p. 23.

51 P. Gries and T. Wang, 'Will China Seize Taiwan? Wishful Thinking in Beijing, Taipei, and Washington Could Spell War in 2019', *Foreign Affairs* (15 February 2019), www.foreignaffairs.com/articles/china/2019-02-15/will-china-seize-taiwan, accessed 9 March 2019.

52 Gries, *China's New Nationalism*.

53 See *China Daily*, 'China Firmly Opposes US Provocation in its Territorial Waters' (28 May 2018), http://global.chinadaily.com.cn/a/201805/28/WS5b0af882a31001b82571c899.html, accessed 14 March 2019.

54 Glaser and Flaherty, 'Hurtling toward a trade war'.

55 CGTN, 'President Xi Calls for Establishment of World-Class Naval Force' (12 April 2018), https://news.cgtn.com/news/7845444d346b7a6333566d54/share_p.html, accessed 8 March 2019.

56 M. D. Swaine, 'The US Can't Afford to Demonize China', *Foreign Policy* (29 June 2018), https://foreignpolicy.com/2018/06/29/the-u-s-cant-afford-to-demonize-china/, accessed 7 March 2019.

3

The Obama administration and India

Christopher K. Colley* and Sumit Ganguly

Introduction

The dawn of the twenty-first century ushered in an era of new opportunity in Indo-US relations. While bilateral ties in the twentieth century were marred by the politics of the Cold War, as well as perceptions of American arrogance and hegemony, the first decade-and-a-half of the new century witnessed the world's two largest democracies come closer together than they had ever been. There are multiple causes for the warming of ties between Washington and New Delhi, which range from shared democratic norms, to real and perceived economic opportunities, to policies based on strategic hedging and the balance of power in the international order. This chapter specifically examines the relationship under the two Obama administrations and the first two years of the Trump administration. It argues that the overriding driver of Indo-US relations during this period was the mutual desire to hedge against the rise of China. Additionally, however, there were other factors influencing ties, chief among these economic considerations. As will be demonstrated, the focus on China and increasing trade links between the United States and India were not always sufficient to prevent domestic obstacles in both the United States and India from posing political challenges to bilateral ties. However, when examining America's relations with India during the Obama era and into the Trump regime, it is nearly impossible to decouple the broader geostrategic situation in which both states have concerns over how Beijing will wield its increasing power.

While China's rise served as a backdrop to expanding ties between Washington and New Delhi, other important (and related) events took place during Obama's eight-year presidency. Specifically, this chapter focuses on three key interrelated

---

*   The opinions expressed in this chapter are those of the author and do not reflect the views of the National Defense College, or the United Arab Emirates government.

aspects of bilateral ties. First, we analyse the diplomatic and political relationship between India and the United States with a focus on the major summits and political meetings at the top levels of government. This section will demonstrate that the honeymoon period of the last three years of the Bush era gave way to a more realistic bilateral relationship with the Obama administration. The second section examines economic ties and highlights the major successes, as well as significant challenges, that confronted both New Delhi and Washington. The final section focuses on the cornerstone of relations, the strategic partnership, and how this is heavily impacted by the rise of China as both a regional and global power. This segment also argues that by the end of Obama's second term, security ties between the two states were robust, but for political reasons were not at the level of a formal alliance. We conclude with a brief discussion of policy changes and continuity under the Trump regime.

Background

Throughout most of the Cold War India and the United States held different worldviews. The United States was determined to maintain its dominant position as a global hegemon and supported its allies while opposing the USSR and other communist states. India's leaders quickly saw the United States as less of a defender of post-colonial states and more of an heir to British imperialism.[1] American support for India's rivals Pakistan, and later China, further divided Washington and New Delhi. Although the United States did support India in its war with China in 1962, and even supplied it with military equipment, Washington did not view New Delhi as a major ally or force in the global war against communism. In fact, America did not view India's policy of "nonalignment" as a form of genuine neutrality.[2] India's 1971 Treaty of Peace, Friendship, and Cooperation with the USSR, where Moscow and New Delhi promised to aid each other in the event of a military conflict, confirmed American suspicions.[3] Washington's ties with Pakistan also posed a significant obstacle between India and the United States. Perhaps the best concrete example of the divergent interests between the United States and India during the Cold War is found in the 1971 USS *Enterprise* incident where the American aircraft carrier entered the Bay of Bengal as a token show of support for Pakistan during the 1971 Indo-Pakistani War. This conflict ended in the dismemberment of Pakistan and the birth of Bangladesh. India's poor economic performance throughout most of the Cold War also led Washington to not take New Delhi seriously. Added to this was India's "peaceful nuclear test" in 1974, which resulted in various legislative acts by the American Congress designed to prevent nuclear proliferation in South Asia, and the 1998 nuclear tests by both Pakistan and India, which resulted in additional American sanctions on both states.[4]

The George W. Bush administration, over the course of two terms, brought about a virtual transformation of Indo-US relations. Specifically, Bush removed one of the most trying elements in the relationship: the US attempt to induce India to abandon its nuclear weapons programme.[5] This policy shift had a transformative effect on the Indo-US relationship. In turn, it benefited from some key initiatives launched in the waning days of the Clinton administration.[6] It is important to note that Bush expended an enormous amount of political capital to assist India. In particular, the administration set out to change domestic American laws in order to accommodate New Delhi. Additionally, Washington worked with friends and allies to alter international regimes in order to allow full civilian nuclear cooperation with India.[7] From a strategic perspective the Bush administration made it clear that it wanted to assist India in joining the ranks of the great powers. As far back as the 2000 American presidential campaign, Condoleezza Rice argued that India had the potential to become a great power, and that the United States would do well to assist in this endeavour. It was also Rice who, in her position as Secretary of State in 2005, put forth a ground-breaking framework for cooperation with India.[8] Consequently, when the Obama administration assumed office in January 2009, the Indo-US relationship was on an extraordinarily secure footing.

Indo-US diplomacy during the Obama years

Despite the significant progress that had been made in Indo-US relations during the 2000s, the Obama administration did not have an auspicious start with India in its first year in office. Almost at the outset the administration caused distress in New Delhi when its Special Representative for Afghanistan and Pakistan, the seasoned diplomat Richard Holbrooke, mentioned that he might include the Kashmir dispute in his portfolio. When rumours about this impending decision emerged from Washington, DC, it invoked a swift and belligerent response from New Delhi. Indian officials felt the new administration was not respecting Indian concerns on a core issue of sovereignty. Interestingly, India even hired lobbyists and used personal connections to keep Holbrooke from including India in his portfolio.[9]

It is crucial to note that upon taking office in 2009, President Obama confronted the worst financial crisis since the Great Depression and preventing the United States from collapsing into a second depression was of paramount importance to the White House. While relations with India were important, they simply did not garner the level of attention that the Bush administration had accorded to India. The lack of focus on India in the first six months of the new administration is illustrated by that fact that Secretary of State Hillary Clinton visited Japan, South Korea, Indonesia and China, but not India.[10] Nicholas Burns, the American Under Secretary of State for Political Affairs from 2005 to 2008, describes a perception in

India that New Delhi was not a priority in Washington. He points out that during Obama's first term the administration was preoccupied with the financial crisis, and its focus in foreign policy was directed at the wars in Iraq and Afghanistan, as well as preventing Iran from acquiring nuclear weapons. Even though strong ties with India were strategically important, India was not a major issue. With regard to India, Burns states, 'it was a classic Washington story of near term crisis crowding out long-term ambitions'. Indian officials privately complained to their American counterparts of the lack of attention Obama was paying to New Delhi.[11] In fact, it would take eight months for the contours of Obama's India policy to emerge.[12]

The first breakthrough in Obama's first term came with Secretary Clinton's four-day trip to India in July 2009. This visit significantly eased concerns in India that the United States no longer viewed New Delhi as a major actor in global affairs. Clinton's trip was the longest ever for a Secretary of State to India.[13] Most importantly, Clinton's trip set the stage for Indian Prime Minister Manmohan Singh's November 2009 visit to Washington.

Singh's visit was significant for multiple reasons. Crucially, by inviting the Indian Prime Minister to the White House for the first state visit of Obama's presidency, Obama was making clear to New Delhi that he attached great importance to bilateral relations, as well as Indian concerns over the threat of terrorism confronting India.[14] Obama openly encouraged India to take a leadership role in Asia by stating, 'In Asia, Indian leadership is expanding prosperity and the security across the region. And the United States welcomes and encourages India's leadership role in helping to shape the rise of a stable, peaceful and prosperous Asia.'[15]

Singh's trip to Washington was followed a year later with a visit by Obama to India. During this visit, Obama announced support for India to become a permanent member of the United Nations Security Council.[16] Obama's support for India on the UNSC is best viewed through the lens of public diplomacy. While his remarks gave face to India and demonstrated to New Delhi that Washington was serious about building robust ties in multiple areas, the fact that China would veto another Asian permanent member on the UNSC made this a somewhat limited diplomatic gesture. In addition to calling for India to get a permanent seat, Obama stated that India was 'an indispensable partner' of the United States in the twenty-first century.[17] A more concrete gesture from Obama was in his announcement that the United States would help India obtain membership in four non-proliferation regimes, these being the Missile Technology Control Regime, the Wassenaar Group, the Australia Group and the Nuclear Suppliers Group.[18]

While there were frequent visits by top diplomats and heads of state on both sides during the period under review, two major events stand out. The first was the visit of Indian Prime Minister Narendra Modi to the United States in September 2014, and the second was President Obama's visit to India in January 2015.

Modi's trip to America

Prior to becoming India's prime minister in the spring of 2014, Modi was banned from entering the United States. The US State Department had refused to issue him a visa by citing the International Religious Freedom Act, which banned foreign officials who were responsible for serious violations of religious freedom from entering the United States. In 2002, an anti-Muslim pogrom had taken place in the Indian state of Gujarat during Modi's term as the chief minister of the state. However, the American position began to change in late 2013 and early 2014 as it became increasingly likely that Modi would be India's next leader. In February 2014, the American government ended its visa ban on Modi and shortly thereafter he became India's prime minister in May. Importantly, Obama was determined to keep Indo-UN relations on stable ground, and personally contacted Modi on the phone after his election victory.[19] While Modi's visa ban meant that he lacked strong ties with Washington, his September 2014 visit went exceedingly well. In New York, Modi sold out Madison Square Garden, he was greeted by thousands of members of the Indian diaspora, and in Washington with Obama, he renewed the 2005 Defense Cooperation Agreement for another ten years. This agreement stated that India and the United States would treat each other at the same level as their closest partners on issues of defence.[20] The Obama–Modi summit surprised many observers in that the two leaders appeared to establish a form of personal rapport with each other. The summit also helped to allay fears in India that the United States was not a reliable partner and that it would be willing to provide vital spare parts to the defence sector in a time of conflict.[21]

Under Obama, the United States enjoyed a relatively high favourability rating with the Indian public, and perhaps more importantly a very low unfavourable rating. As can be seen in Figure 3.1, America's favourability ratings were roughly consistent with those of his predecessor, George W. Bush. Figure 3.2 shows that while unfavourable perceptions declined under Obama, there was a dip in favourable perceptions. In addition, in the years where data is available, Figure 3.3 shows that the Indian public had 'confidence in the US President'.

America's relatively high approval ratings in India, along with Obama's relationship with Modi, help explain why Obama was the chief guest at the sixty-sixth Republic Day on 26 January 2015. This was the first time an American president had this honour, and in making the journey, Obama was the first American president to visit India twice while in office.[22] Obama attached so much importance to the visit to India that he even had to reschedule the annual State of the Union address.[23] A joint statement issued by both Obama and Modi the day before the Republic Day event stated, 'A closer partnership with the United States and India is indispensable to promoting peace, prosperity and stability.' Importantly, this statement mentioned not just the Indian Ocean region, but also the Asia Pacific,

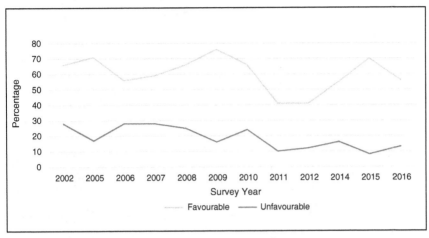

Note: Not shown are the "don't know" and "refuse" answer categories

3.1 Indian favourability ratings of the United States

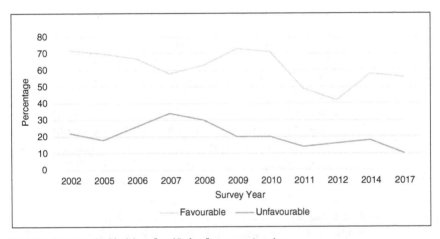

Note: Not shown are the "don't know" and "refuse" answer categories

3.2 Indian favourability ratings of Americans

thus clearly elevating India beyond the domain of a regional power.[24] As will be discussed below, major progress was also made during this visit on a nuclear liability law that stood to benefit American companies. It needs to be noted that Modi's decision to invite Obama to the Republic Day parade constituted a costly signal in that it demonstrated that he was willing to stand up to the Indian left and the America-baiters within India's "attentive public".

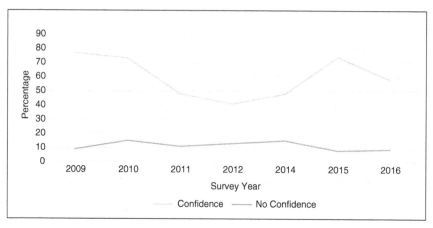

Note: Not shown are the "don't know" and "refuse" answer categories

3.3 Indian confidence in the American president

Political and diplomatic challenges during the Obama era

While Obama and Modi were able to reconcile their differences and come together in Obama's last two years in office, several political/diplomatic challenges showed that as Indo-US relations evolve and mature, significant hurdles remain. While not a major event, it is useful to briefly mention the arrest and strip search in New York of Devyani Khobragade, who was the Deputy Consul General for India, in New York. Mrs Khobragade was charged with visa fraud for bringing to the United States a domestic worker she planned to employ and for failing to pay the worker a minimum wage. The episode demonstrates that Indo-US relations during the Obama period were not strong enough to bypass such events. India retaliated to the arrest by downgrading security at the American Embassy in New Delhi (which could have had serious consequences) and by denying visas to American teachers employed at the American International School in New Delhi.[25] This event also underscores Indian sensitivities towards real and perceived slights by the United States.

A much deeper political challenge is the fact that significant constituencies in India do not wish New Delhi to move towards a closer strategic partnership with the United States. From an ideational standpoint, closer ties to Washington could compromise India's room for political manoeuvre expressed in terms of its commitment to "strategic autonomy". The political left and the communist parties all harbour deep mistrust of the United States and American intentions. This fear of being seen as too close to Washington played a role in scuttling the multi-billion dollar fighter-bomber deal with US defence contractors.[26] At the national level, the Congress Party has concerns that it may lose support from the left, and Muslims, if it is perceived as being too close to America. Additionally, various defence related projects were held up for political reasons. For example, during a three-year period when A. K. Antony was India's Minister of Defence, the United States proposed seventeen defence-related projects, but did not receive a response from the Indian side.[27]

On the issue of diplomacy and foreign policy, the Obama administration had to contend with Indian strategic ties with Iran relating to its role in Afghanistan, and its fraught relationship with Pakistan. Afghanistan is a major concern to India and New Delhi sees it as a strategic rear base for Pakistan. India seeks to limit Pakistani influence in Afghanistan and to that end is the largest regional donor in Afghanistan with over US$2 billion invested in reconstruction and development aid. New Delhi was not consulted or involved with American decision making in regard to pulling out of Afghanistan, which caused significant irritation in India.[28] Washington and New Delhi do not always agree on how to deal with Iran. While a nuclear armed Iran is not in India's interest, Iran plays a significant role in India's energy imports, as well as being a transit point for goods to and from Central Asia. New Delhi is planning to build rail and road links from Afghanistan to the Iranian port of Chabahar to facilitate the flow of raw materials and goods from Afghanistan to India. In addition, India's large Shia Muslim population is a powerful constituency that promotes Indo-Iranian relations. These factors mean that New Delhi does not always endorse American sanctions on Iran.[29]

Overall, the Obama administration's public diplomacy towards India evolved over his two terms in office. While domestic factors and the wars in Iraq and Afghanistan kept India on the back burner in the first six months of his administration, by the end of 2009, relations with New Delhi were back on track. In terms of diplomacy, it is difficult to compare the Obama era with the previous Bush administration. Obama was constrained by the enormity of the financial crisis as well as the two wars he inherited from Bush. As ties between the two states started to mature, the economic links between the two increased, but not without challenges.

Indo-US economic relations under Obama

One of the reasons India was not taken seriously by the United States during much of the twentieth century was because of its anaemic economic record. In 2002, Robert Blackwell, then the American Ambassador to India, described the US trade flow to India as 'flat as chapatti'.[30] However, bilateral trade in goods picked up in the second term of the Bush administration, doubling from US$21 billion in 2004, to US$43 billion in 2008.[31] By the end of Obama's second term, trade ties

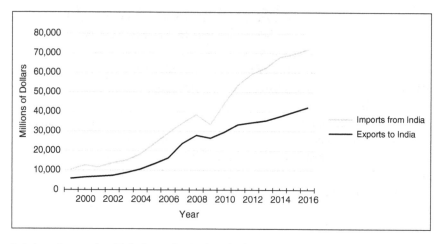

3.4 American trade with India under Bush and Obama

between the two states were rapidly expanding. As Figure 3.4 demonstrates, trade increased by over 600 per cent from 2000–17.

Opportunities for Indo-US bilateral trade

On the surface, the United States and India should have relatively complementary economic ties. India's former Ambassador to the UN, Jaskaran Teja, argues that at the centre of Modi's diplomacy is the need for high technology and capital resources from Western countries, but primarily from the United States.[32] India has an abundance of cheap labour and if it is able to push further economic liberalisation, could become a major source of manufacturing for Western markets. As Tellis and Mohan argue, India must understand that long-term economic growth is based on increasing global trade links, and increasing ties with the United States will enhance this.[33] The United States has also become a major trading partner for India over the past fifteen years. In 2001, India was America's twenty-fifth largest trading partner and by 2014 it had risen to eleventh. While America was India's second largest source of foreign direct investment (FDI) in 2001, it fell to fifth largest in 2014. The overall increase was from 370 million in 2001, to 1.7 billion in 2014.[34] Crucially, when all goods and services are taken into account, the United States is India's largest trading partner.[35]

Links in the form of FDI with the United States have expanded dramatically since 2000. As Figure 3.5 shows, with the exception of the period surrounding the global financial crisis, bilateral FDI steadily increased over the past two American administrations.

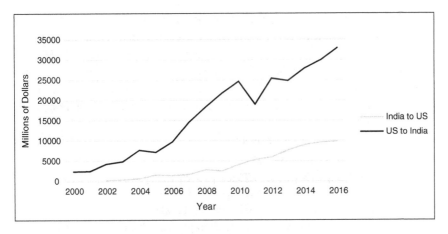

3.5 Bilateral Indo-US FDI

Challenges to Indo-US bilateral trade

While the data shows increasing economic ties between the United States and India, under the Obama administration there was still limited economic interdependence.[36] One of the greatest obstacles to further economic integration during the Obama era stemmed from Indian domestic politics. The difficulties associated with the landmark nuclear deal exemplify this problem. After it was signed in 2008, a nuclear liability law in 2010 made it nearly impossible for American firms to benefit from the deal. Specifically, the new law did not cap liability exposure for nuclear suppliers, thus discouraging private American firms from taking part in a deal established by their own government.[37] Importantly, the legislation was passed in August 2010 just as Indian courts were releasing their final judgments on the horrific Bhopal incident where, in 1984, a chemical leak killed up to 16,000 Indians in the country's worst ever industrial accident.[38] While the courts' concern for the impact that such industries may have on local populations is justified, it has a severe impact on foreign perceptions of doing business and investing in India. What should have been a cornerstone and shining example of Indo-US economic ties, turned out to be a warning and deterrent to American investors in India.[39]

As the Indian economy slowed in 2012–13, New Delhi started to impose discriminatory taxes on foreign investors and began to erect protectionist measures. Trade disputes followed with American firms complaining about Indian protectionism, and both countries filing suits in the World Trade Organization (WTO). The United States banned imports of more than a dozen Indian plants used by the pharmaceutical industry.[40] One basic measure that compares the comparative openness of the US and Indian markets is in the simple average bound tariff. At the start of Obama's second term the tariff for all products in the United States was 3.5 per cent, while in India it was 48.6 per cent. When this is compared to the average GDP per capita in each country, with the United States at US$53,000 and India at US$1,500, the lure of the Indian market is greatly diminished for American firms. New Delhi resists opening the India market because of the political costs and the inability of Indian firms to compete with more efficient American ones.[41]

Under Obama, American firms also frequently complained about violations of intellectual property rights (IPR) by Indian firms. Specifically, the Office of the United States Trade Representative placed India on its priority watch list and scheduled an Out-of-Cycle-Review (OCR) in the autumn of 2014 to look into this issue. Creating an OCR was an escalation because it can lead to recommended sanctions based on the trade representative's report. Realizing the negative impact of such a report, the September 2014 Summit between Obama and Modi addressed issues such as IPR and set up a working group to deal with this issue. In addition, the Indian Ministry of Commerce established a think-tank that focuses on IPR issues.[42] The full impact of these measures has yet to be seen, but it is necessary to note that New Delhi is at least cognizant of American concerns over IPR.

Overall, economic ties between India and the United States increased substantially during the Obama era. Talk of reaching US$500 billion a year in total trade may be premature, but if Washington and New Delhi are able to work out some difficult challenges on a potential free trade agreement, it is possible that bilateral trade would explode. However, there are also severe roadblocks to sustained increases in trade. Domestic Indian political calculations may well tie Modi's or his successor's hands. In addition, some of the structural deficiencies of the Indian economy, such as poor infrastructure and a small middle class, may prevent deeper economic ties.[43] While the structure of the Indian political system and economy may hinder deeper economic ties, the changing dynamics of the international system is driving them closer together.

Indo-US security ties during the Obama era

While America's political and economic ties experienced challenges under Obama, security relations between the two were robust and even strengthened during his eight years in office. This section argues that the best explanation for Washington's strategic embrace of New Delhi is found in an attempt to hedge against a rising China. Both the United States and India are involved in strategic rivalries with China[44] and, over the past decade and a half, these two separate rivalries are increasingly linked together. The expanding assertiveness of the Chinese People's

Liberation Army and Navy (PLA and PLAN), as well as China's overall growing power, is causing states all over Asia to rethink their security strategies vis-à-vis China.[45]

The rise of China provides Washington and New Delhi with both opportunities and strategic threats. The opportunities lie in the potential economic benefits that working and trading with China can deliver. The threats stem from the strategic rivalry that China poses to both the United States and India. For the United States, working with India in the security realm helps to preserve American hegemony while also assisting India in its rivalry with China. While both states are engaged in hedging, they are not aiming to "contain" China. A strategy of containment requires a state to prevent another state's rise by attempting to exclude it from the international community, while also working against it in multiple arenas.[46] Hedging, according to Tunsjo, is:

> The development and implementation of government strategies aimed at reconciling conciliation and confrontation in order to remain reasonably well-positioned regardless of future developments ... States hedge by combining contradictory cooperative and confrontational strategies to produce a balanced approach in order to manage uncertainty.[47]

India is both actively working with China in the economic realm, while also preparing for a worst-case security scenario. Figure 3.6 shows the expanding economic ties between India and China, demonstrating the absence of a clear containment policy.

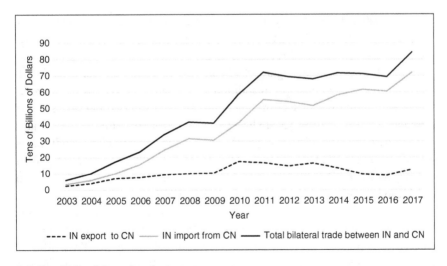

3.6 Sino-Indian bilateral trade

Rivalry dynamics

Indian leaders have harboured deep suspicions about China dating back to the foundations of both states in the late 1940s.[48] The 1962 war between India and China, where mechanised PLA forces quickly defeated the ill-equipped Indian army, had a traumatic impact on leaders in New Delhi. As the Chinese military has recently increased its power and, more importantly, its ability to project power into the Indian Ocean Region (IOR), threat perceptions in India have increased dramatically. The rise of China has the potential to radically alter the geopolitical strategic landscape in ways that may be detrimental to American and India interests. Given these circumstances, it is understandable that Washington and New Delhi work together to deal with a much more powerful and increasingly assertive China. As Paul Kapur argues, India's policies towards the United States and China are interconnected, and it is 'impossible to understand the Indian position on one without understanding its position on the other'.[49]

Obama's Pivot to Asia was a way to shift America's strategic focus to the Asia Pacific region. Behind this was a critical aspect that encouraged American partners and allies to work together to balance the rise of China. A key component of this was to increase military interoperability amongst America and its allies.[50] For American strategists India was an important component of the Pivot. American Secretary of Defense Leon Panetta specifically referred to India as the 'linchpin' of this strategy,[51] while Secretary of State John Kerry spoke of India as playing a critical role.[52]

Arms sales

Between 2009 and 2017, the Obama administration played a key role in providing the Indian military with advanced weapons systems. High profile purchases included C-130JS Super Hercules and ten C-17 transport planes; twenty-four Harpoon Block II missiles; eight P-8Is (vital for anti-submarine warfare); as well as Apache helicopter gunships. In addition, the Pentagon helped the Indian military in ways less visible such as sharing information about key choke points in the IOR where PLAN submarines are likely to transit, working with the Indian navy on undersea sensors, and assisting in the construction of catapults on India's new aircraft carriers.[53] While the United States is not India's largest source of foreign military hardware, as Figure 3.7 demonstrates, during the Obama administration American arms exports to India increased dramatically.

By collaborating with the United States in the security realm, India is able to gain access to not only American technology and know-how, but improve its tactics in military exercises such as Malabar, Salex and RIMPAC (Rim of the Pacific Exercise). (India was an observer to RIMPAC from 2004–10, but

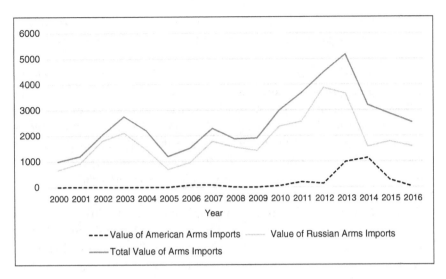

3.7 Indian arms imports in SIPRI's trend indicator values

a participant from 2012.)[54] The Chinese are acutely aware of the strengthening security ties between the United States and India but seem tone deaf to India's concerns of Chinese encirclement. A prime example of this was Xi Jinping's state visit to India in September 2014 during which Chinese forces crossed the Line of Actual Control that separates India and Chinese controlled territory in Tibet. The manoeuvre was viewed as a major insult to Prime Minister Modi and left Indians speculating why the crossing was ordered.[55] This episode along with the Chinese Belt and Road Initiative (BRI), through which hundreds of billions of dollars will be invested in hard infrastructure in the region, increases Indian fears of Chinese encirclement. The BRI's China Pakistan Economic Corridor crosses through disputed territory in Pakistani controlled Kashmir. China did not consult India about this massive project and because New Delhi sees it as a violation of Indian sovereignty in Kashmir, it has boycotted the initiative.

Change or continuity under Trump?

The Obama administration remitted office with Indo-US relations on a mostly even keel. President Trump, during his election campaign, had only focused on India when dealing with the issue of the apparently questionable allotment of H1-B visas which permit foreign professionals to work for specified periods in the United States. Upon assuming office, in the context of unfair trade practices, he mentioned India on a few occasions. His anti-immigrant remarks, though not specifically directed against those of Indian origin, have nevertheless caused some concern in New Delhi.

On the issue of trade, as of early 2019, the Trump administration is considering withdrawing the privileges India was granted under the Generalized System of Privileges. Through this agreement India has been able to export billions of dollars of goods to the United States tax free. The Trump administration's action follows a surprise move by New Delhi in December 2018 that made it more difficult for the American firms Amazon and Walmart to conduct e-commerce in India. India took action out of concern that Indian firms will not be able to compete with the two American companies.[56]

That said, in other areas, most notably regional security, the Trump administration has, for the most part, maintained the policies of his predecessor. To that end, in September 2018 he sent former Secretary of Defense, James Mattis, to India. During his visit Mattis made clear that the administration saw India as a bulwark for regional stability and that the United States was willing to continue weapons sales to India. Also, much to the delight of New Delhi, in early 2018 Trump announced that he was suspending over $2 billion worth of aid to Pakistan, India's nettlesome neighbour, because of its failure to rein in support for terror. In addition, the announcement in mid-2018 of the name change of the US Pacific Command (PACOM) to the US Indo-Pacific Command is an important piece of diplomacy. Even though PACOM had jurisdiction over India since the end of the Second World War, the symbolic renaming demonstrated to New Delhi that India matters in American geostrategic calculations.[57]

Given the Trump administration's significant misgivings about China on a variety of fronts, as of early 2019, it seems reasonable to conclude that it will continue with the trajectory laid out by the George W. Bush and Obama administrations and seek to engage India in an attempt to balance against China. Of course, the scope and dimensions of this engagement to some degree also depend on India's willingness to work with the United States. As argued earlier in this chapter, elements within India's political establishment still remain wary of the prospect of an overly robust strategic partnership with the United States. Unless a significant shift takes place within India's political culture despite the progress that has been made in the recent past, there may be distinct limits to the Indo-US strategic partnership.

Conclusion

Indo-US relations during the Obama era had a fitful start. On the domestic front, the financial crisis was a clear and present danger that the White House had to deal with immediately. In terms of foreign policy, the wars in Iraq and Afghanistan took priority in the first six months of the new administration. However, Hillary

Clinton's July 2009 trip to India and Prime Minister Singh's trip to Washington in November of that year placed the relationship back on track. As bilateral ties increased, challenges that could be ignored, or did not exist during the Bush years, began to demand attention. Concerns over IPR and market accessibility became major impediments in the relationship. These were partially offset by the personal ties between Obama and his Indian counterparts. While economic ties between the United States and India increased dramatically during Obama's two terms, the full potential of economic ties were blocked by both political factors in India and by the structural deficiencies of the Indian economy.

While political and economic ties may not be as robust as they could be, the foundation of the relationship is centred on security ties. Faced with a rising China that exhibits increasingly assertive behaviour, and that is locked in a strategic rivalry with both India and the United States, New Delhi and Washington have found common cause to work together. This is unlikely to change dramatically during the remainder of the Trump administration unless trade and immigration issues really come to the fore and cause the relationship to flounder. Furthermore, as argued earlier in this chapter, significant political constituencies are against a form of direct external balancing and it is not clear how eager India is to join the United States in a strategic alignment specifically designed to confront China.[58] This situation could change in the near future as China continues to make major inroads into the IOR and on India's northern periphery. These developments may induce those within India's political establishment who remain leery about a closer alignment with the United States to reconsider their stance.

Notes

1   A. Tellis, 'US India relations: The struggle for an enduring partnership', in D. M. Malone, C. R. Mohan and S. Raghavan (eds.), *The Oxford Handbook of Indian Foreign Policy* (Oxford: Oxford University Press, 2015), p. 484.

2   *Ibid.*, p. 486.

3   P. S. Kapur, 'India and the United States from World War II to the present: A relationship transformed', in S. Ganguly (ed.), *India's Foreign Policy* (Oxford: Oxford University Press, 2009), pp. 251–74.

4   *Ibid.*, p. 259.

5   S. Ganguly and D. Mistry, 'The case for the US-India nuclear agreement', *World Policy Journal*, 23:2 (2006), pp. 11–19.

6   S. Talbott, *Engaging India: Democracy, Diplomacy and the Bomb* (Washington, DC: Brookings Institution Press, 2004).

7   H. Pant, *India and the United States: An Emerging Partnership* (Manchester: Manchester University Press, 2016), p. 23.

8   *Ibid.*, pp. 24–5.
9   J. Kirk, 'India's season of discontent: US-India relations through the prism of Obama's "Af-Pak" policy, year one', *Asian Affairs*, 37:3 (2010), p. 153.
10 *Ibid.*
11 N. Burns, 'Passage to India', *Foreign Affairs*, 93:5 (2014), p. 134.
12 R. Kumar, 'New potential for US-India relations under Obama', *The International Spectator*, 44:4 (2009), p. 21.
13 C. Mahapatra, 'Obama administration II and India', *Indian Foreign Affairs Journal*, 8:2 (2013), p. 196.
14 Kirk, 'India's season of discontent', p. 148.
15 White House, 'Remarks by President Obama and Prime Minister Singh of India in Joint Press Conference' (24 November 2009), https://obamawhitehouse.archives. gov/the-press-office/remarks-president-obama-and-prime-minister-singh-india-joint-press-conference, accessed 9 March 2019.
16 V. Samson, 'India, China, and the United States in space: Partners, competitors, combatants? A perspective from the United States', *India Review*, 10:4 (2011), p. 429.
17 Mahapatra, 'Obama administration II and India', p. 194.
18 *Ibid.*, p. 431.
19 H. Pant, 'Modi's unexpected boost to India-U.S. relations', *The Washington Quarterly*, 37:3 (2014), pp. 93–6.
20 *Ibid.*, p. 107.
21 J. Teja, 'The new India-US reset', *American Foreign Policy Interests*, 36:6 (2014), p. 382.
22 Brookings India Center, 'The Second Modi-Obama Summit: Building the India-US Partnership', The Brookings Institution (January 2015), www.brookings.edu/wp-content/uploads/2016/06/The-Second-Modi-Obama-Summit-Briefing-Book.pdf, 9 March 2019.
23 A. Tellis and C. R. Mohan, 'The Strategic Rationale for Deeper US-Indian Economic Ties: American and Indian Perspectives', Carnegie Endowment for International Peace (2015), http://carnegieendowment.org/files/US_India_TellisMohan_Final.pdf, p. 73, accessed 9 March 2019.
24 White House, 'US-India Joint Strategic Vision for the Asia-Pacific and the Indian Ocean Region' (25 January 2015), https://obamawhitehouse.archives.gov/the-press-office/2015/01/25/us-india-joint-strategic-vision-asia-pacific-and-indian-ocean-region, accessed 9 March 2019.
25 Burns, 'Passage to India', p. 126.
26 S. Ganguly and W. Thompson, *Ascending India and its State Capacity* (New Haven: Yale University Press, 2017), p. 248 and p. 260.
27 A. Vasudeva, 'US-India Defense Ties: A Delicate Dance', *Foreign Policy* (8 October 2015), http://foreignpolicy.com/2015/10/08/u-s-india-defense-ties-a-delicate-dance/, accessed 9 March 2019.
28 J. D. Schmidt, 'The Asia-Pacific strategic triangle: Unentangling the India, China, US relations on conflict and security in South Asia', *Journal of Asian Security and International Affairs*, 1:2 (2014), p. 214.

29   *Ibid.*, pp. 215–16.

30   E. A. Feigenbaum, 'India's rise, America's interest: The fate of the US-Indian partnership', *Foreign Affairs*, 8:2 (2010), p. 78.

31   US Census Bureau, 'Trade in Goods with India' (2018), www.census.gov/foreign-trade/balance/c5330.html, accessed 10 March 2019.

32   J. Teja, 'The new India-US reset', *American Foreign Policy Interests*, 36:6 (2014), p. 376.

33   Tellis and Mohan, 'The Strategic Rationale', p. 16.

34   *Ibid.*, p. 34.

35   *Ibid.*, p. 73.

36   *Ibid.*, p. 1.

37   Pant, 'Modi's unexpected boost', p. 98.

38   T. C. Schaffer and H. B. Schaffer, *India at the Global High Table: The Quest for Regional Primacy and Strategic Autonomy* (Washington, DC: Brookings Institution Press, 2016), p. 178.

39   Burns, 'Passage to India', p. 134.

40   *Ibid.*, p. 137.

41   Tellis and Mohan, 'The Strategic Rationale', pp. 32–3.

42   Brookings India Center, 'The Second Modi-Obama Summit', p. 27.

43   See Ganguly and Thompson, *Ascending India and its State Capacity*, ch. 6.

44   M. Colaresi, K. Rasler and W. Thompson, *Strategic Rivalries in World Politics* (Cambridge: Cambridge University Press, 2007).

45   A. Liff, 'Wither the balancers? The case for a methodological reset', *Security Studies*, 25:3 (2016), pp. 420–59; R. S. Ross and O. Tunsjø (eds.), *Strategic Adjustment and the Rise of China* (Ithaca: Cornell University Press, 2017).

46   G. Kennan, 'The sources of Soviet conduct', *Foreign Affairs*, 25:4 (1947), pp. 566–82.

47   O. Tunsjø, 'US-China relations: From unipolar hedging toward bipolar balancing', in Ross and Tunsjø, *Strategic Adjustment*, p. 46.

48   J. Garver, *Protracted Contest: Sino-Indian Rivalry in the Twentieth Century* (Seattle: University of Washington Press, 2003).

49   P. Kapur, 'India's relationship with the United States and China', in T. Fingar (ed.), *The New Great Game: China and South and Central Asia in the Era of Reform* (Stanford: Stanford University Press, 2016), p. 54.

50   N. Silove, 'The Pivot before the Pivot: US strategy to preserve the power balance in Asia', *International Security*, 40:4 (2016), pp. 45–88.

51   S. Hu, 'India's rise and China's response', in Fingar, *The New Great Game*, p. 79.

52   Mahapatra, 'Obama administration II and India', p. 200.

53   Interviews conducted by Christopher K. Colley with India defence experts, New Delhi, India (Summer 2016).

54   D. Scott, 'The "India-Pacific": New regional formulations and new maritime frameworks for US-India strategic convergence', *Asia-Pacific Review*, 19:2 (2012), p. 99.

55   Interviews conducted by Christopher K. Colley with Indian security experts, New Delhi, India (Summer 2016).

56   J. Slater, 'Is India the Next Target in the Trump Administration's Trade Wars?',
     The Washington Post (13 February 2019), www.washingtonpost.com/world/
     asia_pacific/is-india-the-next-target-in-the-trump-administrations-trade-
     wars/2019/02/13/d1d7d896-2f90-11e9-ac6c-14eea99d5e24_story.html?utm_
     term=.322d5cf8c9b0, accessed 10 March 2019.

57   K. Parpiani, 'India-US Relations Under Trump: Guarding Against
     Transactionalism by Pivoting to the US Legislature', ORF Issue Brief no. 262
     (October 2018), www.orfonline.org/research/india-us-relations-under-trump-
     guarding-against-transactionalism-by-pivoting-to-the-us-legislature-45058/,
     accessed 10 March 2019.

58   Ganguly and Thompson, *Ascending India and its State Capacity*, p. 261.

4

Obama and Japan: An endangered legacy

Matteo Dian

Introduction

This chapter will discuss the legacy of the Obama administration of 2009–17 for US–Japan relations. It will highlight elements of change and continuity that characterised the Obama years in the realms of security and economic policy, as well as the significance of historical memory and the processes of reconciliation between the two countries. It will also discuss policy shifts promoted by the administration of President Donald Trump at around the halfway mark of his 2017–21 presidential term in office. The Trump presidency, it is argued, has injected a high degree of uncertainty into the bilateral relationship, causing perceptions of declining American influence in the region, especially in the economic realm.

Obama's relations with Japan can be divided into several phases. During the period from January 2009 to March 2011, and particularly the tenure of former Japanese Prime Minister Yukio Hatoyama (September 2009–June 2010), the Obama administration had a difficult relationship with the government led by the Democratic Party of Japan (DPJ). Hatoyama's intention of promoting political equidistance between the United States and China, and to achieve a higher degree of autonomy from Washington, appeared to be a threat to the stability of the US-led regional security architecture.

The crisis generated by the earthquake and tsunami of 11 March 2011 and resultant incident at the Fukushima nuclear power plant, as well as increasing Chinese assertiveness over the maritime and territorial disputes in the East and South China Seas, contributed to what the United States considered a return to normality in its relations with Japan, with a strong emphasis on the centrality of the alliance and a more adversarial relationship with China. Operation Tomodachi, by which Washington provided assistance to Tokyo in the aftermath of the disaster, helped recover and strengthen the foundations of the US–Japan alliance.

The most significant elements of discontinuity and change during the Obama era occurred in the period following the announcement of Obama's Pivot to Asia, not least after the return of Shinzo Abe to power in December 2012. With Abe, Obama found a partner who was particularly eager to embrace the role the Pivot had designed for Japan: that of democratic security provider and main supporter of the US-led regional order. By early 2019, however, some of these progresses appear endangered by the policies promoted by the Trump administration. As we will see, Japan has reacted to Trump's unpredictability and the perceived decline of US influence by upgrading its cooperation with other Asian democracies in the economic and security realms, and promoting a more accommodating policy towards Beijing.

Obama and the Democratic Party of Japan: From Futenma to Tomodachi

Following the 2008 US presidential elections, Washington's relations with Tokyo were not among the most pressing priorities in Obama's foreign policy agenda. Early American policies towards Japan reflected a substantial continuity with the Bush era; in the first months of the presidency, bilateral relations were expected to continue on the established trajectory of incremental progresses towards a closer military and diplomatic partnership.[1] The Japanese general elections, held in September 2009, completely changed this situation. The Obama administration perceived Hatoyama's victory as the beginning of an upheaval of the domestic foundations underlying the security arrangement with Japan, if not the entire US position in East Asia.[2]

Obama vs. Hatoyama

The relations between the Obama administration and Japan suffered a downturn after the 2009 Japanese elections, when the centre-left DPJ achieved an historic success, momentarily ending the five decades-long political hegemony of the Liberal Democratic Party (LDP). The DPJ promoted both a distinctive interpretation of Japanese identity and a different strategic vision of the country's interests. The first rested on fundamental assumptions of Japan's Asian identity. As Hatoyama stated in 2009, 'the Japan–US relationship is an important pillar of our diplomacy. However, at the same time, we must not forget our identity as a nation located in Asia … [T]he East Asian region … must be recognized as Japan's basic sphere of being.'[3] Hatoyama considered the main objectives of his government to be 'restraining US political and economic excesses', as well as to 'maintain [Japan's] political and economic independence, and protect its national interest when caught between the United States … and China'.[4] Consequently, Hatoyama tried to significantly upgrade Tokyo's bilateral relations with Beijing.

The key initiative from this point of view was the creation of the East Asia Community which brought mechanisms for financial and monetary cooperation and a security framework aimed at solving territorial disputes. China and Japan agreed upon negotiations aimed at approving rules for dispute resolution in the East China Sea, and proposed defence dialogues and exchanges, affirming that the Sino-Japanese relationship would advance mutually beneficial economic and strategic ties. These policies, along with Hatoyama's statements on the necessity to 'further enhance the mutually beneficial relationship with China based on common strategic interests',[5] were considered in Washington to be potentially destabilising to the security order based on US hegemony and the centrality of the US-led system of bilateral alliances.

The other crucial problem regarded US military bases in Japan. The Bush administration and the Japanese government had reached an agreement on a revision of the US presence in Japan in 2006, as part of a comprehensive posture review started in 2004.[6] The agreement foresaw the relocation of the Futenma Air Station to Henoko Bay, a less populated area of the Okinawa Prefecture. During his 2009 election campaign, Hatoyama promised the complete relocation of Futenma 'outside of Okinawa Prefecture at the very least'.[7] The Obama administration considered this a major violation of the agreement and a danger for the entire process of the posture review. However, the DPJ made another move that signalled its will to contest established relations and practices in the alliance. In 2009, the Japanese cabinet discussed the idea of calling the US to renounce the policy of first use of nuclear weapons in the event of conflict. This exposed a major disagreement on the centrality of the US nuclear umbrella in East Asia and beyond.[8]

All these policies received a negative response from Washington. Almost for the first since the 1950s, the United States faced a political leadership different from the LDP, which secured a strong majority in the Japanese Diet that appeared willing to reorient the nation's foreign policy. The Obama administration and wider US foreign policy community perceived DPJ policies not as a legitimate reorientation of an allied country priority, but rather as a threat to the foundations of the alliance and consequently to the entire US strategic position in East Asia.[9] The Obama administration's response was to nudge, and if necessary coerce, Japan into adopting a foreign policy aligned with Washington's interests.[10]

Hatoyama resigned in June 2010, nine months after his election. Resistance from the United States over his attempts to reorient Japanese foreign policy was by no means the only cause of his resignation. Disagreements with coalition partners, opposition from the Japanese establishment and the powerful state bureaucracy, and a corruption scandal, all played important roles. However, the Obama administration had demonstrated its disdain for Japan's new course, assuming an uncompromising stance on all the main issues under bilateral negotiation, starting with the relocation of bases in Okinawa. Thus, what McCormack defined as a new 'Battle for Okinawa' played a crucial part in the demise of the Hatoyama government.[11]

Hatoyama's resignation made several realities of US–Japan relations more evident. First, the Obama administration, in continuity with the bipartisan consensus that has characterised US East Asia policy in the post-war period, openly favoured conservative over progressive forces, to the point of questioning their foreign policy credentials and legitimacy. Second, the Obama administration considered Japan's attempt to rebalance its foreign policy towards Asia and China, and to achieve a degree of diplomatic autonomy from Washington, a serious threat to regional American interests. Finally, Obama reminded Japan that, as theorised by Paul Schroeder, alliances are 'tools of management', namely instruments of influence on allies' foreign policy.[12] On this occasion, the United States demonstrated its capacity and will to derail Japanese attempts to promote significant changes in the country's foreign policy orientation.

Tomodachi and the "return to normal"

Hatoyama's resignation and the election of Naoto Kan at Kantei led to an improvement in the alliance. Reignited territorial disputes with China over the Senkaku/Diaoyu Islands led Tokyo to accelerate the return to an alliance-centred foreign policy. A clear sign of this change was the publication of the 2010 National Defense Program Guidelines, a strategic document that introduced the concept of 'dynamic deterrence' which significantly expanded the role of the Japanese armed forces beyond the traditional 'defensive defense'.[13] The document also stressed the strategic value of Japan's anti-submarine warfare capabilities, and the joint US–Japanese Ballistic defence system.[14]

Japan was already returning to an alliance-centred defence policy when it was hit by the earthquake, tsunami and nuclear crisis of 11 March 2011 (3–11 crisis). Aside from the massive human and social damage this triple disaster caused, it had notable political consequences. First, it continued to undermine public confidence in the DPJ government. Second, it contributed to improve the image both of the Japanese Self Defense Forces (JSDF) and US forces in Japan; Operation Tomodachi oversaw unprecedented logistical coordination and integration between American and Japanese forces to help victims, demonstrating to the Japanese public the utility of military cooperation with American forces in the country. US forces in Japan, along with the broader alliance, enjoyed unprecedented approval among the Japanese public.[15] As importantly, members of the JSDF were celebrated as heroes by the Japanese media, arguably for the first time in the entire post-war period. This opened a window of opportunity. For instance, one of the effects of the response to the 3–11 crisis was public acceptance of the dispatch of the JSDF abroad in peacekeeping missions, and the approval of measures aimed at improving interoperability and coordination with US forces.

The prime ministership of Yoshihiko Noda, who succeeded Naoto Kan in September 2011, led to several areas of progress for the US–Japan relationship, such as the decision by Tokyo to purchase the American F-35 fighter jet and to enter discussions for the Trans-Pacific Partnership (TPP).[16] Over the longer period, the legacy of 3–11 and Tomodachi has been palpable, paving the way for a return to power of Shinzo Abe who promoted a narrative of recovery from crisis and national rebirth, together with a return to a foreign policy centred on the US alliance and "special relationship" with Washington.

Obama, Abe and the Pivot to Asia

Abe and the alliance

The election of Shinzo Abe as Japanese Prime Minster in December 2012 instigated a fundamental change in the relationship between the Obama administration and Japan. Abe's vision of national recovery largely coincided with the agenda and the strategic priorities of the Pivot, both in the security and economic realms.

The authors of the Pivot envisaged an expansion of the Japanese security role and a further strengthening of the alliance. On this point, the Pivot did not entail fundamental departures from previous strategies, since the United States had been pressuring Tokyo to "do more" since the early 1950s. The difference was found in the speed and extent of the changes. Abe actively embraced the role of democratic security provider which the Pivot envisaged for Japan, promoting reforms that would enable such an outcome as well as fundamental progresses for the alliance. Indeed, Abe presided over five particular reforms towards the expansion of Japanese security involvement: the creation of a National Security Council, modelled on the American example; the approval of a state secrecy law which allowed enhanced intelligence-sharing with the United States and other friendly countries; the reform of arms export principles that allowed Japan to jointly develop weapon systems with the United States and allies; and the release of the first ever National Security Strategy for Japan.

The most consequential step for the alliance, however, was the re-interpretation of Article 9 of the Constitution which allows Japan to perform "collective self-defence". This interpretation allows Japan to use force not only to defend its territory, but also 'when an armed attack against a foreign country that is in a close relationship with Japan occurs and as a result threatens Japan's survival'.[17] This allows Japan, for example, to protect US forces deployed in East Asia, to intercept missiles directed at the United States, and to expand its role in exercising deterrence autonomously and jointly with the United States towards both China and North Korea.[18] Moreover, the new interpretation allows Japan to jointly exercise deterrence in so-called "grey zone scenarios", namely, situations in which adversaries promote coercion and changes to the status quo, without reaching the threshold of an open conflict.[19]

Overall, these reforms paved the way for the approval of the 2015 Guidelines for the Alliance, which define the division of roles and duties in the bilateral relationship.[20] Previously, they have been modified only twice, in 1978 and 1997. The new guidelines clearly demonstrate both a renewed convergence of strategic interests and the will to reach higher levels of interoperability, intelligence-sharing and coordination. The most important concept they articulate is the idea of "seamless cooperation"; while traditionally the alliance was supposed to work only in case of attack against Japan, the new document announces cooperation in peacetime as well as in "grey zone contingencies" such as in the East and South China Seas where China aims to disrupt the status quo with coercive and hybrid measures short of outright conflict. To deal more effectively with this new type of challenge, the guidelines introduce new coordination mechanisms in the realms of intelligence, surveillance and reconnaissance; missile defence; joint maritime patrolling; outer space and cyberspace; and joint training.[21]

The renewal of the alliance and progresses in the security sphere, however, were unable to prevent disagreement between the Obama administration and the Japanese foreign policy establishment, not least regarding US policy towards China and North Korea. A key moment came in 2013 when senior White House officials, including former National Security Advisors Tom Donilon and Susan Rice, endorsed the Chinese concept of "new type of great power relations", implying the recognition of China's core interests.[22] From a Japanese standpoint that concept entailed the possibility that the United States could sacrifice Tokyo's security interests to achieve a long-term security bargain with Beijing. The Obama administration later dropped all references to the idea, but Donilon and in particular Rice gained the nickname of "Kissingerians", which carries negative connotations in Japan.[23]

The second significant point of disagreement came with Washington's "strategic patience" towards North Korea. This has been judged as weak and ineffective in the Japanese foreign policy community, since it proved ineffective in forcing Pyongyang to stop or even limit its nuclear programme. As with the Obama administration's policies towards China, Susan Rice – who admitted that both Washington and Tokyo need to 'learn to live with a nuclear North Korea'[24] – attracted the focus of Japanese criticism.

TPP and the economics of Obama's Pivot to Asia

The economic dimension of the Pivot, including the promotion of the TPP, represents a key element of discontinuity with previous US strategies towards Japan and East Asia, together with the comprehensive engagement of East Asian multilateral institutions. Such promoters of the Pivot as Assistant Secretary of State for East

Asian and Pacific Affairs Kurt Campbell, his successor Daniel Russell, and Director for Asian Affairs in the National Security Council Evan Medeiros, understood that Washington faced a major strategic problem in Asia, namely, the increasing divergence between US security and economic relations in Asia.[25] In the security realm, the United States remained the "indispensable nation" in East Asia. Yet the rise of China had revolutionised the economic realities of the region, with all of Washington's main regional allies increasingly dependent on China for trade and investment. Moreover, since the arrival of Chinese President Xi Jinping, Beijing has promoted a comprehensive blueprint of economic governance in Asia, based on Chinese leadership, values and rules. The most evident manifestations of this Chinese attempt to build alternative forms of economic governance have been the promotion of the Belt and Road Initiative (BRI) and the Asian Infrastructure Investment Bank (AIIB).

Overall, at least since the beginning of Obama's second term, it appeared clear that the Asian region was facing a competition between two models of economic governance: a Sino-centric model, rooted in Beijing's leadership and hospitable to state capitalist practices, and a trans-Pacific model based on renewed leadership by Washington and advanced via free market capitalism.[26] Here, the fundamental differences are in respective norms and principles. China promotes a state capitalist form of economic integration in which its state-owned enterprises play a key role. The TPP promoted a so-called "gold standard" level of regulation which set a high bar of economic practice, and severely limited the influence of these enterprises (and of the Chinese government) from participating member states. The Abe government, in deciding to participate in the TPP, made a clear strategic choice to re-align Japan's security interests with its economic policies; Japan needed to side with the United States to promote the trans-Pacific model of regional governance, and oppose the rise of a Sino-centric economic order. This in turn revealed two strategic assumptions. First, Japan considered the United States able and willing to continue to shape the regional order in East Asia in the foreseeable future. Second, Japan's best interests were understood to be in resisting, rather than participating in, Chinese initiatives such as the AIIB and BRI.

The fact that these assumptions were considered relatively uncontroversial in Japan, at least up to the 2016 elections, makes the legacy of the Pivot and Obama–Abe cooperation evident. The Pivot prescribed for Japan an active role both as security partner and active promoter of a trans-Pacific, free market-oriented, form of regional economic order. Abe embraced this twin role, considering it essential both to the Japanese economic revival and achievement of the status of "first tier nation" in Asia and beyond.[27]

Hiroshima, Pearl Harbor and the "end of the post war"

The final months of the Obama administration were defined by the president's will to leave a meaningful legacy in the realm of historical reconciliation with Japan, embodied by his visits to Hiroshima and by Abe's visit to Pearl Harbor in 2016. Both leaders considered these visits instrumental to the consolidation of their legacies, albeit in very different ways. For Obama, the Hiroshima visit represented an ideal end point to a path mapped out in the Prague speech of 2009, where Obama envisioned a world characterised by successes in nuclear non-proliferation and international arms control; the creation of the global Nuclear Security Summit; the Iran nuclear deal; and the START ("Strategic Arms Reduction") Treaty with Russia. Moreover, Obama used his speech in Hiroshima to articulate a vision of American exceptionalism. Inspired by the concept of "Christian realism", Obama reasserted the moral and ethical value of US global leadership as well as the need to oppose, even by force, authoritarianism and tyranny in the promotion of peace and freedom.[28]

Obama's aims were also practical. Promoting historical reconciliation with Tokyo meant laying the groundwork for further consolidation of the US–Japan alliance, as well as providing an example for other Asian states such as South Korea and the Philippines. Such partners still limit their cooperation with Japan from disagreements over their warring past and perceptions that Japan has failed to adequately apologise for crimes committed during the Second World War. From the American perspective therefore, historical reconciliation is aimed at promoting the multilateralisation of the San Francisco system, complementing bilateral alliances with new forms of cooperation, and connecting different Asian allies of the United States.[29]

From Abe's perspective, the visits to Hiroshima and Pearl Harbor spoke to another long-standing symbolic objective: the end of "the post war" as the period in which Japan needed to apologise for its wartime behaviour, accept legal constraints such as Article 9 of its Constitution, and limit its role in the regional security order.[30] In practical terms, this would allow Japan to finally and legitimately embrace a role of active regional security provider and even assert its status as "first tier nation" in Asia.[31]

Ultimately, and in stark contrast to their predecessors, as well as to the Trump administration from 2017, Obama and Abe conceived the development of the US–Japan relationship within a comprehensive strategic vision, including the use of different instruments of economic, political and security statecraft to shape the contours of the rise of China and uphold the regional order. The election of Donald Trump, and Washington's decision to leave the TPP in 2017, put Japan into a difficult position by throwing into question its ability to rely upon an American-led rules-based international order.

Japan and Trump: The age of uncertainty

The election to president of Donald Trump in November 2016 introduced uncertainties over the future direction and progress of results achieved by the Obama administration with Japan, as well as over the broader aims of the overarching Pivot to Asia. It is however important to differentiate between the security realm (and the bilateral alliance in particular), and other dimensions of US–Japan relations.

Trump's rhetoric during his election campaign greatly alarmed the Japanese leadership. In April 2016 Trump stated that Tokyo needed to defend itself against North Korea, even suggesting that it should acquire nuclear weapons.[32] Prime Minister Abe, sensing the risks the Trump administration could comport, quickly sought to establish a productive personal relationship with the new president. Abe was the first foreign leader to visit Trump Tower following the late 2016 elections, and the meeting of the two leaders at the Mar-a-Lago resort in February 2017 was one of the first high-profile summits hosted by the new administration. On both occasions, Trump and Abe restated the centrality of the alliance for peace and stability in East Asia. Trump's state visit to Japan in November 2017, together with high-profile visits by Vice President Mike Pence (April 2017, February 2018), Secretary of Defense James Mattis (February 2017) and Secretary of State Rex Tillerson (March 2018), helped reaffirm the US commitment to the region and reassure Japan of the strength of the relationship.

Three other factors momentarily diminished fears of early strategic abandonment by Washington during the first twelve months of the Trump administration. First, many in the Japanese foreign and security policy community appreciated an uncompromising US position on North Korea in the 'fire and fury' period in 2017.[33] This position was often compared with Obama-era statements by Susan Rice on the impossibility of stopping Pyongyang's nuclear programme. Second, Trump's public endorsement of Tokyo's position on Japanese citizens abducted by North Korea was interpreted as another positive signal in this direction.[34] Third, despite Trump's volatile crisis management tactics, most Japanese officials seemed to trust the so-called "adults in the room", particularly such senior cabinet officials as National Security Advisor H. R. McMaster, Secretary of State Rex Tillerson, and Secretary of Defense James Mattis. During the first twelve months of the Trump presidency, a number of scholars were ready to characterise US–Japan relations as returning to "normality" after an initially difficult period.[35] Subsequent events testified how those analyses were, arguably, overly optimistic.

A series of policy choices made by Trump created serious anxieties in Tokyo. In 2018, the Trump administration reversed its previous approach towards North Korea, abandoning the policy of maximum pressure to promote a new period of dialogue, culminating with the summits of Singapore in June 2018 and Hanoi in February 2019. Japan sought to maximise policy coordination on North Korea, and it officially expressed its support for the negotiations. Nevertheless, a number of developments seriously concerned Tokyo. Trump's stated intention of 'ending the wargames with South Korea',[36] as well as his failure to mention the issue of Japanese abductees during the Singapore summit, created doubts over Trump's long-term commitment to US alliances in East Asia. Trump's failure, up to early

2019, to achieve any progress towards the denuclearisation of North Korea, and the subsequent failure of the Hanoi summit, also generated fears in Tokyo of a new cycle of provocation by Kim Jong-un's regime. Moreover, two years after Trump's inauguration, the "adults in the room" had either resigned or were dismissed by the president. The most significant departure in this sense was that of Secretary of Defense Mattis, considered a key guardian of the US security strategy in East Asia.[37]

Overall, the Japanese government remains wary of the Trump administration, not merely in terms of its management of the alliance, but also its willingness and capacity to uphold the current international order and its key pillars, from nuclear non-proliferation to free trade and beyond. These fears were confirmed by the withdrawal from several significant agreements in different policy realms, such as the Paris agreement on climate change, the Joint Comprehensive Plan of Action with Iran, the Intermediate Range Nuclear Forces Treaty, and the TPP. The Trump administration also issued tariffs against China and threatened trade restrictions against Japan, South Korea and others. A good indicator of the Japanese mood at around the halfway point of the 2017–21 Trump presidency is found in the document, 'Towards a Greater Alliance', promoted by a non-partisan commission of policy experts and scholars. The document defines Trump's approach to foreign policy as 'the injection of the highest level of uncertainty to be seen in the world order since the end of the Cold War'.[38]

Across the first two years of the Trump administration, the Abe government reacted to the uncertainty it has generated, and the perceived decline of regional US influence, by advancing three main policy strategies. First, in the security realm, Tokyo promoted the idea of a 'free and open Indo-Pacific', which entailed the expansion of security cooperation between major democracies including India and Australia.[39] This proposal envisages both an American presence and the development of a network of security relations aimed at balancing the rise of China. Further, it underlined the fundamental political and ideological fault lines dividing China from the United States and its allies and partners.[40] This idea gained considerable traction in Washington. Trump, as well as senior members of the administration, quickly began referring to the Indo-Pacific with increasing frequency.[41] From a Japanese perspective this represented a significant success, testifying that Tokyo can effectively exercise the role of thought leader in a moment of US retreat.

Second, something similar happened with the negotiations among the eleven remaining signatories to the TPP. Japan led the negotiations aimed at approving the new version of the agreement, now renamed the Comprehensive and Progressive Agreement for the Trans-Pacific Partnership.[42] The Japanese initiative was motivated by the will to uphold high standards in trade as a key component of the current international order, while shaping the contours of China's rise and limiting its economic and normative influence in the region.[43] Ultimately, however, the Japanese government also assumes that the current protectionist trend in Washington will not endure in the longer term, and that the policies of the Trump administration on trade are likely to be reversed by the administration which follows.[44]

The third line of action regards the bilateral relationship with China. The perceived decline of American influence in the region, the possible escalation of trade wars generated by Trump's protectionist policies, and, above all, the intensification of geopolitical competition between Washington and Beijing, have considerably affected Sino-Japanese relations. As Funabashi and Dempsey recently put it, 'Tokyo has begun serious contemplation of a clean-slate foreign policy absent US primacy. In the case of a recalibration like this, no relationship would be more important to stabilise than that with China.'[45] As a consequence, Abe sought to diminish the tension with Beijing. After June 2017, Abe became open to a Japanese cooperation within the framework of the BRI. In October 2018, on the fortieth anniversary of the Treaty of Peace and Friendship with China, Abe visited Beijing for a summit meeting. Abe's accommodating stance reflected the need to stabilise the relationship with China and the necessity to defuse tensions in the realm of security and uphold the basic foundations of the regional economic order, to reduce the consequences of the instability generated by Trump's policies.[46]

Ultimately, however, the Abe government had up to early 2019 been very aware of the indispensability of the United States. As a consequence, Abe himself appeared ready to ignore even very relevant disagreements, such as those on the TPP and trade policies, to help preserve the overall relationship. Moreover, during the first two years of the Trump presidency the Abe government further intensified its international role, being active both in terms of security relations and economic governance, to try to fill the vacuum generated by the perceived decline of US influence and leadership. Nevertheless, as evidenced by the more accommodating policies towards Beijing, the perceived unreliability of the United States undermined Tokyo's position vis-à-vis China, making any resistance to Beijing's attempts to contest the current rule-based order more difficult.

Conclusion

Obama's legacy on US–Japan relations is a complex one. Many accounts of the relationship in the Obama period tend to overlook the fact that the administration navigated through one of the most severe bilateral crises of the post-war period, during the Hatoyama premiership. The Obama White House demonstrated the extent to which the United States can exercise strong political and diplomatic pressures to avoid unwanted foreign policy changes in Japan. The quick demise of Hatoyama, the aftermath of the 3–11 crisis, the return of the LDP as well as Abe's strong leadership, paved the way for a much more cooperative period.

Between 2012 and 2016 the relationship arguably reached a historical peak in terms of strategic coordination. Despite differences in values, for both leaders the relationship was part of a broader strategy encompassing security, economic and symbolic dimensions. Washington and Tokyo jointly worked to consolidate a trans-Pacific regional order, rooted in an enduring US power and will to provide stability and security as well as a renewed capacity to enforce rules and norms of economic governance. In this order, Japan represented the fundamental ally, both in the exercise of deterrence towards main security threats and in supporting such trans-Pacific forms of economic regionalism as the TPP.

Overall, the Obama era cannot be considered an exception in the history of post-war US–Japan relations. Like previous eras, it included moments of intense friction, especially during the first twelve months, as well as episodes of solidarity, not least after 11 March 2011. Only the period between 2013 and 2016 can be considered somehow exceptional. The two countries actively worked together to make progress in terms of security, economic governance, and around historical reconciliation. This level of comprehensive coordination appears rather rare in the history of a bilateral relationship that has been often affected by frictions either in the economic or in the security realm.

Two years on from Donald Trump's inauguration as president in 2017, the landscape of US–Japan relations had changed markedly. The bilateral relationship survived and adapted to a rapidly evolving East Asian security environment. Nevertheless, Japan remained deeply troubled by Trump's policies towards North Korea, by the trade disputes with China, and by mounting geopolitical competition in the region. Tokyo also remained concerned about his administration's will to uphold key pillars of the current international order, in particular over nuclear proliferation, multilateralism, and free trade. The Abe government, meanwhile, showed itself determined to endure even significant setbacks in the relationship, to preserve the alliance and the rules-based order in Asia. So too did it seek to compensate for a leadership vacuum quickly generated by Trump. With a longer-term view, Tokyo seemed aware that any the alternatives to US leadership would lead to an unwelcome rise of the Chinese influence.

In modern history, Trump's position up to early 2019 seemed unprecedented. Japan navigated its way through intense trade disputes during the Reagan (1981–89) and Bush (1989–93) administrations, as well as periods of strategic uncertainty during the Nixon (1969–74) and first Clinton (1993–97) administrations. What made the situation under Trump different is, first, the magnitude of the challenge posed by China. Unlike in previous eras, twenty-first-century China has ample resources to reshape Japan's surrounding political-economic-security environment in its favour. Second, no administration before Trump ever seriously questioned the basic tenets of American grand strategy in East Asia, or cast the strategic value of security alliances or Washington's commitment to uphold the regional order into doubt. Ultimately, the Trump administration has to this point not just actively worked to tarnish some of the most significant accomplishments of Obama and the Pivot to Asia, it has also threatened the stability of the United States' long-standing hegemonic role throughout the Asia Pacific region.

Notes

1 M. Green and N. Szechenyi, 'US-Japan relations: A fresh start', *Comparative Connections*, 11:1 (2009), pp. 1–9.

2 M. Green, *By More Than Providence: Grand Strategy and American Power in the Asia Pacific Since 1783* (New York: Columbia University Press, 2017); M. Dian, *The Evolution of the US-Japan Alliance: The Eagle and the Chrysanthemum* (Oxford: Chandos Publishing, 2014).

3 Y. Hatoyama, 'In Hatoyama's "Fraternity", People the End, not Means', *Japan Times* (9 September 2009), www.japantimes.co.jp/opinion/2009/09/09/commentary/world-commentary/in-hatoyamas-fraternity-people-the-end-not-means/#.XITnIij7TZs, accessed 9 March 2019.

4 Y. Hatoyama, 'A New Path for Japan', *New York Times* (27 August 2009), www.nytimes.com/2009/08/27/opinion/27iht-edhatoyama.html, accessed 9 March 2019.

5 Japanese Office of the Prime Minister, 'Policy Speech by Prime Minister Yukio Hatoyama at the 174th Session of the Diet' (29 January 2010), https://japan.kantei.go.jp/hatoyama/statement/201001/29siseihousin_e.html, accessed 10 March 2019.

6 US Department of Defense, 'Strengthening US Global Defense Posture' (September 2004), www.dmzhawaii.org/wp-content/uploads/2008/12/global_posture.pdf, accessed 10 March 2019.

7 Japanese Office of the Prime Minister, 'Press Conference by Prime Minister Yukio Hatoyama' (28 May 2010), https://japan.kantei.go.jp/hatoyama/statement/201005/28kaiken_e.html, accessed 10 March 2019.

8 J. A. Bader, *Obama and China's Rise: An Insider's Account of America's Asia Strategy* (Washington, DC: Brookings Institution Press, 2012), p. 43.

9 L. E. Easley, T. Kotani and A. Mori, 'Electing a new Japanese security policy? Examining foreign policy visions within the Democratic Party of Japan', *Asia Policy*, 9:1 (2010), pp. 45–66; M. Green, 'Japan's confused revolution', *Washington Quarterly*, 33:1 (2010), pp. 3–19.

10 C. Hughes, 'The democratic party of Japan's new (but failing) grand security strategy: From "reluctant realism" to "resentful realism"?', *The Journal of Japanese Studies*, 38:1 (2012), pp. 109–40.

11 G. McCormack, 'The battle of Okinawa 2009: Obama vs Hatoyama', *Japan Focus*, 46:1 (2009), pp. 1–16.

12 P. Schroeder, 'Alliances, 1815–1945: Weapons of power and tools of management', in K. Knorr (ed.), *Historical Dimensions of National Security Problems* (Westbrook, KS: University Press of Kansas, 1976), pp. 227–62.

13 The term 'defensive defense', according to Article 9 of the Japanese Constitution adopted in 1955 and 1968, refers to the Japanese Self Defense Forces being authorised to use force only to repel an armed invasion against the national territory.

14 Japanese Ministry of Defense, 'National Defense Program Guidelines for FY 2011 and Beyond', www.mod.go.jp/e/d_act/d_policy/pdf/guidelinesFY2011.pdf, accessed 10 March 2019.

15 R. Samuels, *3.11: Disaster and Change in Japan* (Ithaca: Cornell University Press, 2013).

16 M. Green and N. Szechenyi, 'US-Japan relations: Back to normal?', *Comparative Connections*, 14:1 (2012), pp. 1–10.

17 Japanese Ministry of Foreign Affairs, 'Cabinet Decision on Development of Seamless Security Legislation to Ensure Japan's Survival and Protect its People' (1 July 2014), www.mofa.go.jp/fp/nsp/page23e_000273.html, accessed 10 March 2019.

18 A. Fujishige, 'New Japan Self-Defense Force Missions Under the "Proactive Contribution to Peace" Policy: Significance of the 2015 Legislation for Peace and Security', Center for Strategic and International Studies (21 July 2016), www. csis.org/analysis/new-japan-self-defense-force-missions-under-"proactive-contribution-peace"-policy, accessed 10 March 2019.

19 C. Hughes, *Japan's Foreign and Security Policy Under the 'Abe Doctrine': New Dynamism or New Dead End?* (Basingstoke: Palgrave Macmillan, 2015).

20 Japanese Ministry of Foreign Affairs, 'The Guidelines for Japan-US Defense Cooperation' (27 April 2015), www.mofa.go.jp/files/000078188.pdf, accessed 10 March 2019.

21 *Ibid.*

22 T. Donilon, 'The United States and the Asia-Pacific in 2013', Asia Society (11 March 2013), https://asiasociety.org/new-york/complete-transcript-thomas-donilon-asia-society-new-york, accessed 10 March 2019; White House, 'Remarks as Prepared for Delivery by National Security Advisor Susan E. Rice' (21 November 2013), https://obamawhitehouse.archives.gov/the-press-office/2013/11/21/remarks-prepared-delivery-national-security-advisor-susan-e-rice, accessed 11 March 2019.

23 In Japan, Henry Kissinger is synonymous with the "Nixon Shock" of 1972 when the United States under President Richard Nixon re-established diplomatic ties with China without consultation with Japanese officials.

24 Y. Funabashi, 'Obama's Costly Legacy-Building', *The Japan Times* (9 October 2016), www.japantimes.co.jp/opinion/2016/10/09/commentary/japan-commentary/obamas-costly-legacy-building, accessed 10 March 2019.

25 K. Campbell, *The Pivot: The Future of American Statecraft in Asia* (New York: Twelve, 2016).

26 M. Dian, 'The strategic value of the Trans-Pacific Partnership and the consequences of abandoning it for the US role in Asia', *International Politics*, 54:5 (2017), pp. 583–97.

27   The notion of Japan as a first-tier nation comes from R. Armitage and J. Nye, *The US-Japan Alliance: Anchoring Stability in Asia* (Washington, DC: CSIS, 2012). The idea was employed in the "Abe Manifesto" of 2013. See Ministry of Foreign Affairs of Japan, 'Japan is Back' (22 February 2013), www.mofa.go.jp/announce/pm/abe/us_20130222en.html, accessed 10 March 2019.

28   D. Brooks, 'Obama's Christian Realism', *New York Times* (15 December 2009), www.nytimes.com/2009/12/15/opinion/15brooks.html, accessed 10 March 2019.

29   G. Harris, 'In Obama's Visit to Hiroshima, a Complex Calculus of Asian Politics', *New York Times* (5 May 2016), www.nytimes.com/2016/05/26/world/asia/obama-hiroshima-visit.html, accessed 10 March 2019.

30   Hughes, *Japan's Foreign and Security Policy.*

31   M. Dian, *Contested Memories in Chinese and Japanese Foreign Policy* (Oxford: Elsevier, 2017).

32   CNN, 'Full Rush Transcript: Donald Trump, CNN Milwaukee Republican Presidential Town Hall' (29 March 2016), http://cnnpressroom.blogs.cnn.com/2016/03/29/full-rush-transcript-donald-trump-cnn-milwaukee-republican-presidential-town-hall/, accessed 10 March 2019.

33   M. Dian, 'Trump's mixed signals toward North Korea and US-led alliances in East Asia', *The International Spectator*, 53:4 (2018), pp. 1–17.

34   Tokyo currently demands that North Korea return all Japanese citizens abducted between the 1970s and 1980s. Any diplomatic progress with Pyongyang is subordinated to the resolution of this issue.

35   J. Lind, 'The Art of the Bluff: The US-Japan Alliance under the Trump Administration', *Diplomatic History*, ISSF Policy Series (24 April 2017), https://issforum.org/roundtables/policy/1-5af-japan, accessed 10 March 2019.

36   During a press conference following the Singapore summit, Trump described US-ROK military exercises as 'war games' and 'provocative', mirroring the long-standing North Korean insistence that the US–ROK alliance is 'provocative and destabilizing'. See *New York Times*, '6 Highlights from Trump's News Conference, with a Full Transcript' (12 June 2018), www.nytimes.com/2018/06/12/world/asia/trump-summit-transcript.html, accessed 10 March 2019.

37   *Japan Times*, 'Trump Loses a Guardrail' (25 December 2018), www.japantimes.co.jp/opinion/2018/12/25/editorials/trump-loses-guardrail/, accessed 10 March 2019.

38   Mount Fuji Dialogue, 'Towards a Greater Alliance: A Policy Proposal of the Mt. Fuji Dialogue Special Task Force' (April 2017), www.jcer.or.jp/eng/pdf/Mt.FUJI_DIALOGUE20170405report_e.pdf, accessed 10 March 2019.

39   Japanese Ministry of Foreign Affairs, 'Priority Policy for Development Cooperation FY2017' (April 2017), www.mofa.go.jp/files/000259285.pdf, accessed 10 March 2019.

40   Y. Hosoya, 'The rise and fall of Japan's grand strategy: The "arc of freedom and prosperity" and the future Asian order', *Asia-Pacific Review*, 18:1 (2010), pp. 13–24.

41 Demetri Sevastopulo, 'Trump Gives a Glimpse of Indo Pacific Strategy to Counter China', *Financial Times* (10 November 2017), www.ft.com/content/e6d17fd6-c623-11e7-a1d2-6786f39ef675, accessed 10 March 2019.

42 *Japan Times*, '11 States, Minus US, Sign TPP in Free-Trade Push in Face of Protectionist Trump' (9 March 2018), www.japantimes.co.jp/news/2018/03/09/business/11-states-minus-u-s-sign-tpp-free-trade-push-face-protectionist-trump, accessed 10 March 2019.

43 M. Solìs and J. Mason, 'As the TPP Lives On, The US Abdicates Trade Leadership', The Brookings Institution (9 March 2018), www.brookings.edu/blog/order-from-chaos/2018/03/09/as-the-tpp-lives-on-the-u-s-abdicates-trade-leadership, accessed 10 March 2019.

44 N. Smith, 'Will Trump Rejoin the Trans-Pacific Partnership? Let's Hope So', *Japan Times*, www.japantimes.co.jp/opinion/2018/03/06/commentary/world-commentary/will-trump-rejoin-trans-pacific-partnership-lets-hope/, accessed 10 March 2019.

45 Y. Funabashi and H. Dempsey, 'Trump Threat Drives China and Japan Closer', East Asia Forum, www.eastasiaforum.org/2017/07/09/trump-threat-drives-japan-and-china-closer/, accessed 9 July 2017

46 J. Pollack, 'Abe in Beijing: The Quiet Accommodation in China-Japan Relations', The Brookings Institution (25 October 2018), www.brookings.edu/blog/order-from-chaos/2018/10/25/abe-in-beijing-the-quiet-accommodation-in-china-japan-relations/, accessed 10 March 2019.

5

Obama, Trump and North Korea

Bruce Cumings

Introduction

President Barack Obama's historic "Pivot" to Asia, formally announced in late 2011, would come to have little appreciable effect on US policy towards the Democratic People's Republic of Korea (DPRK), other than a dramatic uptick in Kim Jong-un's nuclear weapons development programme. Obama's "strategic patience" towards Pyongyang failed to halt or slow its development of weapons of mass destruction, but it did manage to initiate greater levels of Sino-US cooperation over sanctioning the regime, the introduction of more US resources and weapons to the region (of which China disapproved), and helped tighten the security relationship between the Republic of South Korea (ROK) and Japan. Frustrations in Washington over North Korea intensified towards the end of Obama's second administration as bipartisan support for a more assertive or aggressive policy grew. Obama therefore set the stage for a more aggressive American stance for his successor to the White House, yet no one anticipated the intensity of the rhetoric which President Donald Trump would employ as he threatened 'fire and fury' and total annihilation on the tiny Asian state. Historic summits with Kim Jong-un in late 2018 and early 2019 brought some hopes of a potential for the denuclearisation of the Korean Peninsula, but familiar underlying patterns in the relationship endured.

North Korea in Obama's Pacific Century

President Barack Obama's initial stance towards North Korea can at least partly be inferred from his inaugural address in January 2009. 'To those who cling to power through corruption and deceit and the silencing of dissent,' he asserted, 'know that you are on the wrong side of history, but that we will extend a hand if you are willing to unclench your fist.'[1] The North Koreans proceeded to fire off a long-range missile in April 2009, and test an atomic bomb on American Memorial Day in May. On 4 July, they tested seven short and medium range missiles. These provocative actions put North Korea on Obama's back-burner for most of his first term, and he instead reached out to other former enemies or pariah states which he felt might be more receptive to overture, including Cuba, Iran, Burma and even Laos.

One might have thought North Korea would have been a bigger concern because it was the most dangerous actor in the region Obama had quickly come to identify as his foreign policy priority, namely the Asia Pacific. Obama's Pivot promoted a series of defence policy moves which, at the time, appeared to foreshadow the most significant transformation of the United States' global military position since the end of the Cold War and the collapse of the Soviet Union. The shift began with Secretary of State Hillary Clinton's declaration of America's 'Pacific Century'. Clinton announced a shift away from the wars in Iraq and Afghanistan and 'a strategic turn' towards the Asia Pacific, a region now said to be 'the key driver of global politics' where nearly half the world's population lives, and where 'key engines' of the world economy reside. The security of those engines, she noted, 'has long been guaranteed by the US military', and their region would be more important and more central to American interests than any other for the remainder of the century.[2]

Meanwhile, Obama's Defense Secretary Leon Panetta expressed preference that the United States voluntarily relinquish the ability to fight large wars along both the central front in Europe and in East Asia. This "two war" posture had defined Pentagon strategy for the past six decades. He also indicated that the defence triad of air, naval and land forces was outmoded.[3] The seemingly endless European crisis over national debt in Greece, Portugal and Spain, with the future of the euro and the European Union itself hanging in the balance, added its own punctuation to the apparent eclipse of Europe and the dawn of a new Pacific era. Still, it may just have been that Panetta had run some new ideas up the flagpole to see what would happen; the Pentagon later appeared to retreat from giving up the two-war strategy and the triad.[4]

The Obama administration was the first since the Cold War ended to pay little or no attention to nuclear-armed North Korea. This was perhaps guided by Colin Powell's warning to Pyongyang that 'you can't eat plutonium. You can't eat enriched uranium', and that those who could help feed poverty-stricken North Korea would not do so until it ceased its development of nuclear weapons.[5] But the White House paid particularly close attention to easing strains both with Tokyo over US bases in Okinawa (which brought down the Hatoyama cabinet in 2010), and with Seoul over changes to the US defence posture in Korea. Indeed, US–South Korea relations had been at an all-time low from 2002 to 2007, with George W. Bush and President Roh Moo Hyun barely on speaking terms throughout that period. More broadly, along a great crescent from Rangoon to Darwin to Manila to Seoul to Tokyo, diplomatic efforts were underway with the permanency of the US Pacific defence posture in mind. That posture, with its political-economic corollary, is now around seventy years old and has provided a remarkably durable regional order for the vast economic exchange taking place in recent decades. A key difference now was the remarkable emergence of China as a leading global actor, and a recognition that the significance of this issue had gone largely unaddressed during the Bush administration.

Obama meets regional historical legacies

For his East Asia policy, Obama from the beginning relied on battle-tested, tried-and-true insiders (that is, inside the Beltway) who typically move in a lockstep, bipartisan fashion – regardless of which president or party happens to be in office – towards their desired policies. Hillary Clinton was the perfect Secretary of State for such people, as a quintessential product of the Beltway herself, beginning with her Watergate investigation days in the early 1970s. And on his arrival to the White House in 2009, Obama found a big problem, a smaller problem, and a clear remedy.

The big problem was the physical rise of China, which needed somehow to be contained, while not disrupting global economic exchange. The remedy was to get Japan and South Korea working together under the umbrella of the American alliance. The smaller problem, however, was that Seoul had been through a fit of "anti-Americanism" as Beltway denizens saw it, under Presidents Kim Dae-jung (1998–2003) and, especially, Roh Moo-hyun (2003–8). Fortune eventually smiled in the form of President Lee Myung-bak (2008–13), a former Hyundai executive who harked back to the days of Korean–American amity when the dictators were in power (1948–87). Even better, they thought, was the subsequent election of Park Geun-hye, a daughter of one such former dictator, who stayed in power until 2017. Also in 2012, however, came Japanese Prime Minister Shinzo Abe yet again, and the best laid Beltway plans went awry.

Abe's grandfather, former Japanese Prime Minister Kishi Nobusuke, was in charge of munitions in Manchukuo when Kim Jong-un's grandfather, Kim Il-sung, was fighting the Japanese in the 1930s. Grandchild Kim and grandchild Abe were thus always likely on a collision course. The arrival of Park Geun-hye stirred the pot, since her father, Park Chung-hee, had been an officer in the Japanese Imperial Army, also in Manchukuo, and had colluded with Kishi in the still-controversial normalisation of Japan–South Korean relations in 1965. Standing behind all this was the United States, which, after momentarily designating Kishi a Class A war criminal and incarcerating him in Sugamo Prison, promoted him as an anti-communist and moderniser. The US Military Government in South Korea (1945–48) guided Manchukuo officer Park through its military academy in 1946, and supported him after he led a successful coup of the national government in 1961. The Americans then pushed hard for a normalisation of Japan–South Korea relations, but have never shown much regard for long-standing Korean hatreds and grievances arising from nearly four decades of Japan's colonial rule (1910–45). Instead, from the 1940s to the present, Americans have urged Koreans to unite under the fabled US–Japan alliance.

This and other important elements of twentieth-century history severely constrained President Park, as she sought to manoeuvre between a voting public that suspected she was pro-Japanese, and an Obama administration that wanted her to ally with Abe to help in the containment of China. But to all appearances Park hated Abe; for years she refused to consent to a summit with him in spite of sustained pressure from Washington and Tokyo to do so. Park denounced visits by Abe and his close aides to the Yasukuni Shrine and was particularly vociferous on the issue of Tokyo's continuing unwillingness to deal honestly with the legacy of its wartime sex slavery and the "comfort women" it abused, the vast majority of whom were Korean. So, while Park would talk to President Xi Jinping of China, and vice versa, she would not talk to Abe or Kim Jong-un. Xi would also not talk to Abe or Kim. That nobody at all talked to Kim was no doubt of great personal consternation.

A former Soviet official who had worked in North Korea once told me that you could try to direct, or cajole, or nudge the leadership in Pyongyang to do something which, to a foreigner, looked to be in their best interests. They would smile, seem to nod assent, or might even say yes. Then they would do the opposite, even when it directly contradicted their presumed interests. You could call it stubbornness or solipsism; they didn't care. But this dogged insistence on going their own way is as much a part of North Korea's historic behaviour pattern as it is a palpable obstacle to international cooperation today.

In March 2013, Obama responded to North Korean threats and intransigence with a US$1 billion acceleration of the American ballistic missile interceptor pro-gramme, adding fourteen new batteries in California and Alaska. (Such anti-missile forces were also recognised as useful against the type of antiquated Intercontinental Ballistic Missiles (ICBMs) held by China.) Later that month, Obama sent B-52 and B-1 Stealth strategic bombers over South Korea to drop dummy bombs. It was a needless and provocative move. In 1951 Washington initiated nuclear blackmail of the North when it launched B-29s on simulated Hiroshima–Nagasaki bombing missions. Operation Hudson Harbor sought to ascertain the feasibility of atomic weapon use on the battlefield, and B-29s were sent over North Korea on practice atomic runs, dropping dummy A-bombs or heavy TNT bombs.[6] Ever since, nuclear weapons have been part of American war planning against the North. They were not used during the Korean War because the US Air Force was able to raze every city in the North with conventional incendiaries. Few Americans are familiar with this horrific experience, but North Koreans are. It is little wonder, then, that some

15,000 underground facilities have been dug in the name of national security. In short, however provocative the North appears, the United States is reaping the whirlwind of historic nuclear bullying.

Failed talks and culture wars

In early 2012 Washington moved to revive local dialogue by tabling a package of proposals aimed at restarting the Six-Party Talks between the United States, the DPRK, South Korea, China, Japan and Russia. The talks had run intermittently from 2003 but collapsed in 2009 when the DPRK withdrew in protest of UN sanctions imposed by its April 2009 missile tests. The result was the so-called Leap Day Deal, signed in Pyongyang on 29 February 2012. The Deal would see food aid to North Korea in return for a moratorium on testing nuclear weapons or launching long-range missiles. Pyongyang claimed the agreement did not prevent it from launching satellites, which DPRK forces claimed they were attempting with the launch of a long-range rocket. Washington argued that this violated the agreement, and the Leap Day Deal was quickly rendered void.[7] The death of Kim Jong-il in December 2012, while the talks were in full swing, disrupted the course of discussion before Kim Jong-un could take his place. The United States, however, treated it as a direct stab in the back, ending any attempts at engagement, while the DPRK claimed it had informed the Americans of the coming launch.

While Obama had been quickly greeted with North Korean bomb and missile tests on entry into office, it was also China's turn to consider the knife sticking out of its own back. PRC forces saved North Korea from oblivion when they intervened in the Korean War in 1950 and has, certainly since the end of the Cold War, represented its closest (arguably only) ally. After the North's third nuclear test in February 2013, however, Beijing was openly critical of Pyongyang's actions and argued that they threatened world peace.[8] Relations between the two countries became unprecedentedly cold. Xi met several times with South Korean President Park, and on the eve of Xi's visit to Seoul in July 2014, Pyongyang showed its pique by launching several short and medium range missiles.

As 2014 came to an end, an unpredictable set of events involving North Korea mingled tragedy and farce in ways that simultaneously reflected both the absurdity and the perils of that country's place and significance in the world. Hackers who may or may not have been North Korean unloaded huge tranches of data from Sony Pictures in protest of the film, *The Interview*, which climaxed with a gruesome assassination of Kim Jong-un. The hackers then threatened to attack any theatres that would show the film. Large theatre chains opted not to screen it, and Sony pulled the movie before later relenting to pressure and releasing it.

Had the film depicted the decapitation of Barack Obama, Xi Jinping, or many other recognised foreign leaders, its makers would have been castigated. But it was aimed at North Korea, a country with no real friends. As such, the American media can say and do anything it wants, and very few protest. Most interesting then, and most typical of any number of crises over North Korea, is that Pyongyang made wild charges – in this case that the US government backed *The Interview* – and media commentators mocked Pyongyang's paranoia. Further examination, however, then reveals that a kernel of truth lay at the bottom of the North Korean claims; the American media was not only wrong, but as usual failed to do any investigative reporting into the matter.

During a US Strategic Command symposium in August 2014, Major General John MacDonald, formerly of US Forces Command in Korea, advocated the assassination of North Korean leaders. The video of this symposium was circulated by the Strategic Command, in the knowledge that officials in Pyongyang watch this periodic symposium every time it airs.[9] Furthermore, Sony emails show that company executives consulted with the State Department and CIA about any backlash that might occur from releasing the film; Bruce Bennett, a consultant with the US government, told Sony in June 2014 that the only way to get rid of the North Korean regime was to assassinate its leader. Bennett also told Sony that the imagery of Kim's gruesome murder in *The Interview* should be kept to be leaked into North Korea as a samizdat DVD to help destabilise the regime.[10] In the midst of this episode, Richard Haass, President of the Council on Foreign Relations, published an editorial in the *Wall Street Journal* which advocated regime change, or as he put it, 'ending North Korea's existence as an independent entity and reunifying the Korean Peninsula'.[11]

If a North Korean leader, including Kim Jong-un, were to be assassinated by American forces, it is very possible that the truce on the Korean Peninsula would break and open war would resume. It seems it did not occur to Americans working for Sony that Pyongyang would naturally see the film not just as an American product but one manufactured in Japan, the North's colonial enemy and *bête noire* for seventy years.

Chinese frustrations and American failure

China's reliance on North Korea as a problematic but useful "buffer" between itself and the South necessitates its uneasy alliance with Pyongyang; no Chinese leader wants the ROK, with 28,000 American troops in its territory, to control the Yalu River border. Indeed, Obama's strategy throughout his time in office of seeking to persuade the leaderships of both South Korea and Japan to leave behind their nations' historical grievances and unite in reinvigorating the United States' regional influence by proxy was not lost on Beijing. To this end, in late 2015, Beijing sent Politburo Standing Committee member Liu Yunshan to Pyongyang on the seventieth anniversary of the founding of its Worker's Party. Liu became the highest-ranking visitor from the PRC in several years. Some analysts surmised that the deal to be struck on the visit was a pledge from the North not to test any more A-bombs or long-range missiles. Liu reportedly asked Kim to stop testing atomic weapons, but more quickly followed.[12] In February 2016 Beijing sent top North Korea specialist Wu Dawei to Pyongyang to request a halt to tests of long-range missiles. Wu was barely back home before reports of more tests.[13]

The key irritant in Sino-North Korean relations, including throughout the Obama era, has been that with every A-bomb or missile test Washington ramps up its deterrence efforts in Northeast Asia. US carrier task forces have been rerouted to the Yellow Sea; B-1 and B-52 bombers have been sent to the Korean theatre; and ever more anti-ballistic missile batteries, which China sees as a threat to its older missiles including its antiquated ICBMs, have been sold to allies or dispatched. On the surface, this would appear to be a problem for Pyongyang. Most goods available in its markets are made in China and it earns significant amounts from Chinese firms exploiting its natural resources. However in recent years China has also become more accepting of UN sanctions on the North. This invites a uniform view of the Chinese Communist Party's attitudes towards North Korea when in fact the leadership, and the general public, are in fact quite split. Many hardliners in the Chinese military and the CCP empathise with the North. This often co-exists with a mistrust or even acrimony for the United States. Xi Jinping is the first Chinese leader to so openly denounce Pyongyang's provocations; his predecessor, Hu Jintao, lauded the North's closed political system for its ability to repel subversive Western ideas and practices.[14]

The general view of North Korea across the American political spectrum, Democrat and Republican, meanwhile, has long been that it *is* an evil regime. Perhaps it is this which inhibits serious US investigative reporting and debate on North Korea. That deficiency, in turn, means that even the highest US officials often know next to nothing about the country. For instance, former Defense Secretary Leon Panetta writes about the Korean War as if he just discovered it, with a boiler-plate description of his visit to Panmunjom that could have been written forty years ago. In passing, Panetta trots out a venerable shibboleth from the Orientalist playbook; he eyeballs an 'inscrutable' North Korean soldier across the DMZ, 'just as inscrutable as the regime behind him'. '[I]t is an exasperatingly difficult culture to observe and understand ...', he writes, '... our insights into the regime were few and shallow ... Still, the regime was infuriatingly hard to penetrate.' Yet he is curiously matter-of-fact in saying that, '[i]f North Korea moved across the border', the United States would command the ROK's military and would 'defend South Korea – including by the use of nuclear weapons, if necessary'.[15]

This is a naïve but telling passage. A small Asian country is seen as 'inscrutable', and that is infuriating; power needs to know, so why don't they let us know everything we want to know? Following the launch of the North Korean rocket which signalled the end of the Leap Day Deal, Panetta asserted that the United States was prepared for 'any contingency' with regard to North Korea. 'We're within an inch of war almost every day in that part of the world', he said, 'and we just have to be very careful about what we say and what we do.'[16] For American presidents and their officials to contemplate unprovoked attacks against the North is both a stunning example of American arrogance and an astonishing admission of failure, the roots of which extend for perhaps seven decades. This has been a failure to remove the risk of war in Korea, and to make peace with an adversary determined to wait the United States out forever, if that is what it takes.

In 2015, an Obama Doctrine seemed finally to have emerged. 'We will engage, but we preserve all our capabilities', he claimed. Engagement while 'meeting core strategic needs', he said, would serve American interests in new relations with Iran, Burma and Cuba.[17] The Obama administration, then, was to end with new relationships with nearly every former pariah state. Yet the most important one, North Korea, remained out in the diplomatic cold. (As of early 2019, battle-torn Syria occupies its own unfortunate political space, clinging precariously to statehood.) Despite, or perhaps because of, this, North Korea arguably remains far more dangerous than the others, not least because of its precisely unquantifiable nuclear arsenal. At the very least, however, it has on occasions shown itself to be receptive to US presidential diplomacy towards its nuclear and missile programmes. This, indeed, has always been a crucial element of its design.

Trump and the return of US unilateralism

The election of Donald Trump in November 2016 brought into the White House a person with no foreign policy experience, riding a swell of opposition to free trade, internationalism, and the rules of the international game since 1945. Trump has shown he is an American nationalist of the first order. His appeals to racism and anti-immigrant sentiment, and opposition to free trade and a determination to set tariffs on exporters to the American market, put him in line with prominent isolationists of the 1930s.[18] During his campaign, Trump complained that 'we defend everybody', and that 'we will not be ripped off anymore'. He then threatened to withdraw American protection from Japan and South Korea, including the nuclear umbrella, asking why they don't defend themselves against North Korean nuclear weapons and missiles.[19] His naïveties had already been illustrated in 2016 when, as a presidential candidate, he announced that he would be willing to meet with Kim Jong-un without preconditions or concessions, a desire he reiterated a year later as president.[20]

Notably, Trump said he wanted to renegotiate security pacts with Japan and South Korea, among others, unless they start 'paying their way'. Asked by the *New York Times* if he was isolationist, he denied this but asserted that he was 'America First. I like the expression'. When asked to point back into history to the peak of American power, he identified the era of Theodore Roosevelt, and said that two of his favourite Americans were generals Douglas MacArthur and George S Patton.[21]

The cunning of history is such that its emissaries sometimes arrive in strange form. Donald Trump is no exception. Andrew Bacevich's 2005 critique of American power coincided with my own sense that a fundamental rethinking of America's relationship to the world is required.[22] Bacevich outlines a number of principles, the first of which is to 'heed the intentions of the founders'. Nothing in the Constitution, he observes, 'commits or even encourages the United States to employ military power to save the rest of humankind or remake the world in its own image'. He argues for Congress to reassert its constitutional obligations in foreign affairs: 'to view force as a last resort'; to limit American dependence on foreign resources; to organise US forces for national defence rather than power projection; and to reconcile the professional military with the realities of American society. These principles, which I share, call for a full rethinking of the many American bases and garrisons abroad, and truly significant reductions in defence spending. This would only bring the United States into consonance with what its advanced industrial allies spend on military power projection.[23] As of early 2019, it does not seem that Donald Trump is serious about bringing the troops home. At the same time, however, he is the only president since 1945 to repeatedly suggest his intentions to do so.

In February 2017 Trump was having dinner at Mar-a-Lago with Japanese Prime Minister Shinzo Abe when it emerged that under Kim Jong-un's direction, North Korea had tested a new, solid-fuel missile fired from a mobile (and therefore difficult to detect) launcher. The president discussed the issue on his own telephone in front of the various people sitting with him.[24] This missile was a pointed nod to history that no American media outlet grasped; as already noted, Shinzo Abe is the grandson of former Japanese Prime Minister Kishi Nobusuke, a political leader in 1930s Manchuria. Kim Jong-un's grandfather, Kim Il-sung, spent a decade fighting the Japanese at the same time in the same place.

The American media appear to live in an eternal present, with each new crisis treated as *sui generis*. Likewise, every episode with the DPRK during the first two years of the Trump administration seemed to be accompanied by the refrain that the country has a history of violating one agreement after another. In fact, Bill Clinton struck a deal which saw Pyongyang cease plutonium production between 1994 and 2002. In October 2000 Washington and Pyongyang reaffirmed their commitment to that Agreed Framework, and another was signed in the White House with General Jo Myong-rok stating that neither country would bear 'hostile intent' towards the other.[25] The Bush administration ignored both agreements and under John Bolton's influence as Under Secretary of State for Arms Control and International Security Affairs, later National Security Advisor under Trump, it set out to destroy the 1994 Framework. The simple fact is that Pyongyang would have no nuclear weapons today if Clinton's agreements had been maintained by Washington.

Breakthroughs and false hope (?)

North Korean technological advancements of weaponry, evident throughout Obama's time in office, continued throughout the first two years of the Trump administration. Indeed, 2017 saw a flurry of long-range missile tests from North Korea, demonstrating its ability to strike the mainland United States. It also saw the tragic death of Otto Warmbier, an American citizen held captive in Pyongyang after being accused of stealing a propaganda sign while on a visit to the country. UN sanctions followed, and in August 2017 Trump asserted that North Korea would be met with 'fire and fury like the world has never seen' if it continued to threaten the United States.[26] In his September 2017 address to the United Nations, he threatened 'to totally destroy' North Korea.[27] Kim Jong-un called Trump a 'dotard' and 'deranged'; Trump nicknamed Kim the 'little rocket man'.[28] US–North Korea relations had become dangerously unstable as two cantankerous and highly egotistical leaders clashed.

In November 2017 Trump declared the era of "strategic patience" over.[29] Trump's early approach to North Korea, then, in almost every respect, could hardly have presented a more striking contrast to that of Obama. Around the same time, the centrist Council on Foreign Relations issued a report stating that 'more assertive military and political actions' towards the DPRK should be considered, 'including those that directly threaten the existence of the regime'.[30] Secretary of State Rex Tillerson had warned of pre-emptive action during his trip in March to East Asia,[31] and a former Obama administration official, Anthony Blinken, wrote that a priority for the Trump administration should be to work with China and South Korea to 'secure the North's nuclear arsenal' in the event of regime change.[32]

The dawn of 2018 saw Kim Jong-un deliver an unusually conciliatory New Year's address. South Korean President Moon Jae-in quickly invited a North Korean team to the PyeongChang Winter Olympic Games in February, in which the delegations competed under a symbolically powerful unified flag. Kim's sister, Kim Yo-jong, and Kim Yong-chol, a former intelligence chief, impressed the crowds with their quiet dignity and apparent rapport with Moon. A concomitant shift in rhetoric followed between Trump and Kim, for which Trump claimed responsibility. Kim made his first foreign trip as leader to Beijing for talks with Xi Jinping in March, before then-CIA Director (and nominated new Secretary of State) Mike Pompeo travelled to Pyongyang in April. In June 2018 Trump and Kim met at a historic summit in Singapore; Trump became the first sitting US president to meet a North Korean leader. From the summit came an eye-catching but vague commitment to denuclearisation, and an equally vague commitment to a new peace regime on the Korean Peninsula.[33] The summit also drew criticism from those who noted that it handed Kim Jong-un a valuable domestic propaganda opportunity he had always craved. Regional governments nonetheless expressed hopes that US–DPRK tensions, which had so recently all-but boiled over, had abated, and that a path towards denuclearisation of the Korean Peninsula and geopolitical stability in Northeast Asia might lie ahead.

Hopes of genuine sea change come rarely around North Korea and so the expectations of experienced observers were understandably cautious. Credible reports nevertheless emerged that the Kim regime was dismantling missile testing and production facilities and that anti-US propaganda materials were being removed from North Korean streets. The DPRK's large, annual "anti-US imperialism" rally was called off in the summer of 2018. Trump, meanwhile, proclaimed that he and Kim Jong-un 'fell in love' in Singapore and joint military exercises with the South were postponed to avoid antagonising the North.[34] Yet, by December Pyongyang made it clear that they would not relinquish their nuclear capabilities until the United States removed its own from the South and the wider region, raising questions about exactly what had been agreed in Singapore.[35] Investigation also indicated that the DPRK maintained numerous active, undeclared missile sites.[36] A second summit between Trump and Kim in February 2019 ended without major agreement. An announcement in March that annual US–South Korea military exercises were being permanently cancelled to aid denuclearisation efforts brought criticism that the tail of Pyongyang was wagging the dog of the United States and its allies, by succeeding in eroding the regional American security presence.[37] In truth, North Korea has to varying extents been steering and manipulating the security environment of East Asia for decades, not least since the end of the Cold War and the collapse of its main communist support structures. In early 2019 it continues to do so, despite the unorthodox theatrics initiated by Trump.

Conclusion

Across President Obama's two terms in office, his "strategic patience" towards the DPRK got very little from Pyongyang besides an ever-growing reliability of its A-bombs and missiles. Still, there was little real choice but to talk to the North Koreans, by broadly adopting the logic of Siegfried Hecker, former Director of the Los Alamos National Laboratory, who argued to sustain a message of "three no's" towards North Korea: 'No more nukes, No better nukes, No proliferation'. In return, Pyongyang would be able to keep its existing stockpiles but expand them no further, in exchange for concessions.[38] Over time Beijing became more active in backing UN sanctions against Pyongyang, though it is an open question as to how much influence Obama exerted on that shift. His Pivot to the region brought more diplomatic and security resources to the region, including the THAAD missile system in Hawaii and Guam, and eventually, in South Korea. It also encouraged closer security ties between Seoul and Tokyo.

To this extent, Obama left a legacy of sorts in Washington's relations with Pyongyang; by embracing regional multilateralism over unilateralism and rejecting the rhetoric of an "Axis of Evil" – both key features of the Bush administration's regional strategy – and even to some extent by simply neglecting North Korea altogether, Obama succeeded in defusing some of the tensions brought by his predecessor's obsession with terror and "rogue states" like North Korea, especially in his first term. The arrival to power of Kim Jong-un in 2012 brought a renewed acceleration of the DPRK's nuclear and long-range missile capabilities. This, combined with Obama's focus on securing a nuclear deal with Iran (achieved in 2015), emboldened Pyongyang. In many ways then the Obama administration kicked the North Korean can down the road. Its aim was to seek closer diplomatic and security agreements with its neighbours, particularly South Korea and Japan, but also China, to reinforce Washington's regional authority and exert indirect influence over Pyongyang. This effort towards "outsourcing" security was a key feature of the Pivot in broad terms. China's increased willingness to support US-led sanctions on North Korea also reflects well on Obama, though this also contributed to frustrations in Pyongyang and its relationship with Washington progressively worsened.

From 2017, Donald Trump took the US–North Korea relationship on a diplomatic rollercoaster up until the time of writing in early 2019. Trump's open admiration for historical figures including Theodore Roosevelt and Douglas MacArthur, as well as his notoriously fragile temperament, help explain his natural recourse to military solutions and markedly aggressive rhetoric towards Pyongyang, especially in his first twelve months in the White House. Trump's fondness for disparaging the record of his presidential predecessor led him to declare an end to Obama's "strategic patience", though this was likely as much for show as a sign of personal conviction. More broadly, by immediately questioning the benefits Washington derives from its alliances and military presence in Asia, and arguing that its closest regional allies needed to "do more", Trump began to erode Obama's two-term project of local trust and consensus-building. Neither president, sadly, has taken at all seriously the plight of the millions of innocent North Koreans starving and/or locked away in prison camps. These are the timeless victims of both a murderous regime and a lack of American leadership on human rights.

The regime in Pyongyang senses an opportunity in Donald Trump; by carefully playing to his curious admiration for authoritarian "strongmen" and questionable commitment to regional security, Kim Jong-un has become closer to an American president than either his father or grandfather managed, yet both Trump and Kim are highly unpredictable characters. The problem for North Korea is that its image among the American public and many of their policy makers (Trump's personal up-down relations with Kim notwithstanding) is so negatively charged, and one of an almost inhuman authoritarian machine the world would be better without. Leon Panetta's observation that the two sides so often come 'within an inch of war' is therefore a result of American politics as well as those of the DPRK. Ultimately, long-term solutions to the challenges posed by North Korea must have the support and participation of neighbouring South Korea, China and Japan. Trump may see America First, but to cement a positive legacy of his own on the peninsula he would need to reach out to those he has already criticised for not contributing enough.

Notes

1   White House, 'President Barack Obama's Inaugural Address' (21 January 2009), https://obamawhitehouse.archives.gov/blog/2009/01/21/president-barack-obamas-inaugural-address, accessed 10 March 2019.

2   H. Clinton, 'America's Pacific Century', *Foreign Policy* (11 October 2011), http://foreignpolicy.com/2011/10/11/americas-pacific-century/, accessed 6 March 2019.

3   P. Goodspeed, 'Obama Looks to Counter China's Influence with Australian Naval Base', *National Post* (15 November 2011), https://nationalpost.com/opinion/peter-goodspeed-u-s-looks-to-assert-itself-in-pacific-region-with-australian-naval-base, accessed 10 March 2019; E. Bumiller and T. Shanker, 'Panetta to Offer Strategy for Cutting Military Budget', *New York Times* (2 January 2012), www.nytimes.com/2012/01/03/us/pentagon-to-present-vision-of-reduced-military.html, accessed 10 March 2019.

4   M. Memmott, 'Pentagon Says Two War Strategy Not Likely to be Scrapped', *NPR* (5 January 2012), www.npr.org/sections/thetwo-way/2012/01/05/144722456/pentagon-says-two-war-strategy-not-likely-to-be-scrapped, accessed 10 March 2019.

5   See S. Snyder, 'US-North Korean negotiating behaviour and the Six Party Talks', in S. Joo and T. Kwak (eds.), *North Korea's Second Nuclear Crisis and Northeast Asia Security* (Aldershot: Ashgate), p. 158.

6   Documents on this project discovered by the author and discussed in B. Cumings, *The Origins of the Korean War*, 2nd edition (Princeton, NJ: Princeton University Press, 1990).

7   See A. Panda, 'A Great Leap to Nowhere: Remembering the US-North Korea "Leap Day" Deal', *The Diplomat* (29 February 2016), https://thediplomat.com/2016/02/a-great-leap-to-nowhere-remembering-the-us-north-korea-leap-day-deal/, accessed 12 March 2019.

8   T. Branigan, 'China's Patience with North Korea Wears Thin After Latest Nuclear Test', *Guardian* (12 February 2013), www.theguardian.com/world/2013/feb/12/china-north-korea-nuclear-test, accessed 11 March 2019.

9 P. Hayes, 'Strategic Negligence and the Sony Sideshow', NAPSNet Policy Forum (22 December 2014), https://nautilus.org/napsnet/napsnet-policy-forum/strategic-negligence-and-the-sony-sideshow/, accessed 10 March 2019.

10 *Ibid.*

11 R. N. Haas, 'Time to End the North Korean Threat', *Wall Street Journal* (23 December 2014), www.wsj.com/articles/richard-haass-time-to-end-the-north-korean-threat-for-good-1419376266, accessed 10 March 2019.

12 J. C. Hernandez, 'Hydrogen Bomb Claim Strains North's Bonds with Beijing', *New York Times* (7 January 2016), www.nytimes.com/2016/01/07/world/asia/north-korea-china-hydrogen-test.html, accessed 10 March 2019.

13 BBC, 'North Korea Fires Long Range Rocket Despite Warning' (7 February 2016), www.bbc.co.uk/news/world-asia-35515207, accessed 12 March 2019.

14 H. McDonald, 'Mutual Interest Binds China to North Korea', *Sydney Morning Herald* (16 December 2006), www.smh.com.au/world/mutual-interest-binds-china-to-north-korea-20061216-gdp2cr.html, accessed 10 March 2019.

15 L. Panetta with J. Newton, *Worthy Fights: A Memoir of Leadership in War and Peace* (New York: Penguin, 2014), pp. 274–6.

16 CNN, 'Panetta: We're Within an Inch of War Almost Every Day' (19 April 2012), https://edition.cnn.com/2012/04/19/politics/pol-clinton-panetta-interview/index.html, accessed 10 March 2019.

17 T. L. Friedman, 'The Obama Doctrine and Iran', *New York Times* (6 April 2015), www.nytimes.com/2015/04/06/opinion/thomas-friedman-the-obama-doctrine-and-iran-interview.html, accessed 10 March 2019.

18 N. Cohn, 'Trump's Secret Weapon: Blue-State Voters', *New York Times* (27 March 2016), www.nytimes.com/2016/03/27/upshot/trumps-secret-weapon-blue-state-voters.html, accessed 10 March 2019.

19 D. Sanger and M. Haberman, 'In Donald Trump's Worldview, America Comes First, and Everybody Else Pays', *New York Times* (27 March 2016), www.nytimes.com/2016/03/27/us/politics/donald-trump-foreign-policy.html, accessed 10 March 2019.

20 BBC, 'Donald Trump: I Would be Honoured to Meet Kim Jong-un' (1 May 2017), www.bbc.co.uk/news/world-asia-39773337, accessed 11 March 2019.

21 *Ibid.*

22 A. Bacevich, *The New American Militarism: How Americans Are Seduced by War* (New York: Basic Books, 2005).

23 *Ibid.*, pp. 208–21.

24 Y. Alcindor, J. Weisman and A. Stevenson, 'Scenes From Mar-a-Lago as Trump and Abe Get News About North Korea', *New York Times* (13 February 2017), www.nytimes.com/2017/02/13/us/politics/donald-trump-administration.html, accessed 10 March 2019.

25 US Department of State, 'US-DPRK Joint Communique' (12 October 2000), https://1997-2001.state.gov/regions/eap/001012_usdprk_jointcom.html, accessed 13 March 2019.

26 J. Pramuk, 'Trump Warns North Korea Threats "Will Be Met with Fire and Fury"', *CNBC* (8 August 2017), www.cnbc.com/2017/08/08/trump-warns-north-korea-threats-will-be-met-with-fire-and-fury.html, accessed 12 March 2019.

27 White House, 'Remarks by President Trump to 72nd Session of the United Nations General Assembly' (19 September 2019), www.whitehouse.gov/briefings-statements/remarks-president-trump-72nd-session-united-nations-general-assembly/, accessed 11 March 2019.

28 M. Stevens, 'Trump and Kim Jong-un, and the Names They've Called Each Other', *New York Times* (9 March 2018), www.nytimes.com/2018/03/09/world/asia/trump-kim-jong-un.html, accessed 14 March 2019.

29 White House, 'Remarks by President Trump and Prime Minister Abe of Japan in Joint Press Conference' (6 November 2017), www.whitehouse.gov/briefings-statements/remarks-president-trump-prime-minister-abe-japan-joint-press-conference-tokyo-japan/, accessed 11 March 2019.

30 Council on Foreign Relations, 'A Sharper Choice on North Korea: Engaging China for a Stable Northeast Asia', Independent Task Force Report no. 74 (3 October 2016), https://cfrd8-files.cfr.org/sites/default/files/pdf/2016/09/TFR74_North%20Korea.pdf, accessed 10 March 2019.

31 M. Fisher, 'The Risks of The Interpreter', *New York Times* (19 March 2017), A-10.

32 A. Blinken, 'The Best Model for a Nuclear Deal with North Korea? Iran', *New York Times* (11 June 2018), www.nytimes.com/2018/06/11/opinion/trump-north-korea-iran-nuclear-deal.html, accessed 12 March 2019.

33 White House, 'Joint Statement of President Donald J. Trump of the United States of America and Chairman Kim Jong Un of the Democratic People's Republic of Korea at the Singapore Summit' (12 June 2018), accessed 13 March 2019.

34 J. Bykowicz and F. Fassihi, 'Trump Says he and Kim Jong-un "Fell in Love"', *Wall Street Journal* (30 September 2018), www.wsj.com/articles/trump-says-he-and-kim-jong-un-fell-in-love-1538336604, accessed 12 March 2019.

35 *Guardian*, 'North Korea Says it Will Not Denuclearize unless US Removes Threat' (20 December 2019), www.theguardian.com/world/2018/dec/20/north-korea-us-kim-jong-un-trump-denuclearize-nuclear-threat, accessed 12 March 2019.

36 Joseph Bermudez, Victor Cha and Lisa Collins, 'Undeclared North Korea: The Sino-ri Missile Operating Base and Strategic Force Facilities' (21 January 2019), https://beyondparallel.csis.org/undeclared-north-korea-the-sino-ri-missile-operating-base-and-strategic-force-facilities/, accessed 23 October 2019.

37 Al Jazeera, 'US, South Korea to End Key Joint Military Exercises' (3 March 2019), www.aljazeera.com/news/2019/03/south-korea-key-joint-military-exercises-190303055241782.html, accessed 13 March 2019.

38 S. Hecker quoted in A. Lankov, *The Real North Korea: Life and Politics in the Failed Stalinist Utopia* (Oxford: Oxford University Press, 2013), p. 280.

6

The United States and Australia: Deepening ties and securitising cyberspace

Maryanne Kelton and Zac Rogers

Introduction: Strengthening the alliance

Obama's politics of liberal internationalism promoted the rule of law, free trade and democratic values throughout the Asia Pacific. At the same time, his pragmatic realism was designed to secure the United States' position in the region. This approach extended to deepening ties with regional allies and fostering the growth and corporatisation of US cyber capability. On both counts, he found a willing ally in Australia. Obama's specific legacy, then, was to consolidate US–Australia political and economic relations while simultaneously strengthening security ties across all strategic domains, with cyber security, space, and maritime collaboration key features.

In these developments, US regional policy was prominent in Australian concerns. Here, long-standing policy principles drove Obama's two-term approach in Asia. These principles included sustaining stability in Asian markets to provide access and conditions conducive to the US commercial sector, technology, and investment. Obama's backing for the Trans-Pacific Partnership (TPP) provided the means by which the United States would underwrite the rules of trade and investment for the new economy and confirm the United States' position as the region's leading trade and investment partner. In the security sector, US policy principles had been to sustain American power and command of the regional commons and advance the position of the dollar, technology, and investment. To do so Obama proposed the "Pivot" strategy, which comprised the focus of sea power and deployments to the region.[1] It also required renewed commitment to US primacy by alliance partners.

For the most part, this strategy was welcomed by Australia. However, Obama was restricted in his reach and effectiveness by the demands of the global financial crisis, the Afghanistan and Iraq Wars, and congressional partisanship. The realisation of the alliance's stated goal of maintaining a regional rules-based order was also becoming both more important and more difficult because of the uncertainty surrounding the re-emergence of China. US frustrations in forging better relations with Beijing also created significant challenges for Canberra,[2] particularly given burgeoning Australian economic ties with China. Obama's Pivot also oversaw a less visible but highly consequential reprioritisation of the cyber domain in allied security ties, which was dependent on the integration of US entrepreneurial, innovative, and technological resources to maximise Washington's position.[3]

If it was clear in the first months of the Trump presidency from January 2017 that Obama's diplomatic legacy was vulnerable to revision, it has become correspondingly evident two years in, that the underlying calculative pragmatism of US foreign policy remains. To date, the US force posture in the Pacific remains largely unaltered, as has Australia's integration into its architecture. So too, the pace of cyber change and the processes of cyberspace securitisation and corporatisation so evident during the Obama administration, are not diminishing under Trump.

This chapter argues that the Obama legacies and the Trump disruptions for Australia are these: first, Australia's diplomatic relations with the United States, which largely flourished during the Obama years, have now become more fraught and unpredictable at the leadership level but remain institutionally strong. Regional uncertainty which was intensifying under Obama and, indeed, which he could not control, has been exacerbated by Trump's unpredictability across his first two years in charge. Second, security ties have been deepened and continue apace despite the change of administration. Third, while a gradual expansion of security ties with Australia characterised the public face of the Obama administration, the alliance's cyber contours, still evolving under Trump, represent a decisive yet publicly under-recognised infusion to the relationship. Nonetheless, the cyberspace remains problematic given the uncertainty surrounding its evolution. Accordingly, the chapter is divided into a three-part analysis of: the US–Australia public diplomacy and internationalism; the traditional security relationship; and the developing processes in securitising the cyberspace.

Obama's cooperative diplomacy; Trump's threat to liberal order

After the stark unilateralism of the Bush administration, Obama's frequent display of liberal internationalism and progressive cosmopolitanism was welcomed in Australia.[4] His support for liberal norms and international regimes drew marked support. From his understanding of America as a Pacific nation, to his repeated visits to the region, his familial connections with Indonesia, and his cooperative diplomacy, Obama's intent to work with the region was clear. In these respects, Australia was reassured by the presidential interest in its immediate region. Emblematic too of the Obama effect in the relationship was Prime Minister

Julia Gillard's 2011 statement to the US Congress, in which she announced that Australia was '[a]n ally for the sixty years past and Australia is an ally for all the years to come'.[5] Obama reciprocated in November 2011 in an address to the Australian parliament where he announced his signature regional policy: the wide-ranging Pivot to Asia. The Pivot would also involve incremental moves towards a US federated Pacific security architecture, where its bilateral alliances would be cross-braced through minilateral relationships. For example, Australia would be party to the continued evolution of a trilateral strategic dialogue with the United States and Japan. Notably, Obama's intent to strategically Rebalance US global policy by upgrading US Asia Pacific regional engagement was met with local bipartisan support. Australia's response, to further upgrade US relations, was aided by Obama's popularity, which by now was intersecting with official concern over China's rising power and the attendant regional uncertainty generated.

Integral to the Pivot was the pursuit of a regional economic agenda to which Australia lent support. Obama argued that the vehicle to do so, the TPP, based on shared liberal values and harmonised standards for the new economy, would facilitate deep economic integration and establish the rules of the new order. Washington's initial intent was to align its economic allies in a liberal venture so successful that China would eventually seek to join and, by doing so, participate in the American-authored economic standards and norms. As a middle power, despite a number of bilateral trade disputes with the United States, Australia traditionally has been well served by the generally cooperative, open, rules-based economic system Washington has sponsored. Bilaterally, between 2009 and 2016, two-way goods and services trade with the United States increased from AUS$49.5 billion to AUS$68.4 billion, and by 2017 the United States was the largest investor in Australia, with AUS$896 billion, or 27.5 per cent of the total.[6] That said, Australia is integrated economically into the region. By far, its largest trade partner is China in both goods and services exports (30 per cent of the total export profile in 2017) and imports (18 per cent) with Japan and South Korea second and third largest export destinations respectively. Despite Obama's resolve, however, the United States struggled to exercise power in shaping the regional and global trading landscape. The World Trade Organization (WTO) had not concluded the Doha Round since negotiations began in 2001, while in the United States itself the Obama administration failed to steer the TPP through Congress. Australian government dismay at the failure to ratify and implement the Partnership was not universally shared however, as some domestic analysts continued to argue the loss of sovereign control in new generation trade agreements in sectors such as health, quarantine, and intellectual property rights.[7]

Early in office too, Obama's vexation with a lack of progress in US–China relations was evident.[8] The East and South China Sea disputes intensified, as did American accusations that China continued its human rights abuses, perpetrated significant theft of US cyber resources, and failed to allow US technology

companies the freedom to operate in China.[9] By 2016, Obama's Pivot in its diplomatic and economic manifestations was compromised. The rules of the new
economy could not be written in Washington, and the United States could do little
to manage instability surrounding the 2014 Thai coup; new Philippine President
Rodrigo Duterte's hostility; and a seeming fracturing of ASEAN with the continental states increasingly leaning towards China. Ostensibly, then, US command
of the regional commons, with Australia in the slipstream, was beginning to
appear more tenuous. Beyond the continuity of Washington's new Strategic and
Economic Dialogue with Beijing, the United States' ineffective attempts to progress Sino-US relations in a way that suited American interests, which reflected
China's strengthening economic position and enhanced capacity to exercise the
tools of economic statecraft, concerned Australian policy makers. They were, however, encouraged by Obama's cooperative diplomacy in maintaining relations with
many regional states. Relations with Indonesia, Japan, South Korea, Vietnam and
Singapore demonstrated the assurance and confidence that underpinned trusting
relations.

These efforts can be more starkly appraised and appreciated with the inauguration of Donald Trump as president in January 2017. Trump's posturing business
tactics were unsuited to the strategy and sophistication of foreign policy, while his
complete disregard for the foundations of the liberal order and international diplomacy provided an immediate disruption to the Obama legacy. So too his failure
to comprehend that the functional cooperation, reciprocity, consistency, and rela-
tional arrangements on which trust is constructed and maintained underpins
the international system.[10] The characteristics of contempt and the influence of
domestic political imperatives were evident at the leadership level of analysis in
the tense telephone discussion of January 2017 between Trump and Australian
PM Malcolm Turnbull surrounding a refugee swap. Nevertheless, the refugee
exchange of sorts eventually proceeded and so too Australia negotiated a steel
tariff exemption in 2018. Both negotiations exemplify Australia's reliance on trust
in the bilateral institutional arrangements and bureaucratic attention to the relationship that have been developed since the Second World War.[11]

Illustrative of Trump's broader disdain, however, included his critiques of Asia
Pacific allies such as Japan and South Korea as free riders on American strength,
his decision to withdraw the United States from the Paris climate negotiations, and
the dismantling of the US State Department's diplomatic capacity. Furthermore,
the region has become awash with uncertainty and concern. Trump's unpredictability was evident in the variations between the dramatic exchange of nuclear
threats with the DPRK's Kim Jong-un in early January 2018 to the fanfare of
the Singapore meeting in June where few details were disclosed. For Australia,
instability on the Korean Peninsula may adversely affect Australia's Northeast
Asian regional friends; jeopardise its extensive trading relations; and raise
questions regarding the appropriate duties for Australia as it is a signatory to the

1953 Korean armistice. In the economic realm, though Obama understood the long-term benefit to the United States of the TPP and sought to realise its benefits institutionally, Trump has so far failed to grasp the bigger picture of its utility beyond the immediacy of the deal and promptly terminated the prospect of a US-led regional trading regime (at least to date). Over and above trade agreements *per se*, disturbingly for Australia, Trump's reticence through to the beginning of 2019 in approving judiciary appointments for the WTO appellate body were commensurate with a broader approach that failed to support the functioning liberal order on which Australia depends.

Continuity in US–Australia alliance strategy

Though Obama's Pivot in its political and economic manifestations was proving increasingly difficult to execute, substantive and enduring changes in the security domain were evident. And as is demonstrated in this section, part of the Obama legacy was the intensification of a hard-headed pragmatism aimed at maintaining US regional primacy through the relocation of US forces and upscaling of assets to the region. Australia, through its part in intensifying relations, further interlinked with US security strategy. In doing so, however, Australia's room to manoeuvre became more limited. As RAAF Air Marshal Leo Davies was later to explain, heightened interoperability fosters a shift in US–Australia ties further along a continuum towards institutional integration.[12]

Obama's plan had been to maintain the regional power balance by dissuading China from seeking regional hegemony. It was a strategy inherited and pursued since 2001, with Washington providing access for regional allies to integrate into key US cyber, space, and electronic warfare technology networks through which it 'would lead a web of more powerful allies and partners with stronger links to one another'.[13] One of the differences between the Bush and Obama administrations, however, was that the former had sought to avoid disclosure of a strategy to which China would object, and indeed respond to by escalating its military modernisation, presence, and regional relations. In Australia during this period, official government documents, including the Australian Defence White Papers of 2009 and 2016, and the 2017 Department of Foreign Affairs and Trade White Paper, acknowledged concerns regarding China's rising power.[14] Australia's continued assertions of the importance of the rules-based order were coupled with statements noting China's rising 'power and influence'[15] and Chinese militarisation of South China Sea islands.[16] Such threat perceptions were critiqued by Beijing.[17] Australia's concerns were manifest because of the complexity of its strategic hand: security connected intimately to the US alliance, with China trade surpluses sustaining Australian prosperity.[18] Although options for Australia are not presented in binary terms, the rising frequency of specific policies embodying choice highlights the challenge.

The 2011 decision to station up to 2,500 US Marines from the Air-Ground Task Force on a rotational basis in Darwin underscored Australia's importance to Obama's Asia Pacific strategy. The agreement was the expression of the evolving upgrade in Washington–Canberra relations and contextualised by Obama's Pivot to Asia. Located on Australia's northern reaches, Darwin is proximal to Southeast Asian waterways and the strategic Pacific–Indian Ocean transit straits of Malacca, Sunda, Lombok and Ombei-Wetar. The Marine contingent was a key manifestation of enhanced bilateral relations and expected to contribute to the strengthening of a cooperative naval posture, particularly towards a much needed amphibious and ship-to-shore capability for the Asian littoral environment. The Enhanced Air Cooperation Initiative also enabled heightened interoperability, the use of fifth generation air capability, and renovated training and air facilities throughout northern Australia including for US strategic bombers.

Elsewhere, the Space Situational Awareness Partnership announced in 2010 provided oversight on the integrity of the US and allied space system, enabling event information and assessment, including tracking satellite orbits, missile launches, space debris, and foreign and adversary space intelligence, including strategies, tactics, intent, and knowledge.[19] A renewal of space surveillance through the Northwest Cape facilities and a modernised Kojarena Australian Defence Satellite Communication Station permitted a more extensive contribution to the US global interception system.[20] The location of these space surveillance and communication assets in Western Australia not only provided better surveillance north to China and through the increasingly contested reaches of maritime East Asia, but also served access to US and Australian operations out to the Middle East. These developments additionally contributed to Obama's aim of securing stability in Iraq and Afghanistan. With the rise of ISIL in Syria and then the fall of Fallujah in 2014, the United States and Australia redeployed defence personnel in the Combined Joint Task Force and, in the process, Australia acquired invaluable interoperable battlefield experience. Australia remained a willing alliance partner in Obama's intent to 'degrade and destroy' ISIL through a light footprint, multilateralised, counter-terrorism approach. Given Australia's promotion of reciprocity in alliance arrangements and the opportunity to institutionalise interoperability, through Operation Okra Australia deployed an Air Task Group, Special Operations Task Group, and the army's Task Group Taji, to respectively conduct airstrikes, and train and assist Iraqi forces. An Australian naval contingent led maritime security.[21] Similarly, Australia's commitments to Afghanistan were shaped by Obama's strategy of deploying 68,000 additional troops there in 2009. Now, around 300 members of the Australian Defence Force (ADF) still remain in Afghanistan as part of Operation HIGHROAD.

Joint US and Australian threat analysis had also progressively linked the Middle East battlefields to the Asian littorals. The return of foreign fighters from Iraq and Syria to the East Asian region was of profound concern to Australia, and as such converged with the US interest in maintaining regional stability. Given Australia was also apprehensive about resurgent nationalisms, military modernisation, and an attendant decline in trust in East Asia, Obama's support for regional cooperation to address transnational security threats was welcome. For instance, and though modest, the 2015 Southeast Asia Maritime Security Initiative, which provides for maritime domain awareness and capacity building, exemplified Washington's interest in fostering functional regional cooperation around issues such as piracy, disaster management and relief, sea lane security, and surveillance of extremist activities. This initiative, however, also sits within a more extensive US and allied strategic plan progressed through Obama's tenure: the construction of a maritime surveillance system extending from Japan through the East Asian archipelagic waters of the Philippines and Indonesia, to the Andaman Islands at the northwestern reaches of the Malacca Strait.[22]

While the Pivot itself was not rolled out in Australia in an entirely smooth fashion (the US Marine rotations were delayed, for example, with a cost sharing agreement for the AUS$1.5 billion project only finalised in 2016 and the entire complement of Marines was estimated to take up residency only by 2020[23]), the theme of Australian territory and assets enhancing US operational reach was consistent. And, what was clearly observable in the Obama era, was the continuity of the realist pragmatic theme in US foreign policy – for example through the military Pivot to Asia, the development of a cyber exploitation strategy, and the increasing use of drone strikes in Western Asia and the Middle East. Similarly, while Obama's overt liberal internationalism may have obscured some of the hard-nosed defence decisions, the publicity around Trump's "America First" policy and its prospects in the demands for increased burden-sharing masked the continuity of US regional defence strategy. Through Trump's first eighteen months in office, continuity remained in the nature of the US and Australian deployments in the Middle East, with 1,100 Australian personnel plus a naval contingent remaining on station there. Undeniably too, the substantive strength of the Pivot was preserved through the first year of the Trump administration, as evident in PACOM's (US Pacific Command) maintenance of its regional strategy.[24] PACOM's threat analysis of both China's military modernisation and the asymmetric threat to US primacy in the western Pacific, and the potential regional instability arising from ISIL-inspired groups or returned fighters from the Middle East to littoral states, continued to inform Trump's strategy of engagement. Events such as the five-month siege in the southern Philippines city of Marawi in 2017 by ISIL-affiliated groups were an acute reminder of the dangers for regional security to which the United States needed to remain responsive.[25]

As such, the Trump administration sustained the pressure on Australia to actively respond to threat analyses. Flights from Australia's RAAF Butterworth base in Malaysia under the Five Powers Defence Arrangements consistently surveilled the regional waterways. However, as of April 2018, and despite US pressure, Australia has refrained from sailing within twelve nautical miles of the new islands created by China's South China Sea terra formation projects in the strategic triangle of the Spratly Islands, Paracel Islands, and Scarborough Shoal. While Australia's decision to lease the port of Darwin to a Chinese commercial entity was criticised stridently by Pentagon officials, more recently Turnbull's conservative government has also progressively reviewed Chinese investment in Australia through a strategic prism. The government, increasingly sensitised to the broader strategic rivalry, has constrained Chinese investment in Australian infrastructure such as power grids, agricultural holdings, and even political parties. Chinese telecommunications firm Huawei continues to be blocked from participation in the new local access broadband network being rolled out across Australia.[26]

Under the radar, however, another development has been taking place of crucial significance for Australia. While commercial innovations and technological development have been assimilated into the realisation of US geopolitical ambitions since the Second World War,[27] recent developments revealed the integration and extant potency of Silicon Valley heavyweights (big Internet and data primes whose commercial substrate is the digital domain) into the fray. Under Obama, these newcomers, with albeit competing and sometimes unruly agendas, began to fly as birds of a feather – flocking together in a fashion to transform and increase American strategic power. As a close US ally with long-standing commitments to technological and institutional interoperability, Australia's strategic comfort is being buffeted by the ongoing effects.

Securitising cyberspace: Origins of a crisis

The cyber age, to quote Lucas Kello, remains in 'a revolutionary condition'.[28] Its inherent uncertainty is generating deeply disruptive strategic and political contours from which even the closest of alliances are not immune. A shift of strategic weight to the cyber domain forced an improvised reappraisal of threats to regional security. Cast from outside the rubric of a post-Bush administration era to which Obama's thinking was initially set in contrast, the ongoing improvisation is marked by uncertainty.[29] Incongruous with an alliance whose stated goals for decades have centred on the certainty brought about by a public commitment to rule-making in international relations, the cyber age to which Obama was inducted, and Australia has followed, permitted no such certainty.

Obama's introduction to America's cyberwar began before he was even sworn in as president. The growth and strategic evolution of American cyber power subsequently advanced more aggressively and rapidly than at any time prior. Shortly after winning the presidential election in November 2008, Obama was briefed by ex-NSA Director and then Director of National Intelligence Mike McConnell, one of the United States' most influential figures in the development of cyber warfare. McConnell outlined to the President-elect the contours of the digital battlefield – America's alarming defensive weaknesses, the efforts already underway to strengthen them – and later, in a transition meeting with President George W. Bush, a snapshot of the growing offensive side of cyber operations. Among these were Operation *Olympic Games* – underway since 2007 – the infiltration and exploitation of computer networks in Iran that would later become known as Stuxnet, and the CIA's drone programme. Bush encouraged the President-elect to continue these operations.[30] Obama not only agreed, he would pursue an even more aggressive agenda in cyberspace. Obama was entering the White House at an inflection point in the short history of cyber warfare. His tenure oversaw the institutionalisation of cyberspace as a legitimate domain of strategic competition and the demise of the idea that the Internet was an apolitical global space. The expansion and development of cyber capabilities and the increasing involvement of a host of actors challenged the very constitutive elements traditionally associated with international security which, for a middle power reliant on stability and predictability such as Australia, was unsettling.

The fundamental insecurity of the digital medium presented Australia with the typical dilemma facing all advanced industrialised nation states, whose economic competitiveness has become increasingly tied to leveraging the advantages in efficiency and innovation offered by the digital age. As a strategic and military ally of the United States, however, Australia's dilemma runs deeper. The digitisation of warfare offered the ADF an attractive pathway to pursue its long-standing goal of regional superiority based on the technical and operational sophistication of small but highly capable armed forces. This was manifest in the late 1990s in the ADF's embrace of Network-Centric Warfare, which closely tracked the American effort with a few minor caveats. Networked warfare is predicated on robust and seamless information flows, which are in turn reliant on the integrity, assurance, and security of data stored in and transiting the platforms and systems embedded in the digital medium. Cyber security, therefore, sits at the centre of Australia's strategic security in both civilian and military terms. In 2008, Australia was underprepared at a tactical and operational level for the age of cyberwar, despite the maximising of self-reliance being a central theme of its defence community. At the strategic level Australia's security remained deeply intertwined with its senior ally, and cyber insecurity was set to introduce a new level of uncertainty.

2007 was a very big year in cyber security. By 2008 it had reached a point of departure. In April and August 2007 Russia launched cyber-attacks against Estonia and Georgia in what are generally understood as the first such instances of interstate attacks;[31] in September four Israeli Air Force F-15s destroyed a half-built nuclear reactor in eastern Syria, evading Syria's Russian-made air-defence systems by hacking its computer network and spoofing the radar systems;[32] and April saw the US National Security Agency (NSA) debut its revolutionary Real Time Regional Gateway (RTRG) in Iraq as part of the "surge". For the first time, NSA operatives were on the battlefield coordinating the use of computer network exploitation ("hacking") to find, arrest or kill terrorists and insurgents in real time. At the operational level, Australia's Signals Intelligence (SIGINT) station at Joint Defence Facility Pine Gap underwent a significant expansion. Embedded cross-institutional rivalry in the US intelligence community was wrestled closer to alignment. The nature and structure of digital computing across global networks, and indeed of the various groups the United States found itself in conflict with in cyberspace, meant any clear demarcation between civil, military, state, non-state, individual, networked, and commercial domains were being erased. The non-ergodic implications of cyberwar hit home at the highest level.

The strategic substance of the ANZUS alliance lies in signals intelligence under the UKUSA agreement,[33] colloquially known as the Five Eyes. Yet SIGINT, the interception of information in transit via the electromagnetic spectrum, was challenged fundamentally by the onset of the digital age. SIGINT was evolving. Unlike an analogue signal, digital information transits a heterogeneous global communications network in packets via the most efficient route and reconfigures at its destination. Since the continental United States hosted some 80 per cent of the network's physical infrastructure and bandwidth, most digital packets at some point travel through the United States on route to their destinations. Yet, they were legally off limits to the foreign intelligence collection activities of the NSA and CIA. The impact of 9/11 was pivotal. If another homeland attack was to be averted, the NSA argued that it required quick access to the phone calls and emails of suspects who may be US citizens and whose data packets may be stored on servers or travelling through networks in the United States; that is, there was no time for warrants. The NSA argued it only required the meta-data to establish "contact chains" that would enable it to identify threats for further attention. President Bush signed the order to give the NSA these powers on 4 October 2001. The NSA's mass meta-data collection programme, known as Stellar Wind, began immediately and grew exponentially. Though contact chaining using meta-data had its limitations, the new laws represented an opening to the goldmine of global digital communications.

Turbulence and the Pine Gap expansion

US Army General Keith Alexander's arrival as NSA Director in 2005 catalysed the NSA's leap into the cyber age. A new system, Turbulence, consisted of a subset of nine systems that penetrated the network from multiple entry points.[34] This approach provided redundancy regarding potential intelligence gaps, granularity by overlaying vectors of analysis, and speed. It gathered and combined SIGINT from satellites, microwave transmissions, mobile phone networks, and packets of data traversing the Internet either via undersea and overland fibre optic cables or at the gateway of Internet service providers. Turbulence spawned numerous specialised programmes, many of which were revealed to the public by Edward Snowden in 2013. One of them, RTRG, focused these tools on a specific region and undertaking. It was commanded from early 2007 by General David Petraeus and used in the Iraq War in unprecedented coordination with the military, to target and remove terrorists and insurgents from the battlefield. NSA equipment and analysts were deployed inside Iraq to enable genuine "real time" operations. Hand-in-glove intelligence–military operations alongside US Special Forces developed, exploiting the digital communications networks of insurgents with lethal efficiency. RTRG heralded a new operational art of warfare with cyber at its core. It also had significant implications for Australia's operational involvement.

Pine Gap among other joint facilities is the primary locale for the US–Australia SIGINT relationship over five decades.[35] The facility underwent significant expansion between 2006 and 2008 with regard to its operational remit, number and depth of multi-agency involvement, and customer base for the 'actionable intelligence' it produced.[36] In sum, this period saw Pine Gap expand its remit beyond ground control of orbital systems (since 1967) and relay station for ballistic missile-defence data (since 1999) into support for real time military operations worldwide.[37] Expansion paralleled significant organisational changes at the US National Reconnaissance Office (NRO), with the above mentioned shifts in operational focus at NSA. The NRO established a Ground Enterprise Directorate with the explicit mandate of transforming Pine Gap and similar Mission Ground Stations into premier providers of integrated real time intelligence tailored for war-fighting, as manifest in the NSA's RTRG.[38] This put Pine Gap's 2006–8 expansion at the fulcrum of developments in cyber warfare, its integration into military and intelligence operations, and their battlefield debut in 2007. It gave Australia, via the Australian Signals Directorate (ASD) co-located with US agencies at Pine Gap, 'access to the heart of frontier advances in information operations'.[39]

Catching up and collective cyber security

In 2008 Australia's civilian and military capacity for both computer network defence and offensive countermeasures in cyberspace were underdeveloped.[40] For the ADF, cyber security was a critical enabler inside broader efforts to stand up a fully networked force that sought to take advantage of competitive opportunities for small but technically sophisticated militaries in the digital age.[41] As strategic, economic and political narratives played out, with many quick to question the forbearance of the alliance under the Trump administration, Australia has been expanding its reach and competency in cyberspace in both the civilian and military spheres. In January 2010 the ASD (then Defence Signals Division) established the Cyber Security Operations Centre, a defence-based centre hosting liaisons with other agencies. In November 2014 it became the Australian Cyber Security Centre housing all contributing agencies[42] under a one roof, whole-of-government approach. In April 2016 the government released its inaugural Cyber Security Strategy,[43] while the 2016 Australian Defence White Paper quietly prioritised cyber security as a key capability area, flagging expansion of the cyber workforce with the intention of establishing a research and development capability to help strengthen the ADF's military information systems.[44] Parliament passed laws introducing mandatory reporting of data breaches for businesses with responsibilities under the Privacy Act which came into force in February 2018. Standards Australia developed a priority list of standards to support development of blockchain technology, a key element in the effort to build security and provenance into Web 2.0.[45] For all of these efforts, Australia draws on its partnership with the United States, leveraging its multi-decade membership of the Five Eyes intelligence sharing agreement. In addition, Australia in 2017 looked to bolster partnerships with established cyber-leaders, including Japan, Israel and Estonia.

By the time Obama handed over the presidency to Trump in January 2017, the reality of cyberspace was that the constitutive elements of international security were effectively garbled. Cyberspace emerged as a ubiquitous yet opaque battlefield. Its physical attributes are as tangible as any other, but do not conform to a typical pre-twenty-first-century geopolitical outline. This does not mean that states are not competing to control it. Similarly, the status and functions attributed to cyberwarfare remain very much in their infancy. Obama's legacy to Trump is that the race to secure the US strategic stake in the physical and institutional realities of cyber warfare is very much on. Perhaps no geographical region is more strategically consequential in this race than the Indo-Pacific – a region in which Australia is 'top-centre', no longer 'down-under'.[46]

Conclusion

Obama's progressive and persuasive expression of liberal internationalism found resonance in Australia. The rules-based order Obama promoted overtly was one which Australia necessarily endorsed and has supported both publicly and consistently. As such it marked a departure from the Bush administration that preceded it and the Trump administration that would follow. In its vocal nationalism, the Trump administration's derision for international norms, including a ready failure to support the international trading system, climate change regimes and international organisations more generally, coupled with a diminution of the State Department's influence, generated concerns in Australia regarding the sustainability of the liberal international order. Regionally, a spiral of distrust,[47] unable to be moderated by Obama and exacerbated in 2017 by the variations in the DPRK–US relationship, aggravates the discomfort currently experienced in Australia, as indeed elsewhere in the region.

And yet, two years into the Trump presidency in early 2019, these observations of the public divergence between US administrations and the repercussions for Australia belie the continuity of a realist pragmatism in US foreign policy: a pragmatism to which Australia also subscribes.[48] Arguably, if Trump is inclined to any arm of government, he appears most disposed to the Pentagon's hierarchy and strategy. Though presidential rhetoric in 2017–18 was more dramatic, inconsistent, and risk laden, few substantive changes were made to the US force posture in the Asia Pacific. Cold War-era security agreements have thus far been maintained, and some reweighting of US forces to the region continued, defining the continuity of the US military presence. Divergences between Trump's diplomacy and US military strategy, however, revealed to Australia that as it marks the southern anchor of US presence in East Asia, it must work to reconstitute trust with regional states as they reassess their great power hedging strategies.

As argued in this chapter, Obama rigorously pursued policies to maximise US authority at an inflection point of an emerging and rapidly developing cyberspace commons. Moreover, the United States did so in the full embrace of state power as constituted by the entirety of its public and private resources. The weight of its innovative technological resources was central to its pursuit of cyber exploitation and in maintaining primacy in the Asia Pacific. Thus, US security policy was increasingly cyber and corporatised, and as such more exposed to attendant uncertainty as it was by necessity interlinked with the big Internet and data primes. Australia, as a US ally and middle power with a vital interest in the vanguard of high-tech advancement, is a willing partner but unsupported by indigenous capacity. Yet the more significant implications for Australia at a time of dynamic change in the international system arise from the tapering of Australian choices in and beyond the strategic setting, as it progressively integrates with US technologies and systems. Australia's discomfort, which has also risen with the unpredictability of the Trump policy choices, is now more likely to be accelerated as rapid and far-reaching technological change generates greater uncertainty.

Notes

1   M. Wesley, 'Living in a post-American Asia', *Australian Financial Review* (4 August 2017).

2   K. Campbell and E. Ratner, 'The China reckoning: How Beijing defied American expectations', *Foreign Affairs*, 97:2 (2018), pp. 60–70.

3   A. Tellis, 'Overview: Power and ideas in the making of strategy', in A. Tellis, A. Szalwinski and M. Wills (eds.), *Strategic Asia 2017–18: Power, Ideas, and Military Strategy in the Asia-Pacific* (Washington, DC: National Bureau of Asian Research, 2017), pp. 6–7.

4   See for example Lowy Institute, The Lowy Institute Polls 2005–2017, The Diplomacy and Public Opinion Program, Sydney, www.lowyinstitute.org/about/programs-and-projects/polling, accessed 11 March 2019.

5   Australian Department of the Prime Minister and Cabinet, 'Address to the Congress of the United States, Washington' (9 March 2011), http://pmtranscripts. pmc.gov.au/release/transcript-17726, accessed 11 March 2019. See also N. Bisley, '"An ally for all the years to come": Why Australia is not a conflicted US ally', *Australian Journal of International Affairs*, 67:4 (2013), pp. 403–18.

6   Australian Department of Foreign Affairs and Trade, 'Australia's Direction of Goods and Services Trade – Calendar Years from 1987 to Present' (September 2018), http://dfat.gov.au/trade/resources/trade-statistics/Pages/trade-time-series-data.aspx, accessed 11 March 2019; Australian Department of Foreign Affairs and Trade, 'Statistics on Who Invests in Australia' (June 2018), http://dfat.gov.au/trade/topics/investment/Pages/which-countries-invest-in-australia.aspx, accessed 11 March 2019.

7   On the issue of health policy in the Australia–US Free Trade Agreement see T. Faunce, 'How the Australia–US free trade agreement compromised the pharmaceutical benefits scheme', *Australian Journal of International Affairs*, 69:5 (2015), pp. 473–8.

8   J. Bader, *Obama and China's Rise: An Insider's Account of America's Asia Strategy* (Washington, DC: Brookings Institution Press, 2012).

9   S. Harris, *@war: The Rise of the Military-Internet Complex* (Boston: Mariner, 2014), pp. 52–3.

10 E. Bienvenue, Japan's and China's Strategies for Maritime Diplomacy in Southeast Asia, 1945–2009: Identifying Prospects for Maritime Cooperation (PhD dissertation, Flinders University, 2015).

11 E. Bienvenue *et al.*, 'Monitoring the Effectiveness of International Engagement and the Health of Trust-Based Bilateral Relationships: A Trust-Based Framework', Defence Science and Technology Group Discussion Paper, Flinders University (forthcoming).

12 L. Davies, 'A Fifth-Generation Air Force: Alliance Structures and Networked Capabilities from an Australian Perspective', Centre for Strategic and International Studies (11 May 2017), www.csis.org/events/fifth-generation-air-force-alliance-structures-and-networked-capabilities-australian, accessed 11 March 2019.

13 N. Silove, 'The pivot before the pivot: US strategy to preserve the power balance in Asia', *International Security*, 40:4 (2016), p. 47.

14 Australian Department of Defence, 'Defending Australia in the Asia Pacific Century: Force 2030' (2009), www.defence.gov.au/whitepaper/2009/docs/defence_white_paper_2009.pdf, accessed 11 March 2019; Australian Department of

Defence, '2016 Defence White Paper' (2016), www.defence.gov.au/whitepaper/docs/2016-defence-white-paper.pdf, accessed 11 March 2019; Australian Government, '2017 Foreign Policy White Paper' (2017), www.fpwhitepaper.gov.au, accessed 11 March 2019.

15 Australian Government, '2017 Foreign Policy White Paper', p. 25.

16 *Ibid.*, p. 47.

17 Chinese Ministry of National Defense, 'Defense Ministry's Regular Press Conference on November 30' (30 November 2017), http://eng.mod.gov.cn/focus/2017-11/30/content_4798766.htm, accessed 11 March 2019.

18 H. White, 'Powershift: Australia's future between Washington and Beijing', *Quarterly Essay*, 39 (2010), pp. 39–74.

19 United States Government Accountability Office, 'Report to the Subcommittee on Strategic Forces, Committee on Armed Services, House of Representatives' (May 2011), p. 5.

20 R. Tanter, 'Pine Gap: An Introduction', Nautilus Institute (24 January 2017), https://nautilus.org/publications/books/australian-forces-abroad/defence-facilities/pine-gap/pine-gap-intro/, accessed 11 March 2019.

21 Australian Department of Defence, 'Transcript – Press Conference with Chief of Joint Operations VADM David Johnston and CO Task Group Taji COL Matthew Galton – Update on Australian Defence Force Operations – 18 December 2015', https://news.defence.gov.au/media/transcripts/transcript-press-conference-chief-joint-operations-vadm-david-johnston-and-co-task, accessed 11 March 2019; Australian Department of Defence, 'Press Conference with Vice Admiral David Johnston and Air Commodore Vincent "Joe" Iervasi – Update on Australian Defence Force Operations' (30 March 2016), https://news.defence.gov.au/media/transcripts/press-conference-vice-admiral-david-johnston-and-air-commodore-vincent-joe-ierva-0, accessed 11 March 2019.

22 D. Ball and R. Tanter, *The Tools of Owatatsumi: Japan's Ocean Surveillance and Coastal Defence Capabilities* (Canberra: ANU Press, 2015), p. 54.

23 B. Gill, 'Pivotal Days: US-Asia Pacific Alliances in the Early Stages of the Trump Administration', Chatham House, Asia Programme Research Paper (June 2017), p. 17, www.chathamhouse.org/sites/default/files/publications/research/2017-06-23-pivotal-days-us-asia-pacific.pdf, accessed 11 March 2019.

24 A. Connelly, 'Autopilot: East Asia Policy under Trump', Lowy Institute (31 October 2017), www.lowyinstitute.org/publications/autopilot-east-asia-policy-under-trump, accessed 11 March 2019.

25 C. Cronin, 'The Overlooked Gap in the Southeast Asia Maritime Security Initiative', Centre for Strategic and International Studies (28 April 2016), https://csis-prod.s3.amazonaws.com/s3fs-public/publication/160428_SoutheastAsia_Vol_7_Issue_9.pdf, accessed 11 March 2019.

26 Australian Department of Defence, 'International Relations 10, Darwin Port Privatisation', Senate Estimates Brief, www.defence.gov.au/FOI/Docs/Disclosures/361_1516_Documents.pdf, accessed 11 March 2019.

27 L. Weiss, *America Inc.: Innovation and Enterprise in the National Security State* (Ithaca: Cornell University Press, 2014).

28 L. Kello, *The Virtual Weapon and International Order* (New Haven: Yale University Press, 2017), p. 1.

29 P. Katzenstein and L. Seybert, *Protean Power: Exploring the Uncertain and Unexpected in World Politics* (Cambridge: Cambridge University Press, 2018).

30 F. Kaplan, *Dark Territory: The Secret History of Cyber War* (New York: Simon & Schuster), p. 203.

31 *Ibid.*, pp. 162–5.

32 *Ibid.*, pp. 160–1.

33 D. Ball, 'The strategic essence', *Australian Journal of International Affairs* 55:2 (2001), pp. 235–48.

34 Kaplan, *Dark Territory*, p. 157.

35 D. Ball, *Pine Gap: Australia and the US Geostationary Signals Intelligence Satellite Program* (Sydney: Allen & Unwin, 1988); D. Ball, *A Suitable Piece of Real Estate: American Installations in Australia* (Sydney: Hale & Iremonger, 1980).

36 D. Ball, B. Robinson and R. Tanter, 'Management of Operations at Pine Gap', Nautilus Institute (24 November 2015), p. 7, http://nautilus.org/wp-content/uploads/2015/11/PG-Managing-Operations-18-November-2015.v2.pdf, accessed 11 March 2019.

37 D. Ball, B. Robinson and R. Tanter, 'The Militarisation of Pine Gap: Organisations and Personnel', Nautilus Institute (14 August 2015), p. 5, http://nautilus.org/wp-content/uploads/2015/08/The-militarisation-of-Pine-Gap.pdf, accessed 11 March 2019.

38 Harris, *@War*, pp. 34–6; Ball *et al.*, 'Management of Operations at Pine Gap', p. 9.

39 K. Beazley, 'Foreword', in G. Waters, D. Ball and I. Dudgeon (eds.), *Australia and Cyber-Warfare* (Canberra: ANU Press, 2008), p. xix.

40 See Waters *et al.*, *Australia and Cyber-Warfare*.

41 See Australian Department of Defence, 'NCW Roadmap 2009' (Canberra: Commonwealth of Australia, 2009), www.defence.gov.au/capability/_pubs/NCW%20Roadmap%202009.pdf; Australian Defence Force, 'Force 2020' (2002), www.defence.gov.au/publications/f2020.pdf, accessed 11 March 2019.

42 These include the Department of Defence; the Attorney-General's Department, the Australian Security Intelligence Organisation, Australian Federal Police, and the Australian Crime Commission.

43 Australian Department of the Prime Minister and Cabinet, 'Australia's Cyber Security Strategy: Enabling Innovation, Growth, and Prosperity' (2016), https://cybersecuritystrategy.pmc.gov.au/assets/img/PMC-Cyber-Strategy.pdf.

44 Australian Department of Defence, '2016 Defence White Paper'.

45 See Z. Rogers, 'Blockchain and the state: Vehicle or vice?', *Australian Quarterly*, 1:89 (2018), pp. 3–9.

46 I. Rehman, 'From Down Under to Top Center: Australia, the United States and this Century's Special Relationship', The German Marshall Fund of the United States

(26 May 2011), www.gmfus.org/publications/down-under-top-center-australia-united-states-and-centurys-special-relationship, accessed 11 March 2019.

47   W. S. Bateman, 'Building cooperation for managing the South China Sea without strategic trust', *Asia & the Pacific Policy Studies*, 4:2 (2017), pp. 251–9.

48   B. O'Connor and C. Wakefield, 'No-Drama Obama's Foreign Policy Legacy', *Australian Outlook* (19 January 2017) www.internationalaffairs.org.au/australianoutlook/no-drama-obamas-foreign-policy-legacy/, accessed 11 March 2019.

7

Obama's legacy in US–ASEAN relations: Promises and perils

Prashanth Parameswaran

Introduction

Southeast Asia has traditionally occupied a marginal role in US foreign policy in general and US Asia policy in particular, and American commitment to the region has remained quite ambivalent since the end of the Cold War. But during his time in office, US President Barack Obama raised the level of US attention given to Southeast Asia and the Association of South East Asian Nations (ASEAN) to a level not seen since the end of the Vietnam War.[1] Seeing Southeast Asia and ASEAN as vital to preserving what it referred to as the rules-based international order, the Obama administration made the region and the regional grouping a vital part of its so-called "Rebalance" to the Asia Pacific and took measures to concretise this across countries and realms.

Yet as this chapter will show, by the end of his second term, Obama's legacy in US–ASEAN relations in fact remained quite mixed. On the one hand, the administration achieved some notable success in increasing and institutionalising a higher level of attention to Southeast Asia, committing Washington to Asia's multilateral diplomatic framework, and improving relations with Southeast Asia's people. But on the other hand, it faced challenges in confronting the reality of China's growing influence in Southeast Asia, crafting an economic approach for the region, and articulating a clear and comprehensive approach to dealing with democracy and human rights questions. The Trump administration added another layer of complexity to assessing Obama's legacy in this respect, because while it continued or built on some aspects, it also departed from, and in some cases undermined, others as well.

The legacy of US–Southeast Asia relations

Southeast Asia has traditionally occupied a marginal role in US foreign policy in general and US Asia policy in particular, unlike China or Japan, which both loomed much larger and much earlier. Even though there was some level of US involvement in some Southeast Asian states previously, the region really first rose to prominence in the context of threats to the United States and to its European and Asian allies and partners during the Second World War and then the Cold War.[2] That prominence was followed by a pattern of waxing and waning of US commitment after the end of the Vietnam War and continued from the end of the Cold War and thereafter, which some characterise as various forms of neglect.[3]

As a result, by the late 1990s and early 2000s, a clear gap had emerged where Southeast Asia's importance as a region had grown significantly, but US policy had not become correspondingly focused on the region. Despite ongoing challenges ranging from human rights to underdevelopment, economic growth among the original ASEAN Five (of Indonesia, Malaysia, the Philippines, Singapore and Thailand), Southeast Asia's centrality in addressing challenges from maritime security to China's rise, and ASEAN's transformation from an anti-communist bloc to a forum for major powers to engage made the region's importance clear. Yet US attention tended to be in reaction to particular crises rather than a focus on the region for its own sake, be it the Asian financial crisis of 1997 or the war on terrorism in the early 2000s. Though this pattern had long been evident, it also prevented the rise of a more strategic, region-wide, and balanced approach to Southeast Asia.

Despite the traditional interpretation of being consumed by distractions in the Middle East and sceptical about multilateralism, the George W. Bush years actually saw some movement in the direction of more robust engagement with Southeast Asia. Some of this was evident in the usual building block work that tends to make up the continuity between administrations, be it expanding the scope of security cooperation with partners or contributing to the development of multi-lateral institutions in the ASEAN-led diplomatic framework.[4] But there were also initiatives that were to serve as precursors to some of the Obama administration's priorities, including the appointment in 2008 of the first resident US ambassador to ASEAN,[5] and joining the Trans-Pacific Partnership (TPP, then known as the Trans-Pacific Strategic Economic Partnership).[6] Yet, at the same time, it was not until the Obama administration that we saw the true development of a clear and comprehensive approach to engaging Southeast Asia more specifically articulated.

Obama's approach to ASEAN and Southeast Asia

From the outset, the Obama administration made clear that the basis for its approach to engagement with Southeast Asia and ASEAN was that it saw a greater investment in the region as being a vital part of preserving what it had referred to as the rules-based international order. As a result, it is no surprise that his administration made the region a vital part of its Rebalance to the Asia Pacific and undertook a series of initiatives to try to make that happen across the economic, security, and people-to-people realms of the relationship.

The Obama administration saw Southeast Asia and ASEAN as key to the preservation of the rules-based international order, which was emphasised as an enduring US national interest from the outset.[7] From the administration's perspective, if Washington wanted to preserve the post-Second World War US-led international order that would promote peace and prosperity, engaging emerging regions and regional institutions would be critical to solving collective action problems.[8] Southeast Asia and ASEAN served as a good example in this respect: the region, for all its limitations, and in contrast to other parts of the world, had emerged as peaceful and prosperous since ASEAN's founding in 1967 despite its tremendous diversity.[9]

The administration's thinking reflected the realities it faced in Asia as well. Within the Asia Pacific, Washington's attempts to preserve a rules-based international order – from advancing freedom of navigation to promoting economic openness and competitiveness to advancing the rule of law, good governance, and human rights and democracy – would largely play out in Southeast Asia.[10] The region was the hub of multilateralism in the Asia Pacific, comprising a diverse array of states at various levels of political and economic development, and was at the centre of Chinese attempts to undermine aspects of the rules-based international order.[11] As Obama himself put it during his last year of office, 'engagement with Southeast Asia and ASEAN ... is central to the region's peace and prosperity, and to our shared goal of building a regional order where all nations play by the same rules'.[12]

Therefore, it is no surprise that Southeast Asia and ASEAN was a centrepiece of the Rebalance to the Asia Pacific. Even in early articulations of the Rebalance, administration officials admitted privately that arguably the most significant part of the administration's Rebalance was the greater share of attention devoted to Southeast Asia as a region and ASEAN as a multilateral grouping within US Asia policy, the so-called "Rebalance within the Rebalance". Officials also referred to ASEAN as a fulcrum of the region's emerging architecture, reflecting what Hillary Clinton during her time as secretary of state referred to as the grouping's 'indispensable' role on a host of political, economic and strategic issues.[13]

The administration's approach to Southeast Asia and ASEAN itself was centred on four aspects: strengthening security alliances and partnerships; investing in multilateral institutions; advancing economic engagement; and promoting democracy and human rights. Though these general objectives were of course not new to US Asia policy, there were distinguishing features in each of these that were reflective of the Obama administration's approach.

First, the Obama administration focused on strengthening alliances and partnerships. While this had long been a key part of advancing US policy, the Obama administration took a much more comprehensive view, focusing not only on treaty allies such as Thailand and the Philippines, but inking a series of strategic and comprehensive partnerships with key Southeast Asian states such as Vietnam, Indonesia and Malaysia and opening up new partnerships with countries like Myanmar.[14] The content of these partnerships was significant too in that they reflected the administration's comprehensive approach – security realms of these alliances and partnerships, for example, were focused not just on terrorism or maritime security, but more broadly on humanitarian assistance and disaster relief, as well as climate change.

Second, the administration invested significantly in multilateral institutions in addition to bilateral partnerships. This was evident in a series of steps undertaken during its tenure, including ratifying the Treaty of Amity and Cooperation; becoming the first non-ASEAN country to appoint a resident ambassador to ASEAN in 2011; joining the East Asia Summit (EAS); institutionalising annual US–ASEAN summits, inking a strategic partnership with ASEAN; and even holding the first ever US–ASEAN summit on US soil at Sunnylands. Taken together, this investment in multilateralism was particularly notable for a US Asia bureaucracy that had long been largely dominated by North East Asian concerns. These were also steps that the Bush administration did not take during its time in office.

Third, the Obama administration sought to boost US economic engagement in the region. This occurred for example through US-led efforts such as the Lower Mekong Initiative (LMI) and ones in partnership with regional states like Singapore such as the Third Country Training Program, whereby the Obama administration demonstrated a commitment to building the capacity of lesser developed regional states.[15] The administration also rolled out the region-wide US–ASEAN Connect Initiative which sought to better coordinate existing US government programmes in the region around business, energy, innovation and policy.[16] And while not a solely Southeast Asia-based initiative, the TPP comprised four ASEAN countries – Brunei, Malaysia, Singapore and Vietnam. With several other Southeast Asian countries that had considered joining as well, the TPP was pitched by the administration as representative of the kind of rules that Southeast Asian states should aspire to.[17]

Fourth and lastly, the administration sought to advance democracy and human rights. Part of this was accomplished indirectly through attempts to address rule of law challenges in Southeast Asian states, through such efforts as the Open Government Partnership to promote good governance and transparency, and democracy programmes in individual Southeast Asian states such as the Philippines and Myanmar.[18] An important element of this strategy was investment in the young people of Southeast Asia, which Obama himself saw as part of the growth and dynamism in Southeast Asia and a source of change in the future. The signature investment in this realm was in the Young Southeast Asian Leaders Initiative (YSEALI), launched in 2013, to strengthen partnerships with emerging leaders in the region.[19]

Assessing Obama's approach

An evaluation of the Obama administration's approach suggests that the legacy is in fact quite a mixed one. On some counts, the administration's approach was a success. First and most clearly, the Obama administration raised, sustained and institutionalised a high level of attention to Southeast Asia after years of ambivalence.[20] Following decades of ebbs and flows in US attention to Southeast Asia, the Obama years saw a sustained effort to increase the focus on the region across countries and realms, led not only by bureaucracies or high-level officials but by Obama himself, who visited Southeast Asia eight times during his time in office – more than two times the number of any sitting US president – and held the first US–ASEAN Summit on US soil.

As it intensified the focus on Southeast Asia, and mindful of the episodic attention it had previously been afforded in Washington, the Obama administration worked assiduously to institutionalise the growing momentum with the region. In the administration's view this would help ensure lock-in that would be difficult to reverse by any subsequent administrations.[21] In that sense, though often a lot of the media attention was placed on flashier initiatives like the Sunnylands Summit, it was measures such as the formulation of new strategic and comprehensive partnerships or the establishment of a new Office of Multilateral Affairs at the State Department's Bureau of East Asian and Pacific Affairs, that were the more significant initiatives because they helped produce the lock-in effect that the administration sought.

Second, the Obama administration firmly committed the United States to the ASEAN multilateral framework and clearly articulated the bipartisan case for US investment in the regional grouping. While US ambivalence to multilateral institutions in Asia had long been evident, the George W. Bush years had seen a clear trend where Washington's lukewarm attitude stood in marked contrast to ASEAN's enhanced role in the regional order and the attention it received from other powers. As ASEAN's role in the regional security architecture had increased significantly with the emergence of forums such as the EAS in 2005 and the ASEAN Defence Ministers' Meeting Plus, major powers in the Asia Pacific such as China, Japan and India had moved to solidify their ties with the regional grouping even as the United States remained ambivalent about its own commitment for various reasons.[22] By firmly committing the United States to the ASEAN multilateral framework, the Obama administration effectively resolved a long debate about the extent to which the region should commit to the multilateral framework.

As it went forward with that commitment, the Obama administration also clearly articulated why investing in ASEAN was directly related to US national interests. Previous administrations had advanced various reasons why Washington ought to be *indirectly* engaged in the ASEAN multilateral framework, whether to back an anti-communist bloc against the Cold War Soviet Union or support Asian prosperity in the early to mid-1990s after the fall of the Berlin Wall. Yet the Obama administration specifically tied ASEAN to the fate of the rules-based order and the US role in preserving and shaping that order in Asia. As Michael Fuchs, Obama's former deputy assistant secretary of state for East Asian and Pacific Affairs, has put it, the administration's commitment to ASEAN was rooted not only in recognising the grouping's centrality, but its commitment to the norms of the liberal international order and ensuring that Washington would be at the table in discussions where the future shape of those norms would be debated in the region.[23]

Third, the Obama years saw an improvement in perceptions of the United States among Southeast Asia's population. Though opinion polls tend to be quite fickle and cannot tell the whole story, and while the trend was less evident during Obama's second term, polls revealed a clear increase in positive views of the United States even in countries where levels of anti-Americanism had previously been quite high, such as Indonesia and Malaysia.[24] While some of this is owed to positive perceptions of Obama himself, the administration's policies as well as initiatives such as YSEALI no doubt also contributed to more benign perceptions of the United States. This was particularly notable relative to the initial years of the Bush administration, where issues such as US foreign policy in the Middle East and an overemphasis on the terrorism threat had led to initial negative perceptions in some regional states.

Administration officials, including Obama himself, repeatedly and publicly emphasised the importance of improving America's image among Southeast Asia's populations as a key part of its engagement with the region. Part of this rested in the oft-cited fact that this represented a long-term investment, since the younger generation would become the region's future leaders. But the additional reality that the Obama administration understood was that in order for Southeast Asian governments to have the right environment to expand ties with Washington, they needed the support of their populations. Some of these governments still recall periods where negative perceptions of US foreign policy had led to diminished popular support for the United States, restricting the ability for policy makers to publicly support Washington's initiatives.

But the Obama administration's approach also confronted several major challenges. The first and clearest was managing relations with a rising China, whose influence was increasing in Southeast Asia and becoming manifested in ways detrimental to US interests and those of some regional states. Despite being cognizant of this trend and its manifestations, the administration's desire to ease Beijing's insecurities and collaborate on issues, ranging from addressing global climate change to managing the Iran nuclear issue, repeatedly trumped the necessity to confront China on aspects of its assertive behaviour, leading to greater anxieties in the region as well as on the broader question of the reliability of the United States.[25]

There are several cases that illustrate this point, but nowhere was this clearer than in the South China Sea. Though the South China Sea disputes themselves are long-standing and chiefly among China and four Southeast Asian claimants – the

Philippines, Vietnam, Malaysia and Brunei – the issue had nonetheless come to be viewed as a test of US and Chinese resolve; Beijing's assertive and at times unlawful moves, including seizing geographical features, harassing vessels, and constructing artificial islands directly threatened the rules-based order the Obama administration sought to defend.[26] Yet while the administration continued to rhetorically emphasise the importance of the South China Sea in this context and tried to ward off more aggressive forms of Chinese behaviour, it did not take the more forward-leaning measures that would have clearly deterred Beijing. 'The net result', concludes one regional observer, 'is a sense of a shifting power balance in Southeast Asia and a feeling of a China on the march forward as the US has looked weak and was in disarray, whatever the objective economic and military facts of the region may be.'[27]

Second, and turning to the economic realm, the Obama administration ultimately failed to engage the region in a manner which accommodated the diversity of Southeast Asian economies. The elephant in the room here is the fact that the TPP, repeatedly framed by Obama administration officials and observers as not just having economic benefits but able to catalyse a "race to the top" among Southeast Asian states, via the provision of common, high-level standards, was left unratified.[28] Though there were several reasons behind this, including legislative opposition and popular discontent, the administration shares the blame for not spending more of its political capital sooner to overcome the obstacles to see it through.

Beyond the TPP, other initiatives were articulated but not adequately resourced or sufficiently fleshed out before the administration's end in early 2017. Capacity-building efforts like the LMI continued, but faced immense resourcing difficulties even as new initiatives from China such as the Lancang-Mekong Cooperation developed later but gained steam more quickly.[29] Other initiatives were considered and had begun to be articulated in areas like infrastructure, innovation and entrepreneurship, but were not advanced by the end of Obama's second term. Even though officials had indicated that concerns behind some of these initiatives, like inadequate staffing and resources, may have been addressed had there been more continuity within administrations, the underdevelopment of initiatives during Obama's time in office means that even a generous grading of his legacy would register as an incomplete.[30]

Third and finally, the administration failed to articulate a clear and comprehensive vision for democracy and human rights in the region even as it saw growing challenges on this front. Officials were correct when they argued that US policy had to depart from the lecturing of Southeast Asian states seen in the past, including during the Clinton and Bush years, and that such an approach may be less effective relative to privately conveying concerns to individual countries. But despite repeated requests and complaints by rights groups and critics, the administration did not present a coherent policy for balancing interests and values.[31] Administration officials instead repeatedly cited the merits of treating each country on a case-by-case basis and making distinctions accordingly, such as between democracy and good governance or private and public forms of concern.

The restrictions brought by the lack of a clear vision in this area were illustrated when democratic backsliding in the region began to take hold during the Obama administration's later years, particularly with the military coup in Thailand in 2014 and the election of Philippine President Rodrigo Duterte in 2016. Though the administration dealt with the issues on a case-by-case basis and continued to advance other elements of its people-to-people engagement, like YSEALI, the lack of a comprehensive approach in this realm gave way to the perception that this was not a major priority relative to other US interests.

What Trump means for Obama's legacy in Southeast Asia

It is important to emphasise that, irrespective of who was to take office after Obama, questions surrounded the durability of his legacy in Southeast Asia even before he departed.[32] Part of that rested on the uniqueness of Obama's personal commitment to Southeast Asia and ASEAN, including his experience of living in Indonesia. Indeed, with the exception of Hillary Clinton – the first secretary of state to visit all ten ASEAN countries – there was no guarantee that any of the other American presidential candidates would demonstrate the same regard for the region. On top of that, there was a sense that with the next US president having to face a divided country at home and a more tumultuous and fractured world, there was a risk that Washington may have much less patience for multilateralism and may engage selectively with individual ASEAN states rather than the region as a whole.

After two years in office by early 2019, the US administration of President Donald Trump had not clearly articulated a discernible approach towards Southeast Asia. This is not uncommon to see, even in more conventional administrations: for instance, it took the Obama administration more than two years to begin to publicly and actively roll out its Rebalance policy for the Asia Pacific.[33] Nonetheless, the general tendencies evident so far under Trump suggest a mix of continuity from elements of Obama's legacy, and change that may either tackle issues that went unaddressed or undermine progress already made.

The elements of continuity are most evident in the organising principle the Trump administration articulated for the region, as well as in the security and diplomatic realms of its engagement. Thus for example, though the Trump administration has been reluctant to employ the Obama administration's "Rebalance" term, which is fairly common for new administrations to do, administration officials have nonetheless referred to the rules-based order and similar notions with different concepts, most prominently the 'free and open Indo-Pacific'.[34] Such visions are rooted in essentially the same organising principle, dating back to the rules-based international order the United States helped build and lead after the end of the Second World War with allies and partners to advance peace, prosperity and freedom and looking ahead to how Washington can work to address the current strains in that order.[35]

In the realm of security, continuity can be seen in the vision mentioned by Defense Secretary James Mattis and others. The insistence that the United States, together with allies and partners, will focus not only on individual threats like terrorism and North Korea, but also the broader challenge that authoritarian states, chiefly China, pose to the rules-based international order such as in the South China Sea, sounds much like the 'principled security network' that Mattis' predecessor Ash Carter had indicated previously.[36] Further, the Trump administration to date has either continued or reinforced existing attempts over multiple administrations to solidify defence ties with Southeast Asian allies and partners like Indonesia, the Philippines, Thailand and Vietnam.

Of course, there appear to be limits to that continuity in other related areas. There is a harder edge to the administration's line on China's role in the regional security environment at the outset relative to the Obama years. And while this may change further down the line, the early perception among Southeast Asian states has been of the Trump administration attempting to address a narrower list of security concerns, such as North Korea and counterterrorism rather than taking a broader and more comprehensive approach as the Obama administration did. On the more positive side of the ledger, the Trump administration's commitment to raise defence spending has been welcomed in Southeast Asian capitals as evidence that Washington is overcoming budgetary challenges that dogged the Obama era, even as concerns remain about how that military power will be deployed.

Some continuity is also evident on the diplomatic side. Though the new US administration has not been as embracing in its rhetoric about multilateralism compared to its predecessor, Trump did show that he is personally willing to attend Asian summitry by showing up at his first round in the Philippines, even though he did depart early from the EAS. While it is unclear how Trump's attendance record will play out for the remainder of his term, the openness to attending the meetings, which was announced well in advance of the trip itself and largely followed through on despite other priorities, was nonetheless clear. Beyond that episode itself, the characterisation of Trump's attendance as a 'test' for US commitment is itself testament to the importance of the Obama administration's institutionalising of presidential-level travel to Southeast Asia and the enduring power of these binding commitments.[37]

The major discontinuities lie in the economic, rights, and people-to-people dimensions of US engagement with the region. On economics, though the Obama administration had its own issues with realising new economic opportunities for US policy towards the region, the Trump administration compounded Southeast Asian anxieties by taking a strong protectionist and transactional stance in his first two years in charge. Trump's decision to withdraw from the TPP was seen by Southeast Asian member states as being not just a missed opportunity for US leadership on trade, but a reflection of trends that could take years to reverse.[38] Though the administration could reverse or at least moderate its course later on, the discontinuity was quite clear at the outset.

On the human rights front, the Trump administration itself has so far evinced little interest in the advancement of American ideals and instead appears focused more on advancing narrow US interests in a transactional way. The Obama administration was similarly focused more on interests rather than values, and other institutions like the State Department and Congress continue to exercise their role on issues such as the Rohingya crisis in Myanmar. Trump has been less averse to working with Asian strongmen than Obama, as evidenced by the White House visits granted to Philippine President Rodrigo Duterte and Thai Prime Minister Prayut Chan-o-cha during his first year in office. And as the scholar Thomas Carothers has noted, Trump's personal record on rights has also complicated things, from his mocking of the United States as a democratic exemplar, to engaging in the tactics of strongmen leaders such as personally attacking journalists.[39]

Discontinuity is evident in the people-to-people realm as well. There have been basic elements of continuity, such as in the bureaucratic work of running important outreach initiatives that tends to continue across administrations, to Trump's commitment thus far to preserve some Obama-era initiatives like the YSEALI programme. But other developments suggest that change or even reversal is underway. On public opinion for instance, there is early evidence of Southeast Asian discontent with the image of the United States in the world, the extent of American commitment to the region, and with some of the Trump administration's "America First" policies.[40] This was matched by realities on the ground in some Southeast Asian countries, where policies ranging from the travel ban to the decision to move the US embassy to Jerusalem sparked anti-American sentiment and protest.

Conclusions

As this chapter has shown, the Obama administration's legacy in Southeast Asia is a mixed one. The administration achieved some notable successes, including increasing and institutionalising a higher level of attention to Southeast Asia, committing Washington to Asia's multilateral diplomatic framework, and improving relations with Southeast Asia's people. But on the other hand, it also failed to manage some challenges that continue to bedevil the Trump administration, most notably confronting the reality of China's growing influence in Southeast Asia, crafting an economic approach for the subregion, and articulating a clear and comprehensive approach to dealing with democracy and human rights questions.

Though this mixed record is far from surprising, it nonetheless speaks to the more enduring difficulties that US policy makers have always faced in crafting a policy towards the region. Indeed, perhaps the most sobering lesson of Obama's legacy in Southeast Asia and ASEAN is the fact that even with such a high level of presidential commitment and sustained attention by the administration, overcoming some of the key challenges that have long dogged US policy towards the region proved extremely difficult. Those which remain for Washington include fashioning an economic agenda for such a diverse array of states despite resource constraints, and maintaining a regional focus amidst wider threats and challenges in other parts of Asia and the wider world.

At a more granular level, Obama's record also speaks to the question of relative durability of policy. Though Obama's engagement with Southeast Asia's young people was the element of his legacy which attracted most headlines, popular perception is also among the least durable aspects of US policy relative to more underappreciated parts of his legacy such as the institutionalisation of meetings or binding Washington to Southeast Asia's multilateral diplomatic framework. Relatedly, Trump's time in office to early 2019 further underlined the fact that the durability of a president's legacy can be shaped to a significant degree by not just his own record, but that of his successor as well. While Obama's failure to finalise the TPP during his time in office was viewed as a failure as he left, Trump's withdrawal from the agreement and subsequent approach to economic policy has made Obama's record on this count seem much more favourable relatively speaking. And depending on how Trump's tougher approach to China plays out, it could either expose the folly of the overly cautious approach to China during the Obama years, or in fact reinforce the necessity of that more careful orientation towards Beijing.

Finally, it speaks to the importance of recalling the interactive nature of the relationship between Southeast Asia and the United States. Though the Obama administration crafted its own approach to Southeast Asia, as might be expected, the success or failure of that policy was contingent not just on what the United States did or how other major powers reacted, but also on how the region's elites and people responded and on the other regional developments simultaneously occurring. American presidents and US administrations are often remembered not so much for their early or instinctive approach, but for how they respond to the events they encounter during their watch. Obama's legacy in Southeast Asia and ASEAN will not be an exception to that, and nor will Trump's.

Notes

1 Though Southeast Asia and ASEAN are often employed interchangeably for ease of use, including here, it is important to note the distinction between the two terms. "Southeast Asia" refers to the subregion itself, while "ASEAN" refers to the regional grouping of Southeast Asian states founded in 1967.

2   P. Parameswaran, 'Understanding US Policy in Southeast Asia', Remarks at Georgetown University, Washington, DC (22 March 2017).

3   For an example of this line of thinking, see: D. K. Mauzy and B. L. Job, 'US policy in Southeast Asia: Limited re-engagement after years of benign neglect', *Asian Survey*, 47:4 (2007), pp. 622–41.

4   US Department of State, 'US Engagement in Southeast Asia' (25 September 2008), https://2001-2009.state.gov/p/eap/rls/rm/2008/09/110494.htm, accessed 15 March 2019.

5   The Bush administration appointed Scot Marciel as the first US Ambassador to ASEAN, in 2008. The Obama administration is credited with appointing the first *resident* US ambassador to the organisation in Jakarta.

6   Office of the US Trade Representative, 'Trans Pacific Partners and United States Launch FTA Negotiations' (22 September 2008), https://ustr.gov/trans-pacific-partners-and-united-states-launch-fta-negotiations, accessed 13 March 2019.

7   White House, 'National Security Strategy' (May 2010), http://nssarchive.us/NSSR/2010.pdf, accessed 13 March 2019.

8   White House, 'Fact Sheet: Advancing the Rebalance to Asia and the Pacific' (16 November 2015), https://obamawhitehouse.archives.gov/the-press-office/2015/11/16/fact-sheet-advancing-rebalance-asia-and-pacific, accessed 13 March 2019.

9   Center for a New American Century, 'US Policy in Southeast Asia: A Conversation with Deputy National Security Advisor Ben Rhodes' (17 May 2016), www.cnas.org/events/u-s-policy-in-southeast-asia-a-conversation-with-deputy-national-security-advisor-ben-rhodes, accessed 13 March 2019.

10 Author conversation with US official, Washington, DC (February 2016).

11 K. Campbell, *The Pivot: The Future of American Statecraft in Asia* (New York: Twelve, 2016).

12 White House, 'Remarks by President Obama at Opening Session of the US-ASEAN Summit' (15 February 2016), https://obamawhitehouse.archives.gov/the-press-office/2016/02/15/remarks-president-obama-opening-session-us-asean-summit, accessed 13 March 2019.

13 US Department of State, 'America's Engagement in the Asia-Pacific' (28 October 2010), https://2009-2017.state.gov/secretary/20092013clinton/rm/2010/10/150141.htm, accessed 13 March 2019.

14 P. Parameswaran, 'Explaining US strategic partnerships in the Asia-Pacific', *Contemporary Southeast Asia*, 36:2 (2014), pp. 262–89.

15 P. Parameswaran, 'Strengthening US-Singapore Strategic Partnership: Opportunities and Challenges', S. Rajaratnam School of International Studies Commentary (8 August 2016).

16 White House, 'Fact Sheet: US-ASEAN Connect' (8 September 2016), https://obamawhitehouse.archives.gov/the-press-office/2016/09/08/fact-sheet-us-asean-connect, accessed 13 March 2019.

17 Author conversation with US official, Washington, DC (March 2015).

18 White House, 'Fact Sheet: The Open Government Partnership' (20 September 2011), https://obamawhitehouse.archives.gov/the-press-office/2011/09/20/fact-sheet-open-government-partnership, accessed 13 March 2019.

19   Several administration officials interviewed by the author noted that of all the Southeast Asia-related initiatives in the administration, YSEALI was the initiative that Obama was most personally invested in.

20   Mauzy and Job, 'US Policy in Southeast Asia'.

21   D. Kritenbrink, 'Remarks at US-ASEAN Business Council Gala Dinner', Washington, DC (October 2016).

22   For the roots of this ambivalence, see: V. Cha, *Powerplay: The Origins of the American Alliance System in Asia* (Oxford: Princeton University Press, 2016). For the Bush administration's approach, see: M. Green, *By More Than Providence: Grand Strategy and American Power in the Asia-Pacific Since 1783* (New York: Columbia University Press, 2017).

23   M. H. Fuchs, 'Obama's Asia Pivot Has Been a Historic Success', *The New Republic* (31 August 2016), https://newrepublic.com/article/136432/obamas-asia-pivot-historic-success, accessed 13 March 2019.

24   P. Parameswaran, 'The Obama era: The view from Indonesia', in M. Maass (ed.), *The World Views of the Obama Era: From Hope to Disillusionment* (New York: Palgrave Macmillan, 2017).

25   K. Campbell and E. Ratner, 'The China reckoning: How Beijing defied American expectations', *Foreign Affairs*, 97:2 (2018), pp. 60–70.

26   P. Parameswaran, 'US South China Sea After the Ruling: Opportunities and Challenges', The Brookings Institution (22 July 2016), www.brookings.edu/opinions/u-s-south-china-sea-policy-after-the-ruling-opportunities-and-challenges/, accessed 13 March 2019.

27   D. Singh, 'Obama's Mixed Legacy in Southeast Asia', *The Straits Times* (17 January 2017), www.straitstimes.com/opinion/obamas-mixed-legacy-in-south-east-asia, accessed 14 March 2019.

28   For a discussion of rules-based arguments and rule-making in the TPP, see: B. Dolven *et al.*, *The Trans-Pacific Partnership: Strategic Implications*, Congressional Research Service (3 February 2016); T. Allee and A. Lugg, 'Who wrote the rules for the Trans Pacific Partnership?', *Research and Politics* (September 2016), pp. 1–9. For a discussion on the economic effects of the TPP, see: P. Petri and M. Plummer, *The Economic Effects of the Trans-Pacific Partnership: New Estimates*, Peterson Institute of International Economics working paper 16-2 (January 2016).

29   P. Sothirak, 'Lancang Mekong Cooperation and the Future of the Mekong River', Remarks at the 31st Asia-Pacific Roundtable, Kuala Lumpur (23–24 May 2017).

30   Author conversation with Obama administration official, Washington, DC (June 2016).

31   For an example, see: J. Kurlantzick, 'The Pivot in Southeast Asia: Balancing Interests and Values', Council on Foreign Relations (8 January 2015), www.cfr.org/report/pivot-southeast-asia, accessed 14 March 2019.

32   P. Parameswaran, 'Trump or Clinton, Challenges Ahead for US' Asia Policy', *The Straits Times* (11 August 2016), www.straitstimes.com/opinion/trump-or-clinton-challenges-ahead-for-us-asia-policy, accessed 13 March 2019.

33   The official public rollout of the administration's Rebalance policy is often said to have begun with Hillary Clinton's *Foreign Policy* article. See H. Clinton, 'Americas

Pacific Century', *Foreign Policy* (11 October 2011), https://foreignpolicy.com/2011/10/11/americas-pacific-century/, accessed 14 March 2019. Governmental discussions of the approach predate that article, however.

34   Though new administrations are fond of changing these conceptions, the first time that a departure from the Rebalance was publicly signaled during the Trump administration came from Deputy Assistant Secretary of State Susan Thornton in March 2017. See: US Department of State, 'A Preview of Secretary Tillerson's Upcoming Travel to Asia' (13 March 2017), https://fpc.state.gov/268444.htm, accessed 14 March 2019. For an initial articulation of the Free and Open Indo-Pacific concept, see: White House, 'Remarks by President Trump at APEC CEO Summit' (10 November 2017), www.whitehouse.gov/briefings-statements/remarks-president-trump-apec-ceo-summit-da-nang-vietnam/, accessed 13 March 2019.

35   P. Parameswaran, 'Trump's Indo-Pacific Strategy Challenge', *The Diplomat* (27 October 2017), https://thediplomat.com/2017/10/trumps-indo-pacific-strategy-challenge/, accessed 13 March 2019.

36   US Department of Defense, 'Remarks by Secretary Mattis at 2017 Shangri-La Dialogue' (3 June 2017), https://dod.defense.gov/News/Transcripts/Transcript-View/Article/1201780/remarks-by-secretary-mattis-at-shangri-la-dialogue/, accessed 13 March 2019.

37   P. Parameswaran, 'Would a Trump EAS Philippines Miss Really Matter for US Asia Policy', *The Diplomat* (27 October 2017), https://thediplomat.com/2017/04/why-trump-must-go-to-asean-and-apec-in-the-philippines-and-vietnam/, accessed 14 March 2019.

38   Council on Foreign Relations, 'A Conversation with Lee Hsien Loong' (25 October 2017), www.cfr.org/event/conversation-lee-hsien-loong, accessed 14 March 2019.

39   T. Carothers, 'Prospects for US Democracy Promotion Under Trump', Carnegie Endowment for International Peace (5 January 2017), https://carnegieendowment.org/2017/01/05/prospects-for-u.s.-democracy-promotion-under-trump-pub-66588, accessed 14 March 2019.

40   See, for instance: R. Wike, B. Stokes, J. Poushter and J. Fetterolf, 'US Image Suffers as Publics Around World Question Trump's Leadership', Pew Research Center (26 June 2017), www.pewglobal.org/2017/06/26/u-s-image-suffers-as-publics-around-world-question-trumps-leadership/, accessed 14 March 2019; ASEAN Studies Center, 'How Do Southeast Asians View the Trump Administration?', ISEAS Yusof Ishak Institute (4 May 2017), www.iseas.edu.sg/images/centres/asc/pdf/ASCSurvey40517.pdf, accessed 14 March 2019.

8

The Obama administration and the East Asia Summit: Exception, not transformation

Malcolm Cook

Introduction

The Obama administration was the first to put ASEAN at the centre of its Asia diplomacy. Gaining membership to the ASEAN-created and ASEAN-led East Asia Summit (EAS), achieved in 2011, was deemed a particularly important milestone. It is quite possible that the Obama administration may well become the only American administration to prioritise the EAS to such an extent. Up until the time of writing in early 2019, the Trump administration from 2017 reverted to a more typical US approach to Asia focused on Northeast Asia, bilateral relations and American unilateralism.

The contrast between the initial engagements of the first Obama administration in particular and those evident across the two years of the Trump administration both with ASEAN and the EAS provides strong support for the above conclusion. When Barack Obama became president in January 2009, the United States was not a member of the EAS, the most important ASEAN-led regional forum. However, his incoming administration was strongly committed to US membership. In his first year in office Secretary of State Hillary Clinton signed the ASEAN Treaty of Amity and Cooperation. This was the only prerequisite for an ASEAN invitation to the EAS that the United States did not fulfil in 2005, when the Summit was established.

When Donald Trump became president in January 2017, the United States was already a well-established EAS participant. However, the Trump administration's commitment to the institution, the only ASEAN-led leaders-level mechanism that includes the United States, has so far remained unclear. When Vice President Mike Pence made his first visit to Asia in April 2017, it included a brief visit to the ASEAN Secretariat in Jakarta. There, he announced that in November President Trump would attend the APEC Summit in Hanoi, as well as the fifth ASEAN–US Summit and the twelfth EAS in Manila (both scheduled to follow a few days after

APEC), as a sign of continued, if not enhanced, American commitment. Pence was the first US Vice President and the most senior US political leader ever to visit the Secretariat.

Three weeks before the November US–ASEAN Summit, however, the Trump White House indicated that he would skip the EAS which was scheduled to be the last event on his long inaugural trip to Asia. Trump did not attend the Summit and sent his Secretary of State Rex Tillerson in his place instead. The Trump White House claimed that the President did attend the EAS on 14 November 2017.[1] However, this is a case of stretching, if not breaking, the diplomatic truth. President Trump only attended the lunch organised by the ASEAN chair President Duterte of the Philippines, prior to the delayed EAS plenary session itself. This working lunch also included leaders from countries and groupings not in the EAS. The official Summit group photo features a smiling Rex Tillerson; President Trump was already on his plane home.[2] Trump was once again absent from the Summit in November 2018, this time sending Vice President Mike Pence in his place.

These two different approaches to the EAS and their inferred, if not implied, messages about US presidential commitment to ASEAN, provided early insights into the contrasting approaches to Southeast Asia of the Obama administration of 2009–17 and the Trump administration during its first two years in Washington.

On the American side, the first Obama administration came to power with a clear strategy for enhanced US engagement in Asia, in which ASEAN and the EAS had a clear and central role which endured throughout both of Obama's terms in office. The Trump administration did not. On the ASEAN side, the EAS so far has failed to live up to the expectations of the Obama administration. It still fails to occupy a clear or leading role in the ASEAN-led regional architecture. Efforts to strengthen the institution and focus its attention on issues of primary US concern have been constrained due to disagreements over its future among ASEAN member states, and among the eight ASEAN dialogue partners currently invited to the EAS by ASEAN.

By themselves, these ASEAN-based constraints on the development and centrality of the Summit likely would have moderated any post-Obama commitment in Washington to the EAS. The contrasting approach to Southeast Asia in particular, and to diplomacy in general, of the Trump administration suggest a decline of interest from Washington. The Obama administration will likely come to represent an exceptional high-water mark in relation to US engagement with ASEAN and the EAS, and not the beginning of a sustained bipartisan period of commitment.

This chapter begins by setting out the Obama administration's reasons for a strong commitment to ASEAN and the EAS, and what they hoped they would gain from participation. The second part looks at the constraints to the development of the EAS along the lines desired by the Obama administration. The third section looks at the differences in engagement with ASEAN and the EAS in the first two years of the Trump administration, and why they suggest that the Obama years should be considered exceptional rather than transformative when it comes to US engagement with ASEAN.

The ASEAN Rebalance

In 2009, the Obama administration came into office with the outlines of a new strategy for American engagement in Asia that were quickly acted upon. This new strategy, labelled the "Pivot" then the "Rebalance" to Asia, had one major political goal and one major strategic goal. The political goal was to sharply, at least rhetorically, differentiate the new Democratic Obama administration from the prior Republican George W. Bush administration of 2001–09. The widespread criticism of the Bush government and its approach to Asia from US Asia watchers (and from many in Asia as well) made such a differentiation both more important and more beneficial. Many ASEAN and Southeast Asian officials were particularly critical of the Bush administration for its lack of adequate commitment to ASEAN. In 2005, US Secretary of State Condoleezza Rice skipped the ASEAN Regional Forum (ARF), the only ASEAN-led wider regional grouping that included the United States, becoming the first Secretary of State to do so since its formation in 1994.[3] In 2007, Rice again chose to not attend the Forum, despite the storm of protest her 2005 absence had fomented.

The grand strategic goal of Obama's Rebalance was to maintain the United States' leading position in East Asia in the face of growing Chinese power, wealth and assertion. This reassurance effort aimed to assuage concerns from worried Asian allies and partners about the willingness and capability of Washington to maintain its traditionally hegemonic position in East Asia in ways they supported.

The diplomatic pillar of the Rebalance was the only one which brought a marked contrast between the Obama administration and that of George W. Bush. Southeast Asia was the geographical focus of this differentiation and ASEAN the institutional one. The list of diplomatic firsts for the United States in relation to ASEAN under the Obama administration is impressive, both in number and as a cumulative sign of sustained commitment:

- In February 2009 (less than a month after taking office), Secretary of State Hillary Clinton became the first person in her role to visit the ASEAN Secretariat in Jakarta.
- On that same trip, Secretary Clinton expressed for the first time official US plans to sign the ASEAN Treaty of Amity and Cooperation.
- On 22 July 2009, in Thailand, the United States signed the ASEAN Treaty of Amity and Cooperation, becoming the fifteenth non-ASEAN member and the eighth ASEAN dialogue partner to do so.

- In November 2009, the first US–ASEAN Leaders' Meeting was held in Singapore.
- In October 2010, Secretary of State Clinton became the first US senior official invited (as a guest of the host, Vietnam) to the lunch before the EAS.
- In October 2010, Secretary of Defense Robert Gates attended the inaugural ASEAN Defense Ministers Meeting Plus (ADMM+). The sitting Secretary of Defense has attended every ADMM+ Meeting since.
- In September 2010, the United States became the first ASEAN dialogue partner to appoint a resident ambassador to ASEAN. Ambassador David Carden presented his credentials to the ASEAN Secretary-General on 26 April 2011. Now, all ten ASEAN dialogue partners have appointed resident ambassadors to ASEAN.
- In November 2011, Obama became the first US president to attend the EAS. He only missed one Summit gathering in 2013 due to a domestic government shutdown. Secretary of State John Kelly represented the United States that year.
- In 2012, Obama became the first US president to visit Cambodia. He went to Phnom Penh to attend the EAS and the US–ASEAN Leaders' Meeting.
- In 2013, the annual US–ASEAN Leaders' Meeting was elevated to an annual US–ASEAN Leaders' Summit.
- In 2015, the US–ASEAN relationship was elevated to a Strategic Partnership.
- In February 2016, Obama hosted the first US–ASEAN Leaders' Summit to be held in the United States at Sunnylands, California.
- In September 2016, Obama became the first US president to visit Laos. He went to Vientiane to attend the EAS and ASEAN–US Leaders' Summit.

Former Secretary of State Hillary Clinton's November 2011 *Foreign Policy* article entitled 'America's Pacific Century' provides an extensive elaboration of the Asia Rebalance policy. After listing planned enhancements in all the key bilateral relations in the region, Clinton states that:

> Even as we strengthen these bilateral relationships, we have emphasized the importance of multilateral cooperation, for we believe that addressing complex transnational challenges of the sort now faced by Asia requires a set of institutions capable of mustering collective action. And a more robust and coherent regional architecture in Asia would reinforce the system of rules and responsibilities, from protecting intellectual property to ensuring freedom of navigation, that form the basis of an effective international order.[4]

ASEAN and greater US engagement with ASEAN is deemed critical to this 'more robust and coherent regional architecture', with Clinton justifying the intended focus on the regional grouping:

That is why President Obama will participate in the East Asia Summit for the first time in November. To pave the way, the United States has opened a new US Mission to ASEAN in Jakarta and signed the Treaty of Amity and Cooperation with ASEAN. Our focus on developing a more results-oriented agenda has been instrumental in efforts to address disputes in the South China Sea ... [o]ver the past year, we have made strides in protecting our vital interests in stability and freedom of navigation and have paved the way for sustained multilateral diplomacy among the many parties with claims in the South China Sea, seeking to ensure disputes are settled peacefully and in accordance with established principles of international law.[5]

The Obama White House repeated the same themes and hopes for the EAS. Its 'Fact Sheet on Unprecedented US-ASEAN Relations', released in February 2016, states:

In 2009, the United States became a party to the Treaty of Amity and Cooperation in Southeast Asia – the bedrock diplomatic document of ASEAN – opening the door for the United States to join the East Asia Summit (EAS). President Obama participated in the EAS for the first time in 2011 and has attended three of the four Summits since. With strong U.S. support, the EAS has become the Asia Pacific's premier leaders-level forum on political and security issues, helping to advance a rules-based order and spur cooperation on pressing challenges, including maritime security, countering violent extremism, and transnational cyber cooperation.[6]

This presidential support for a strong, more 'results-oriented' EAS focused on security issues also featured in Washington's bilateral diplomacy in Asia throughout the duration of the Obama administration. A US–Japan joint statement from 2014 stated that 'the two countries view the East Asia Summit as the premier political and security forum in the region'.[7] A joint statement from the United States and India in 2015 went further, asserting that 'we commit to strengthening the East Asia Summit ... to promote regional dialogue on key political and security issues, and to work harder to strengthen it'.[8]

The Obama administration's interest and subsequent commitment to the EAS and the ADMM+ process went beyond simply joining and showing up. The ADMM+ process was established in 2010 as a wider regional extension of the ASEAN Defence Ministers (ADMM) process. The ADMM was founded in 2006 as 'the highest ministerial defence and security consultative and cooperative mechanism among ASEAN defence establishments'.[9] The ADMM+ process brings together the ministers of defence of ASEAN member states with those of the eight dialogue partners also invited to the EAS. The United States under Obama, along with Japan and Australia, saw closer engagement with ASEAN and membership in the EAS and the ADMM+ process as a means to strengthen regional security cooperation.

These shared ASEAN interests among the United States and its two most important Asia Pacific allies manifested themselves in three key institutional preferences. The first was to bolster the ADMM+ process which, when it was announced in 2010, was to meet only once every three years. Washington, Tokyo and Canberra supported more frequent meetings, and in 2013 it was decided that the ADMM+ process would meet every two years. In 2017, it was decided that the ADMM+ should henceforth become an annual event.

The second institutional preference was for the EAS to focus predominantly on political and security issues, including contentious ones like the maritime rights disputes in the South China Sea. APEC, along with the Trans-Pacific Partnership (TPP), was seen as the key regional forum for economic diplomacy. This second preference has had more mixed results. The founding document for the EAS, *The Kuala Lumpur Declaration on the East Asia Summit*, released after the inaugural meeting in December 2005, states that 'we have established the East Asia Summit as a forum for dialogue on broad strategic, political and economic issues of common interest and concern with the aim of promoting peace, stability and economic prosperity in East Asia'.[10] The identification of EAS priority areas, as well as the contents of the Chairman Statements released at the end of each annual Summit meeting, have stayed true to this broad, inclusive beginning.

By the end of Obama's first term in office in 2013, six priority cooperation areas had been agreed to for the EAS: energy; education; finance; global health including pandemics; environment and disaster management; and ASEAN connectivity. This list is far from being perfectly aligned with the notion of the Summit as that 'premier political and security forum in the region'.[11] The first components overlap significantly with the agenda of APEC as the Asia Pacific's primary forum for the promotion of economic cooperation and free trade. The final component is focused on public infrastructure development in Southeast Asia, where Japan and China have long represented the major external partners. The breadth and diversity of these priority areas, as well as the lack of a traditional security focus, reflects how the EAS is an ASEAN-led consensus-based body. A such, it always had a limited ability to fulfil the Obama administration's stated goal to 'advance a rules-based order and spur cooperation on pressing challenges, including maritime security, countering violent extremism, and transnational cyber cooperation'.[12]

The third preference also led to mixed and uncertain results. Under the Obama administration, Washington wanted ASEAN-led forums which accommodated the United States to focus on maritime security. In 2010, Secretary of State Hillary Clinton used her presence at the ARF to repeat, to the great chagrin of Beijing, the US national interest in the South China Sea disputes.[13] In 2015, ASEAN's Malaysian Chair announced plans for an ADMM+ joint statement, which came to nothing from a Chinese insistence that no mention be made of the South China Sea disputes.[14] The US goal for the EAS was to have maritime security identified as one of the priority areas of cooperation. The 2015 EAS Statement on Enhancing Regional Maritime Cooperation noted that 'maritime cooperation has increasingly featured in East Asia Summit discussions, its inclusion as a priority area of cooperation merits further consideration'.[15] In 2017, "maritime cooperation" – a softer and broader term than "security" – was added as a 'new area of cooperation'.[16]

EAS constraints

There are three main constraints to the EAS achieving the United States' goal – at least as it was outlined under the Obama administration – of becoming the foremost political and security forum in the region,[17] and in particular to becoming equipped to exert a positive influence on maritime security challenges like those found in the territorial disputes of the South China Sea. These three constraints cannot be moderated by the United States and are behind the relatively limited achievements of the Obama administration in relation to the Summit addressed already.

The first is that the EAS, even after the United States and Russia were invited to join in 2011, is not the most important and best attended leaders' meeting in the region. The APEC Leaders' Meeting (an annual event initiated by the Clinton administration in 1993) includes both the Chinese and Russian Presidents. The EAS, despite claims of ASEAN centrality, makes do with the Chinese premier and either the Russian prime minister or foreign affairs minister. Xi Jinping has never attended the EAS. With the personalisation of political power in the hands of both Putin and Xi, their continued absence from the EAS is a growing problem. This problem is only partly offset by the participation of the current Indian prime minister Narendra Modi, and the leaders of Myanmar, Cambodia and Laos. The Summit may have a more suitable collection of participating states to discuss political and security issues in the Indo-Pacific than APEC, but it does not have a more suitable collection of state leaders at the table.

Second, the EAS is an ASEAN-led and ASEAN-controlled grouping. ASEAN member states determined the criteria by which non-ASEAN states are invited to the Summit, as exemplified by the United States' absence from 2005 to 2010. The United States is invited to the EAS along with the other seven non-ASEAN participants in their capacities as dialogue partners. The prerequisite of signing the ASEAN Treaty of Amity and Cooperation for EAS participation is the clearest example of this institutional power imbalance.

ASEAN's agenda-setting predominance in the EAS, along with its commitment to using the Summit to support ASEAN initiatives, is clearly reflected in the 2011 Chairman's Statement. This statement reiterates that ASEAN should 'remain as the driving force working in partnership with the other participants of the East Asia Summit'. In 2011, ASEAN connectivity – a major focus of Indonesia's chairmanship of the institution that year – was adopted 'as an additional area of cooperation in the EAS, together with the existing five priority areas of cooperation'.[18] ASEAN connectivity is of direct interest to all ASEAN member states, but certainly not all EAS participants.

ASEAN's status as the EAS' foundation and driving force means that any change in the Summit's focus or function requires prior ASEAN agreement. In 2015, on its tenth anniversary, Malaysia as Chair launched a review of the EAS with the idea of strengthening its institutional basis within ASEAN, clarifying the Summit's position within the growing suite of ASEAN-led and controlled regional institutions involving dialogue partners, and reviewing the EAS' increasingly diffuse agenda. With Malaysia as a claimant state in the South China Sea and a strong supporter of ASEAN centrality, hopes were raised that the Summit may move in the direction desired by the Obama administration. A Malaysian "non-paper" on EAS reform was circulated to members.

However, no consensus among ASEAN member states was reached, no major EAS reforms were introduced, and the issue of Summit reform was not an ASEAN Chair priority in 2016, 2017 or 2018. Issues of particular debate within ASEAN in relation to the EAS include whether Canada and the European Union, as the two ASEAN dialogue partners not included as participants, should be asked to join (as the two have in fact requested), and whether the Summit should remain a broadly-based functional body or a more narrowly-focused strategic one.

ASEAN's strong commitment to maintaining its driving force status in the EAS means that Southeast Asian states do not welcome dialogue partner suggestions on how the Summit might be reformed or become more "results-oriented" as the Obama administration in particular suggested. In 2014, Japanese Prime Minister Shinzo Abe gave the keynote speech at the Shangri-La Dialogue in Singapore. Abe proposed the creation of 'a permanent committee comprised of permanent representatives to ASEAN ... and then prepare a road map to bring renewed vitality to the Summit itself, while also making the Summit along with the ARF and the ADMM+ function in a multi-layered fashion'.[19] These ideas are very much in line with the Obama administrations' EAS goals. While there is now an ad hoc committee of representatives to ASEAN in Jakarta, there is still no roadmap for renewed vitality and better coordination among ASEAN-led institutions.

The third EAS constraint is its nature as an inclusive, consensus-based body reflecting the so-called ASEAN Way in a broader ASEAN-led institutional context. In reality, this means that even if ASEAN consensus can be reached on reforming the EAS, consensus among the dialogue partners invited to the Summit also is required. Not surprisingly, China's interests in the EAS are not the same as those of the United States, Japan or Australia. China prefers a functionally-focused institution with a broad mandate, rather than a strategic and political forum focused on maritime security issues. China's stance in the ADMM+ process on the South China Sea, which led to the failed joint statement in 2015, is consistent with Beijing's approach to the Summit. China also has close and asymmetric diplomatic relations with some ASEAN member states that influence their positions on issues of concern to China, like the South China Sea maritime rights disputes and the nature and focus of the EAS. The broad scope of the Summit's priority areas and their focus on economic and non-traditional security issues suited China's interests within the institution better than those of the Obama administrations.

The contrast between US and ASEAN diplomacy towards the 2016 ruling against China's land reclamation activities in the South China Sea, from the case filed by the Philippines under the United Nations Convention on the Law of the Sea, revealed the significant disconnect between the two parties on this core maritime security issue. The unanimous ruling, which Beijing rejected (and still rejects), deemed that China had interfered with the Philippines' sovereign rights in the area and invalidated its own regional nine-dash line claims. Washington coordinated with Canberra and Tokyo, with each issuing statements in support of the decision. Facing pressure from Beijing, ASEAN statements have remained silent on the landmark ruling. In the end, Washington's alliance system in East Asia proved more useful than ASEAN and the EAS for this issue.

The Trump administration

One of President Trump's first executive actions in January 2017 was to withdraw the United States from the TPP. This gave a clear and early indication that Washington's policy to Asia under Trump would at least in part bring a break from the Obama era. Yet no overarching blueprint for American policy in Asia was offered until October 2017, when Secretary of State Tillerson announced the new 'free and open Indo-Pacific' framework in a speech in Washington, DC on US–India relations. The lack of clarity over what this concept means in policy terms, and the absence of nominees and appointments to key Asia positions in the administration, made it difficult up until the time of writing in early 2019 to divine a clear approach to Asia by the Trump administration. At this time the most senior appointment in the US Mission to ASEAN for example was a Chargé d'affaires appointed during Obama's term in office. There were similarly no full US ambassadors to Thailand or Singapore, with the posts being vacant since January 2017, and despite the latter being Washington's most important economic, diplomatic and security partner in Southeast Asia. Australia only received a US ambassador in March 2019.

The first three months of the Trump administration aggravated Southeast Asian and ASEAN concerns about reduced US commitment. According to White House public records, neither the ASEAN Secretary-General nor any Southeast

Asian leader were among either the first fifty telephone calls or fifteen meetings between President Trump and foreign leaders.[20] From April 2017 onwards, however, the Trump administration began paying more attention to Southeast Asia. Vice President Pence's one-day visit to Jakarta and to the ASEAN Secretariat on 20 April that year, along with Secretary of State Tillerson's meeting with the foreign ministers of the ten ASEAN members in Washington, DC on 4 May, helped assuage Southeast Asian fears of abandonment. Tillerson attended the ARF and the EAS Ministerial Meeting in early August 2017 in the Philippines. On the sidelines, the foreign ministers of the United States, Australia and Japan held the first Trilateral Strategic Dialogue since Donald Trump took office. The joint statement issued after this gathering addressed one ASEAN-related maritime security issue in particular:

> The ministers urged ASEAN member states and China to fully and effectively implement the 2002 Declaration on the Conduct of Parties in the South China Sea (DOC). The ministers acknowledged the announced consensus on a framework for the Code of Conduct for the South China Sea (COC). The ministers further urged ASEAN member states and China to ensure that the COC be finalized in a timely manner, and that it be legally binding, meaningful, effective, and consistent with international law.[21]

Secretary of Defense James Mattis attended the ADMM+ meeting in the Philippines in late October 2017, where he proposed a US–ASEAN maritime exercise that would be the first of its kind.[22] (The first China–ASEAN maritime exercise took place in October 2018.[23]) At the 2017 EAS meeting which President Trump missed, a Leaders' Statement on chemical weapons (not a major issue in Southeast Asia) co-sponsored by the United States and Singapore was issued.[24] The Joint Statement released for the fifth ASEAN–US Summit is a boilerplate document with no new initiatives announced.[25]

The degree of American commitment to ASEAN and ASEAN-led processes across the first two years of the Trump administration suggests no precipitate drop-off in American engagement with the key institutions of Southeast Asia in the post-Obama era, notwithstanding the personal absence of President Trump from the East Asia Summits of both 2017 and 2018. In both these years Washington officials attended the expected meetings, proposed new initiatives, and coordinated with close partners including Japan and Australia on ASEAN-related issues. Maritime security in general, and the maritime rights disputes in the South China Sea in particular, remain a focus of US engagement with ASEAN as well.

Yet, the overall approach of the Trump administration to foreign policy, the 'free and open Indo-Pacific' framework for US Asia policy, and the priority issue of US engagement with Southeast Asia since 2017, collectively suggest a very different Asia policy than that of the Obama administrations' Rebalance in which ASEAN and the EAS have come to occupy a less clear and central role.

Recent developments in the US administration's emerging approach to foreign policy appear to run counter to closer engagement with ASEAN and the EAS. President Trump's decision to withdraw the United States from the TPP and the Paris Agreement on Climate Change, along with his criticisms of NATO, are indicative of his defensive, "America First" view of multilateral institutions. (The same can be said of his last-minute withdrawal from participating in the Summit of the Americas sponsored by the Organization of American States, as Trump is the first US president to have done so.) As discussed above, the United States, as an invited ASEAN dialogue partner, is far from first among equals in the ASEAN-led EAS.

The 2017 US National Security Strategy adopts a much stronger and hawkish view of the challenge posed by China and Russia to global and regional American leadership, security and prosperity. In it, the Trump administration contends that 'we will compete and lead in multilateral organizations so that American interests and principles are protected'.[26] As the EAS is a consensus-based body that includes both Russia and China as invited ASEAN dialogue partners, the United States cannot lead the Summit and attempts by Washington to compete with Beijing and Moscow inside it would paralyse the institution. American attempts to "compete and lead" in the Summit would also be counterproductive to engagement with ASEAN; member states have long guarded against their institution becoming a platform for extra-regional major power rivalry and against having to choose between the United States and China. If the Trump administration tries to "compete and lead" in the EAS, it will aggravate both of these existential fears.

Rex Tillerson's October 2017 speech at CSIS is seen as the most extensive explanation by a senior US official of the new 'free and open Indo-Pacific' framework for US Asia policy under the Trump administration.[27] This speech, entitled *Defining Our Relationship with India for the Next Century*, in fact makes no mention of ASEAN or the EAS. At the APEC CEO Summit in Vietnam in November 2017, President Trump gave his first speech on this new framework. He again made no mention of ASEAN or the EAS.[28] The most developed policy coordination mechanisms for this new regional framework are the revived quadrilateral meetings between the United States, Japan, India and Australia and the existing trilateral arrangements between the United States, Japan and Australia, and the United States, Japan and India. No Southeast Asian state is included in these minilateral mechanisms that are in many ways the institutional opposite to ASEAN-led institutions. Brad Glosserman is correct that, 'while there are repeated references to an "Indo-Pacific strategy", there is little more than a set of ideas and nostrums'.[29] These ideas and nostrums will also be very difficult to integrate with the existing suite of inclusive ASEAN-led institutions and the concept of ASEAN centrality.

Across the first two years of the Trump administration, the nuclear and missile threat emanating from North Korea, along with Washington's trade disputes with China, topped the US policy agenda in the Asia Pacific. The Trump administration chose to adopt a "maximum pressure" approach against Pyongyang to try to change its threatening behaviour. Gaining active ASEAN support for this strategy was an aim of American officials with Southeast Asian counterparts at meetings in both 2017 and 2018.[30] Yet, individual Southeast Asian states such as Cambodia, Laos and Myanmar have long-established ties with North Korea, restricting both their own and ASEAN's ability to adopt a maximum pressure strategy. North Korea signed the ASEAN Treaty of Amity and Cooperation before the United States, and is one of twenty-seven states and regional groupings participating in the ARF. It is reported that US efforts to have North Korea excluded from the 2017 ARF attended by Tillerson did not succeed.[31]

Conclusions

If the broad focus and frameworks of US foreign policy in Asia of the Trump administration, up until early 2019, persist, then the level of commitment to ASEAN and the EAS demonstrated by the Obama administration will likely not be maintained. Clear indications of this were found in Trump's absences from the East Asia Summits of 2017 and 2018. The Obama administration of 2009–17 pursued greater engagement with both of Southeast Asia's key institutions, with ASEAN reciprocating by inviting the United States to participate and adopt a more influential role. The Trump administration seems willing to participate in ASEAN-led institutions, of which the United States is now an established member, but seeks new substantive forms of policy coordination outside of inclusive institutions led by others. This means that while Obama represents an exception within the roll call of American presidents, by the degree to which he intensified Washington's commitments to the EAS, he failed to set a sufficient precedent which would make it impossible for the administration of his successor to ignore. Of course, it can also be argued that Trump – as uniquely inexperienced and unorthodox within the pantheon of American leaders – is in fact the exception whose natural tendencies towards unilateralism mean that the lessons of the Obama administration were always to some extent destined to be rejected.

The legacy Obama leaves in US engagement with the East Asia Summit, then, is one of exception rather than transformation. Washington's participation within ASEAN and the EAS will certainly not disappear, and they remain tied in ways closer than before Obama took office in 2009. Yet the high-water mark of the Obama administration has at least for the moment, in early 2019, begun to recede. The Trump administration's escalation of trade disputes with China in 2018 brought the potential for negative economic consequences for Southeast Asian economies, via impacts on tightly interconnected regional production chains. The prospect of instability and even conflict in East Asia also became less unthinkable during Trump's dramatic diplomatic clashes with Kim Jong-un and the North

Korean regime over nuclear and missile technology development the same year.[32] Whether through economic or security fallout, then, or the possibility of neglect as other policy issues are seen to consume Trump's attention, many in the region throughout the first two years of his administration saw evidence of the United States' commitment to both ASEAN and the EAS to be waning.

Notes

1   White House, 'Inside President Trump's Trip to Asia' (15 November 2017), www.whitehouse.gov/articles/president-trumps-trip-asia/, accessed 14 March 2019.

2   ASEAN Secretariat, 'Chairman's Statement of the 12th East Asia Summit' (21 November 2017), http://asean.org/chairmans-statement-of-the-12th-east-asia-summit/, accessed 14 March 2019.

3   G. Kessler, 'In Asia, Rice is Criticized for Plan to Skip Summit', *The Washington Post* (12 July 2005), www.washingtonpost.com/wp-dyn/content/article/2005/07/11/AR2005071100680.html, accessed 14 March 2019.

4   H. Clinton, 'America's Pacific Century', *Foreign Policy* (11 October 2011), http://foreignpolicy.com/2011/10/11/americas-pacific-century/, accessed 6 March 2019.

5   *Ibid.*

6   White House, 'Fact Sheet: Unprecedented US-ASEAN Relations' (12 February 2016), https://obamawhitehouse.archives.gov/the-press-office/2016/02/12/fact-sheet-unprecedented-us-asean-relations, accessed 14 March 2019.

7   White House, 'US-Japan Joint Statement: The United States and Japan: Shaping the Future of the Asia-Pacific and Beyond' (25 April 2014), https://obamawhitehouse.archives.gov/the-press-office/2014/04/25/us-japan-joint-statement-united-states-and-japan-shaping-future-asia-pac, accessed 14 March 2019.

8   White House, 'US-India Joint Strategic Vision for the Asia-Pacific and Indian Ocean Region' (25 January 2015), https://obamawhitehouse.archives.gov/the-press-office/2015/01/25/us-india-joint-strategic-vision-asia-pacific-and-indian-ocean-region, accessed 14 March 2019.

9   ASEAN, 'Joint Declaration of the ASEAN Defence Minsters on Partnering for Change, Engaging the World' (24 October 2017), https://asean.org/storage/2017/10/11th-ADMM-Joint-Declaration-as-of-23-Oct-20172.pdf, accessed 12 March 2019.

10 ASEAN Secretariat, Kuala Lumpur Declaration on the East Asia Summit (14 December 2005), http://asean.org/?static_post=kuala-lumpur-declaration-on-the-east-asia-summit-kuala-lumpur-14-december-2005, accessed 14 March 2019.

11 White House, 'US-Japan Joint Statement'.

12 White House, 'Fact Sheet: Unprecedented US-ASEAN Relations'.

13 M. Landler, 'Offering to Aid Talks, US Challenges China on Disputed Islands', *New York Times* (23 July 2010), www.nytimes.com/2010/07/24/world/asia/24diplo.html, accessed 14 March 2019.

14 *Today*, 'No Joint Statement as US, China Clash over Wording on South China Sea' (4 November 2015), www.todayonline.com/world/no-signing-joint-declaration-asean-defense-forum, accessed 14 March 2019.

15 ASEAN Secretariat, 'EAS Statement on Enhancing Regional Maritime Cooperation' (22 November 2015).

16 ASEAN Secretariat, 'Chairman's Statement of the 12th East Asia Summit' (21 November 2017), http://asean.org/chairmans-statement-of-the-12th-east-asia-summit/, accessed 14 March 2019.

17 White House, 'US-Japan Joint Statement'.

18 ASEAN Secretariat, 'Chairman's Statement of the 6th East Asia Summit' (19 November 2011).

19 Ministry of Foreign Affairs of Japan, 'The 13th IISS Asian Security Summit – The Shangri-La Dialogue – Keynote Address by Shinzo ABE, Prime Minister, Japan' (30 May 2014), www.mofa.go.jp/fp/nsp/page4e_000086.html, accessed 14 March 2019.

20 M. Cook and I. Storey, 'The Trump Administration and Southeast Asia: Limited Engagement Thus Far', ISEAS Perspective No. 27 (27 April 2017), p. 3, www.iseas.edu.sg/images/pdf/ISEAS_Perspective_2017_27.pdf, accessed 14 March 2019.

21 US State Department, 'Australia-Japan-United States Trilateral Strategic Dialogue Ministerial Joint Statement' (6 August 2017) www.state.gov/r/pa/prs/ps/2017/08/273216.htm, accessed 14 March 2019.

22 US Department of Defense, 'Readout of Secretary of Defense Jim Mattis' ADMM-Plus Meeting' (24 October 2017), https://dod.defense.gov/News/News-Releases/News-Release-View/Article/1352288/readout-of-secretary-of-defense-jim-mattis-admm-plus-meeting/, accessed 14 March 2019.

23 L. Min Zhang, 'China, ASEAN Kick Off Inaugural Maritime Field Training Exercise in Zhanjiang, Guangdong', *Straits Times* (22 October 2018), www.straitstimes.com/asia/east-asia/china-asean-kick-off-inaugural-maritime-field-training-exercise-in-zhanjiang, accessed 14 March 2019.

24 White House, 'President Donald J. Trump's Trip to the Philippines' (14 November 2017), www.whitehouse.gov/briefings-statements/president-donald-j-trumps-trip-philippines/, accessed 14 March 2019.

25 ASEAN Secretariat, 'Joint Statement of the ASEAN-US Commemorative Summit on the 40th Anniversary of ASEAN-US Dialogue Relations' (13 November 2017), http://asean.org/joint-statement-of-the-asean-u-s-commemorative-summit-on-the-40th-anniversary-of-the-asean-u-s-dialogue-relations/, accessed 14 March 2019.

26 White House, 'National Security Strategy of the United States of America' (December 2017), p. 4.

27 CSIS, 'Defining Our Relationship with India for the Next Century: An Address by US Secretary of State Rex Tillerson' (18 October 2017), www.csis.org/analysis/defining-our-relationship-india-next-century-address-us-secretary-state-rex-tillerson, accessed 14 March 2019.

28   White House, 'Remarks by President Trump at APEC CEO Summit, Danang, Vietnam' (10 November 2017), www.whitehouse.gov/briefings-statements/ remarks-president-trump-apec-ceo-summit-da-nang-vietnam/, accessed 14 March 2019.

29   B. Glosserman, 'Making the Indo-Pacific Real', *PacNet* (7 March 2018), www.csis. org/analysis/pacnet-18-making-indo-pacific-real, accessed 14 March 2019.

30   N. Ghosh, 'US Courts ASEAN, Wants Help on North Korea', *The Straits Times* (5 May 2017), www.straitstimes.com/world/united-states/us-secretary-of-state-rex-tillerson-hosts-asean-foreign-ministers-in-washington, accessed 14 March 2019; S. Palma, 'Pomeo Seeks South-East Asia Support for Iran and N Korea Policies', *Financial Times* (3 August 2018), www.ft.com/content/157b2f78-96bf-11e8-b747-fb1e803ee64e, accessed 14 March 2019.

31   C. de Guzman and R. Cabato, 'North Korea to Remain in ASEAN Regional Forum', CNN (5 August 2017), http://cnnphilippines.com/news/2017/08/05/North-Korea-ASEAN-Regional-Forum.html, accessed 14 March 2019.

32   See Arms Control Association, 'Chronology of US-North Korean Nuclear and Missile Diplomacy' (March 2019), www.armscontrol.org/factsheets/ dprkchron#2019, accessed 12 March 2019.

Part II

The United States in Asia and the Pacific under Trump

9

Obama, Trump and US politics and diplomacy towards Asia

Robert Sutter

Introduction

As both candidate and throughout his first two years as president to early 2019, Donald Trump employed unilateral actions and flamboyant posturing in upending the strong commitment to positive diplomacy and political engagement of regional governments and organisations of the previous administrations of Barack Obama. Two years into his presidential term, Trump remained avowedly unpredictable as he junked related policy transparency, carefully measured responses, and avoidance of dramatic action, linkage or spill-over among competing interests that characterised Obama government diplomacy.

On the one hand, his approach had the advantage of keeping opponents (like China) as well as allies and partners on the defensive in dealing with the new President. Trump came to see the wisdom of abandoning his earlier cavalier treatment of allies Japan, South Korea and Australia. He built cordial personal ties with most important regional leaders. On the other hand, American engagement in the region remained episodic, featuring intense pressure beginning in 2017 to prevent North Korea's nuclear weapons development and strong actions in 2018 on trade disputes with China that widely impacted other states. Drift characterised his dealing with most other issues. That the President used the pressure to conclude deals with opponents advantageous to the United States seemed to explain his abrupt acceptance of a summit meeting with North Korea's leader and the Trump government's ongoing negotiations with China as it applied tariffs and investment restrictions punishing Beijing.[1]

The administration laid out a dark view of the world in authoritative documents calling for a well-integrated strategy that saw economic, diplomatic and other international strengths as important to overall American national security. China and Russia were the leading opponents. The Trump government followed through with an increase in the defence budget along with strong action defending America from predatory trade and investment from China. The administration's remarkable pragmatism on human rights issues showed that the American leadership would not allow these issues to complicate the pursuit of broadly defined elements of American national strategy. Remaining unpredictable, President Trump rarely used the language of the published strategies and continued cordial interchange with the Russian and Chinese leaders.

Trump versus Obama: Diplomacy in Asia

Soon after taking power in January 2017, the Trump administration unceremoniously announced the end of the Obama administration's signature "Rebalance" policy in Asia.[2] Launched in 2011, that multifaceted policy was widely welcomed in Asia except notably by China, which took assertive and expansive actions in response that the Obama government was less than successful in countering.

The Rebalance policy accompanied US military pullbacks from Iraq and Afghanistan, with greater attention to a broad range of countries in Asia from India in the west, to Japan in the northeast, to the Pacific Island states in the southeast. US diplomatic activism increased; existing, substantial military deployments were maintained and strengthened in some areas; and trade and investment remained open and were poised to increase, notably via the Trans-Pacific Partnership (TPP), a twelve-nation Asia Pacific economic pact that represented the centrepiece of the economic dimension of the Obama administration's Rebalance policy in Asia.[3]

After assuming leadership in 2012, President Xi Jinping showed a much bolder and more assertive posture than previous Chinese leaders in pursuing its interests in Asia and elsewhere at odds with American interests. Xi used economic enticements on the one hand and coercive and intimidating means short of direct military force on the other hand, to compel neighbours to accept Chinese claims to disputed territories and to side with Beijing against American foreign policy initiatives.

President Obama and his administration representatives maintained that their carefully measured, transparent and moderate responses to China's challenges throughout their time in office led to successful outcomes that reflected well on their historical legacy. They were particularly pleased with US–China agreements on such important global issues as climate change. In contrast, a hardening of opinion about China's growing challenges among mainstream US foreign policy elites showed in the 2016 election campaigns, and across a variety of think tank studies and media commentary. Obama's approach appeared too reactive and solicitous towards China. It was viewed to allow Beijing to repeatedly advance in coercive and illegal ways at the expense of others, notably the United States, without appropriate reprisal.

Indeed, President Obama's frustrations grew with China's expansionism and "bullying" in disputed maritime areas such as the South China Sea; cyber theft of US economic and industrial property and other grossly unfair economic practices; continued support for North Korea as it flagrantly violated international sanctions and endangered South Korea and neighbouring states; and other matters. Obama broke with his practice of avoiding negative public comments about China in the first six years of his administration, and in 2014 began to more frequently complain about Beijing's infractions.

Xi Jinping largely ignored the complaints. After many strident warnings, the Obama government eventually took some actions, notably on cyber theft and Chinese bullying and expansionism in the South China Sea. But they were each treated in transparent and measured ways that signalled to Beijing US intent to avoid broader negative consequences for China or US–China relations. The results were mixed; widely publicised offensive Chinese behaviour in the South China Sea and other egregious challenges appeared to meet with an ineffective US response, which American and regional critics saw weakening the US position in the region.[4]

The complaints against the Obama government's ineffectiveness against Chinese challenges fed into a much broader American debate on foreign policy leading up to the 2016 presidential election campaign. Republican leaders in Congress and supporting think tanks and interest groups joined media and other commentators in depicting major shortcomings in the Obama government's policies in Europe, the Middle East and Asia. One target was the so-called Obama Doctrine laid out in the President's speech to graduating West Point cadets in 2014 that showed greater administration wariness regarding security engagements abroad.[5]

In Asia, congressional and other American critics of Obama's Rebalance claimed that Washington was not resolute enough in defending the United States' regional role as security guarantor, and not active enough in promoting greater American trade, investment and diplomatic engagement in competition with China's state-directed efforts. The Republican-leaning Heritage Foundation summed up the critics' concerns by offering far-reaching political-security recommendations for Asia. They included more robust military spending to allow for a long-term goal of 350 naval ships (there are now about 280 ships in the Navy); increased support for allies and partners; expanded involvement with the Association of South East Asian Nations (ASEAN) and other regional groups; and greater firmness in dealing with Chinese challenges to regional and American interests.[6]

Asia, candidate Trump, and 2016 election debates

Most of the 2016 US presidential candidates talked about eroding or challenged US international power and influence, and the need to reaffirm America's role in the world. Candidates Hillary Clinton, Ted Cruz, John Kasich, Marco Rubio and Donald Trump in varying ways favoured strengthening American power and leadership. Bernie Sanders favoured less muscular approaches than the other candidates, emphasising negotiations over military means and pressure. Most advocated strengthened relations with allies, without much emphasis on greater reciprocity on their part.

On specific issues involving US leadership, John Kasich joined free trade advocates in Congress like House Speaker Paul Ryan to support the TPP. Clinton, Cruz, Sanders and Trump voiced varying opposition to the trade pact, but Trump was alone in insisting that allies do more to offset American costs in maintaining their security and overall regional stability or face American withdrawal. He also accepted the possibility that, without support from Washington, allies like Japan and South Korea might be compelled to develop nuclear weapons to protect themselves. All the candidates agreed with overwhelming majorities in Congress that pressure should be applied, including on Beijing, to see a denuclearised North Korea. Yet Trump was alone in also calling for direct talks with North Korea's Kim Jong-un.

China remained the main country of concern regarding challenging US leadership in Asia. Relevant election discourse focused on how China was an unfair partner, and how the United States needed to counter negative features of its rise. Clinton, Rubio and Cruz argued for greater firmness against Beijing, with Clinton and Rubio advocating tougher specific policies, and Cruz favouring a more robust overall approach. In contrast, Sanders urged negotiations. So did Trump, though he also favoured military build-up and large trade sanctions if needed.[7]

Concern with China remained active throughout the campaigns, but secondary within the rhetoric about Asia. China as an issue was overshadowed by strong debate on international trade and the proposed TPP, and on Trump's controversial proposals on allied burden sharing, nuclear weapons proliferation and North Korea. Trump's strong opposition to the TPP and other US trade efforts was at odds with the free trade policies favoured by Republican congressional leaders, but his position had strong appeal among both Republican and Democratic voters. He and Sanders reinforced each other's arguments, and both rode the surprise wave of populist discontent over globalisation to unexpected success in the primaries. Clinton, Cruz and others reversed or modified their positions to accord with the changed politics surrounding the TPP.

Candidate Trump's unique emphasis on getting Japan, South Korea and other allies to compensate the United States for its role as regional security guarantor prompted serious negative reactions that promised significant complications for US alliance relations in the event of his election as president. His calls for Japan and South Korea to compensate the United States for security support it provided were at odds with proposals by Speaker Ryan, Senator John McCain and other Republican congressional leaders, as well as many Republican-leaning think tanks and media. Some of these congressional Republicans vocally opposed such policies.

Trump's acceptance of Japan or South Korea developing nuclear weapons for self-defence, following a US pullback, was a major departure from long-standing policies of Republican and Democratic governments, and one widely seen to add to the danger of war in Northeast Asia. His abrupt announcement that he would seek direct talks with North Korea's leader undermined existing American, South Korean and Japanese policy. It also deviated sharply from the tough posture favoured by the Obama government and by Republican and Democratic congressional leaders and rank and file.[8] Ultimately, these three sets of controversial proposals by Trump garnered little support in the United States and prompted opposition, including from prominent congressional Republicans.

Meanwhile, candidate Trump's flamboyant and often vulgar campaign attacks were widely seen as diminishing American authority abroad, prompting concern from foreign policy specialists within the United States. His populist appeal came from a style of campaigning that featured repeated personal attacks, gross language, and salacious accusations which degraded America's image, providing fodder for Chinese and other opinion stressing the weaknesses of US democracy.[9]

On policy issues, the success of the Sanders and Trump campaign attacks on the TPP surprised congressional leaders, along with most American and Asian commentators. Their success underlined seemingly weak popular support for this important component of US policy in the region, which Ryan, McCain and other Republican congressional leaders continued to back. The fact that the Republican Party – widely seen in the region as strongly committed to US defence ties with Asia – selected Trump despite his controversial views on military disengagement from Asia and Europe, and his acceptance of nuclear proliferation, raised serious doubts about America's future regional role.

Among Asian countries dependent on military support from the United States, non-governmental Japanese commentators seemed the most concerned. On the other side of the spectrum, Chinese commentators saw opportunities for leadership gains in competition with the United States in Asia, following the election's negative impact on the credibility of regional American commitment. This development reinforced the determination of Senator McCain and a large bipartisan group of colleagues to travel to the region prior to the election to reassure allies and partners of continued US support.[10]

President Trump's policies and practices in Asia

President Trump in 2017 came to see the need for altering his policies towards allies and joining congressional and other leaders in pressuring North Korea on nuclear weapons proliferation. However, his overall approach to Asian and other international diplomacy – what New York City police detectives would call his mode of operation – continued to feature dramatic and often crude initiatives that were hard to predict and that raised international tensions, with himself at the centre of attention. The United States is a superpower with many powerful levers of possible use in seeking international advantage. Across his first two years in office it became clear that Trump was much more likely than the more measured and predictable Obama to use those levers in surprising ways, notably by linking issues, and using one source of power in one issue area to gain advantages in another area of policy concern. Whereas the Obama government seemed to prioritise carefully managing differences and resulting tensions, President Trump sought advantage in stoking tensions and exacerbating differences in diplomacy in Asia and beyond. Such behaviour mimicked the controversial and unconventional behaviour of his remarkable and unexpected presidential election victory against more experienced "Establishment" political candidates.

Early Trump administration initiatives upset regional stability, complicating the foreign policies of Asian partners and opponents alike, including China. Subsequent pragmatic summitry eased regional anxiety and clarified the new government's security and political objectives. An effective American strategy remained elusive, especially because of deep divisions in the American administration on trade and economic policy. In 2018, tariffs and restrictions on Chinese investments showed a harder line compatible with an overall toughening of diplomacy, consistent with the administration's National Security Strategy (NSS) and National Defense Strategy (NDS).[11] However, they were implemented along with concurrent high-level negotiations with China to reach a compromise over trade and other economic differences.[12]

There was considerable domestic support, notably in Congress, for the new President's security plans which were generally in line with the priorities of Republican congressional leaders stressing the need to reinforce the American military presence in the region. The omnibus spending bill signed by the President in March 2018 included the first instalment of a planned increase of US$160 billion in defence spending over two years, to improve US military readiness and advance its capabilities in the Asia Pacific and other key theatres of operations.[13]

The President's personal engagement with Chinese and other Asian leaders between 2017 and 2019 detailed below was generally supported in Congress. As discussed shortly, few public complaints were seen in Congress, albeit more in the media and among concerned interest groups, about the new US government's reduced emphasis on human rights and good governance in high-level meetings with Asian leaders. Congress generally supported the efforts by Republican congressional leader, and later Vice President, Mike Pence and other administration leaders including Defense Secretary James Mattis, National Security Advisor H. R. McMaster, and Secretary of State Rex Tillerson to steer President Trump towards supporting US alliance relationships with Japan, South Korea, Australia and others, which had been seriously questioned by Trump when presidential candidate. The turnover in senior administration leaders, with Tillerson, McMaster and Mattis leaving in 2018 and being replaced by proponents of a harder line in US foreign policy, notably Mike Pompeo and John Bolton, raised congressional concern about the absence of senior administration leaders prepared to moderate Trump's inclinations for more aggressive American diplomacy.

Congress remained overwhelmingly supportive of greater US pressure on North Korea, including on China to help manipulate the policies of Pyongyang. Thus, there was little objection to the high priority the President and his staff gave to responding to North Korean weapons tests. North Korean missile launches increased in frequency in 2017, before slowing dramatically in late 2018, and in that time showed recently unprecedented demonstrations of military power and resolve. The tension featured strident rhetoric from the President that caused a few congressional leaders to register concerns about a possible impulsive move from the White House that could start a nuclear war.[14] Caveats in this tough US posture included President Trump's avowed unpredictability in the newly fluid situation on the Korean Peninsula in 2018, which led to his remarkable acceptance of a summit meeting with North Korea's leader in Singapore in June 2018 and another in Hanoi in February 2019.[15]

Regarding US diplomacy and interchange with foreign governments on economic issues – notably the massive American trade deficit with Asia and particularly China – congressional Republican leaders continued to favour free trade. Congressional Democrats, meanwhile, often were associated with proposed government efforts to do more to protect the United States from unfair trade practices of China, as well as some other countries. The Trump government had a hard time formulating a coherent diplomatic approach with Asian governments regarding sensitive economic disputes; administration leaders articulated widely different perspectives, with some favouring a traditional Republican free trade approach and others favouring the approach advocated by candidate Trump of protecting American jobs from China's improper practices.

Where President Trump would come down on this important matter was not clarified by his friendly visit to China in November 2017, followed by a strong declaration against unfair trade during a speech at the APEC Summit attended by the Chinese leader in Hanoi.[16] The administration's diplomatic line on these issues became more consistent and harder in 2018, and was accompanied by substantial tariffs and investment restrictions which specifically targeted Beijing. Nevertheless, the administration continued negotiations with China, presumably seeking a deal advantageous for the United States.

Disagreements within the administration on economic policy delayed a clear US government strategy towards China and the broader Asia Pacific region. Adding to that problem was the fact that the administration was slow in filling key policy-making positions for China, Korea and other Asian issues, especially in the Defense and State departments. The difficulty in selecting qualified staff came in part from the surprising populist upsurge against globalisation and foreign engagement during the 2016 presidential election campaign. This side-lined Republican and Democratic Party elites who supported continued constructive American engagement with the Asia Pacific, rather than the President's emphasis on "America First". Trump's unpredictability in foreign affairs, his demands for intense personal loyalty, and his repeated, public use of vulgar and personal attacks seemed to appeal to his populist base, but most experienced Republican Asian specialists were alienated from the new President.[17]

The Defense Department eventually filled its Asia policy positions, but the departure of Secretary of State Tillerson in March 2018 meant his selected candidate for Asian Assistant Secretary was put aside. The absence of a strong cohort of political appointees in Washington agencies and ambassadors abroad did not prevent Donald Trump from interacting effectively with a wide range of Asian leaders and multilateral inter-governmental groups during his summitry in Washington and his extended trip to Asia in late 2017. And the administration was successful in crafting a coordinated and coherent NSS and NDS. Nonetheless, the absence of diplomatic expertise on North Korea seemed to be a significant weakness as the Trump government prepared for previously unexpected talks with North Korea's leader without the benefit of experienced officials in key positions. It took until July 2018 for the appointments of Trump's ambassador to South Korea and an acting Assistant Secretary of State for East Asian and Pacific Affairs. Trump's US Special Representative for North Korean Policy was appointed the following month.

In general, congressional or other American concern about the absence of a coherent administration policy towards Asia remained the focus of foreign policy specialists concerned with Asian affairs. The crisis over nuclear weapons development in North Korea, beginning in 2017, and tensions caused by tough US tariffs and other economic measures against China in 2018, were high priority issues for the administration, the Congress, the media and non-government organisations dealing with American policy. But they competed for attention with pressing domestic issues including health care reform; tax reform; disaster relief; control of immigration; the role of Russia in influencing US domestic politics and the investigation into possible collusion with the Trump campaign during the 2016 election; and such international issues as the wars in Syria and Afghanistan and the challenges posed by Russian and Iranian assertiveness and expansionism in Europe and the Middle East.

The Trump administration's NSS and NDS provided a well-integrated message for American diplomacy in Asia and the rest of the world. While focused on threats from North Korea, terrorism and Iran, the approach zeroed-in on China and Russia. It employed strong language not seen in authoritative US government commentary on China since before the Nixon administration's opening to China of the early 1970s, to warn in no uncertain terms of China's ambitions to undermine

US economic, security and political interests and displace the United States and its leadership in the Asia Pacific. It clearly sided with those in the administration seeking a much tougher policy towards China on economic issues.

As already noted, the administration followed through with diplomacy highlighting defence build-ups and economic actions in support of the American strategy. The diplomacy generally meshed with congressional concerns regarding North Korea and China. The United States also began closer collaboration in diplomatic negotiations with Japan, India and Australia to foster military cooperation to secure interests challenged by China in the broader Indo-Pacific region. How far the United States would go in countering perceived adverse Chinese actions throughout the first two years of the Trump administration was determined in part by the region's uncertain priority in the very full international White House agenda. On a personal level, President Trump carried out cordial interchange with Chinese leaders seemingly at odds with the harder approach of his administration's avowed strategy.

Early diplomatic successes

President Trump's unconventional personal style in foreign affairs added to uncertainty in US relations with China and the broader Asia Pacific region. He strongly opposed President Obama's predictable, transparent and carefully measured policy-making that had been broadly welcomed in the region. The new President favoured unpredictability; he sought advantage in employing dramatic gestures and rhetoric along with military and economic leverage to benefit from resulting tensions, just as he did at the expense of more conventional candidates in his election campaign. Notably, Trump repeatedly inserted himself into the policy process through bluntly worded tweets and other initiatives that exacerbated frictions over important issues both at home and abroad in ways that appealed to his populist constituency, but which upset foreign partners and opponents.[18]

In January 2017, President Trump quickly followed through on his campaign pledge to withdraw from the twelve-nation TPP. Then came the announcement that the Obama government's overall Asian engagement policy known as the Rebalance policy was ended, with little indication of the Trump administration's regional approach.[19] Both moves reinforced anxiety and dismay among regional allies and partners over the direction of American policy.

The new President's national security leaders, along with Vice President Pence, however, led the administration's reversal of candidate Trump's low regard for American alliances, notably those with Japan, South Korea and Australia. Their travels to the region reassured allies and partners of Washington's security commitments. In June, Secretary Mattis pointedly reassured allies and partners in a measured and strongly-worded affirmation of American support for its security commitments in Asia at the annual defence ministers meeting at the Shangri-La Forum in Singapore.[20] Economic relations remain in question as President Trump continued his complaints about US trade agreements with South Korea and its trade deficits with China and other Asian countries.[21]

North Korea crises and China policy

North Korea's threatening rhetoric, repeated ballistic missile launches, and nuclear weapons testing saw the early Trump government adopt a more assertive diplomatic approach framed by far more tension than Obama's more moderate and reactive policy of "strategic patience". President Trump and senior administration officials repeatedly warned of unspecified US military options to unilaterally deal with the North Korean threat, while increasing public pressure on China to use its influence to get Pyongyang to halt its nuclear weapons programme. Trump's remarks on China's willingness and ability to get North Korea to stop varied from optimism, to warnings that the United States was prepared to take unilateral military actions.[22]

The crisis over North Korea saw Washington devote careful handling to relations with Beijing. During the campaign, Chinese specialists judged that Trump was a pragmatic businessman who could be "shaped" to align with Chinese interests and would be easier to deal with than Hillary Clinton, had she won the 2016 election.[23] President-elect Trump up-ended these sanguine views when he accepted a congratulatory phone call from Taiwan's President Tsai Ing-wen in December 2016. When Beijing complained, Trump criticised Chinese economic policies and military advances in disputed islands in the South China Sea, and questioned why the United States should retain support for the One China policy and avoid improved contacts with Taiwan. Trump was eventually persuaded to endorse – at least in general terms – the American view of the One China policy. His informal summit meeting with President Xi Jinping in Florida in early April 2017 went well. The two leaders met again on the side-lines of the G-20 summit in July that year and held repeated phone conversations over North Korea and other issues before Trump's visit to Beijing in November. Despite serious differences between the two countries, both leaders seemed to value their personal rapport, with Xi promising Trump a 'wonderful' visit in China; that remarkable visit prompted the US President's personal gratitude and appreciation.[24]

After the Florida summit, the Trump government kept strong political pressure on China to use its leverage to halt North Korea's nuclear weapons development. Planned arms sales to Taiwan, freedom of navigation exercises in the South China Sea and other US initiatives that might complicate America's search for leverage to stop North Korea's nuclear weapons development were temporarily put on hold. The United States and China also reached agreement on a 100-day action plan to further bilateral economic cooperation prior to the first US–China Comprehensive Economic Dialogue, set for July 2017.[25]

The conditionality of Trump's positive stance towards Xi showed when he registered dissatisfaction with China's efforts on North Korea in June. This was followed by the announcement of arms sales to Taiwan. Freedom of navigation exercises in the South China Sea also went ahead. China responded with routine complaints, and July's economic dialogue produced no agreement on actionable steps to reduce the US trade deficit with China, ending in failure with a cancelled press conference and no joint statement.

Washington opted against harsh economic measures in the lead-up to, and during, the President's trip to China in November 2017. However, Secretary of State Tillerson and Secretary of Defense James Mattis registered the administration's first criticism of China's widely publicised Belt and Road Initiative. The administration also objected to the World Bank's continuing practice of providing a couple of billion dollars a year in development loans to China, and it joined the EU in opposing China's market economy status at the World Trade Organization.[26] China's uncertainty over the American President also partly explained why, at least temporarily, it avoided controversial expansion in the disputed South China Sea. Beijing also avoided controversial expansions in South China Sea areas claimed by the Philippines because it was seeking to court Philippines President Rodrigo Duterte away from the United States.[27]

Building close ties with Asian leaders

In the first twelve months of his presidency, Trump made progress in advancing diplomatic, security and economic relations with other important Asian countries. The approach featured summit meetings, even with leaders previously shunned by the United States because of concerns over democracy (e.g. Thailand), human rights (e.g. the Philippines) and corruption (e.g. Malaysia). By and large, these leaders responded positively to the high-level attention by the new American President, which many of them actively sought; they reciprocated with economic concessions and positive treatment of Trump.

Japan's long-serving Prime Minister Shinzo Abe sought a position as the President's closest regional partner. He arranged and attended a remarkable meeting in New York in November 2016 with President-elect Trump. This was followed by a summit in Washington in February 2017 that included a full weekend at the President's Mar-a-Lago resort. The two leaders remained on the same page throughout the tensions over North Korea, though Japan worried about the negative consequences of Trump's abrupt shift towards summitry with North Korea.[28]

On a trip to Indonesia in April 2017, Vice President Pence told officials that Trump would attend the APEC Summit in Vietnam and the US–ASEAN and East

Asian summits in the Philippines in November. The White House announced the long trip in October that year. Pence's stop to Australia in April 2017 helped to set the stage for a cordial May meeting in New York between Trump and Australian Prime Minister Malcolm Turnbull. The two leaders put aside an earlier heated telephone argument regarding the United States accepting over 1,000 refugees in Australian custody.[29]

In late April 2017, Trump called the leaders of Singapore, the Philippines and Thailand, inviting them to visit the White House. The invitations to the latter two, along with a separate invitation to the Prime Minister of Malaysia, represented a break from the Obama government's arm's-length treatment of these governments, because of concerns over human rights and corruption. The invitations built personal ties with all three leaders that helped to establish top-level US connections, allowing for President Trump's successful visit to the region and interchange at regional leadership meetings in November 2017.[30]

Vietnam carried out previously agreed visits to the United States of its senior leaders – the Prime Minister, the Foreign Minister, and the Deputy Defense Minister. Prime Minister Nguyen Xuan Phuc was the first Southeast Asian head of government to meet with President Trump in late May. The Vietnamese premier seemed successful in forging a personal relationship with President Trump.[31] Newly-inaugurated South Korean President Moon Jae-in travelled to a summit with Trump in late June. He gave top priority to allied cooperation in dealing with the North Korean threat. The South Korean government also followed through with the deployment of Washington's THAAD anti-missile system in South Korea, despite vocal objection from China.[32]

In late June 2017, Indian Prime Minister Narendra Modi was warmly welcomed at the White House. India's importance in neighbouring Afghanistan grew with Trump's decision in August to add 4,000 American troops to the 8,000 stationed in Afghanistan, endeavouring to counter Taliban combatants seeking to overthrow the US-backed Afghan government. Defense Secretary Mattis made his first visit to India in September, with the Pentagon stressing 'US appreciation of India's important contributions toward Afghanistan's democracy, stability, prosperity and security'.[33]

By mid-2017 Malaysian Prime Minister Najib Razak had become mired in a major corruption scandal involving billions of dollars in investment funds that came under investigation by the US Justice Department. Nevertheless, Najib found Washington fully welcoming during a cordial meeting with Trump in September that year. The Trump administration refused to comment on the government investigation. The Malaysian government said it would buy US$10 billion in US commercial aircraft over five years, and invest close to US$4 billion in the American economy.[34]

The leader of Thailand's 2014 military coup, and resulting Prime Minister Prayuth Chan-ocha, visited the White House with his wife in early October.

This marked the first such visit by a Thai leader since 2005.[35] Singaporean Prime Minister Lee Hsien Loong also made a six-day trip to Washington in late October, just prior to Trump's inaugural visit to the region. He promised large purchases of US commercial airplanes and offered advice on China following the Singapore leader's recent talks with Xi Jinping.[36]

Philippines President Rodrigo Duterte's Draconian crackdown on drug traffickers, beginning almost immediately from when he entered office in mid-2016, resulted in thousands of extra-legal killings that were strongly criticised by the Obama government and others. The White House put aside such concerns when, in April 2017, Trump invited Duterte to meet in Washington. Duterte demurred but by late September was publicly conciliatory towards the United States before welcoming Trump to the Philippines for talks on bilateral relations and ASEAN related meetings, in his role as chairman of the institution in 2017.[37]

Overall, capping American diplomatic efforts in 2017, the results of the Trump visit to Asia appeared successful. Familiar with Trump because of earlier cordial meetings in the United States, important Asian leaders were attentive and solicitous, seeking improved relations. The American President's concerns about the threat from North Korea, US trade imbalances, and other economic complaints were evident throughout. While Trump continued to reject multilateral economic agreements, he participated fully in the APEC and US–ASEAN summit.[38] The President's attentiveness throughout his remarkably long and demanding schedule in the region signalled strong top-level US commitment of continued active engagement in regional affairs. There was little in the trip for administration critics in the United States or elsewhere to complain about.[39]

Recent developments, uncertain strategy

President Trump's 2017 activism in Asia was not repeated in 2018. North Korea and China got high-level attention, but other regional priorities received more episodic treatment. Developments showed some clear and consistent elements of American strategy, notably on defence and in a diminished American profile on human rights, democracy and promotion of good governance.[40] Trump's dramatic move towards summitry with North Korea came in close consultations with leaders of South Korea and Japan. South Korean President Moon Jae-in played an instrumental mediating role between Trump and Kim Jong-un before the Trump–Kim summit in Singapore on 12 June, and in managing US–North Korean disputes that followed. President Trump also praised China's role in facilitating the summit.

Apart from the Singapore trip in June, however, Trump did not travel to Asia; and he avoided the diplomatic bonhomie that characterised his 2017 trip to the region and his meetings with Asian leaders in Washington and Florida. He overrode differences among his senior leaders on trade policy to launch punitive tariffs and political pressure on various Asian and other partners, to compel changes in economic relations advantageous to the United States. South Korea agreed to a revised free trade agreement with the United States, and Japan agreed to talks on a bilateral trade accord. These came in tandem with US pressure on trade with Mexico and Canada, leading to the conclusion of a new trade agreement to replace NAFTA, which Trump had long criticised.

China received the lion's share of administration pressure on trade and it responded in kind. The trade war was accompanied by the Trump government targeting Chinese policies and practices on a wide range of economic, political and security issues, bringing relations to their lowest point in decades. The US hardening on China was in line with the administration's declared national security strategy.

In Asia, administration officials began to flesh out the contents of their avowed Indo-Pacific strategy which showed a clear focus on China as the prime US concern. In June 2018, Secretary of Defense James Mattis described the Trump administration's emerging Indo-Pacific strategy as deepening alliances and partnerships, stressing that ASEAN remained central to regional stability, and affirming openness to cooperation with China 'wherever possible'.[41] In August, Secretary of State Mike Pompeo announced nearly US$300 million in new US funding to strengthen maritime security, develop humanitarian assistance and peacekeeping capabilities, and enhance programmes that counter transnational threats.

Trump also highlighted a US$113 million fund that will promote public–private partnerships as a down payment on a larger project to reorganise and rationalise the US development aid bureaucracy to be better able to mobilise and guide private-sector capital. This project, manifest in the Better Utilization of Investments Leading to Development (BUILD) Act, passed by Congress and signed by the President in October, more than doubled the US government's development-finance capacity, to US$60 billion, in order to support US private investment in strategic opportunities abroad. These measures complemented efforts by Japan, Australia and India, often in cooperation with the United States, to provide funding for infrastructure and investment needed in the Indo-Pacific in competition with China's expansive international infrastructure, lending and investment in the so-called Belt and Road Initiative.

Despite such measures, regional officials looked in vain for a coherent American strategy. Indeed, in March 2019 the US Government Accountability Office released a report which pointed to staff shortages in key positions of the foreign services. While comparable to shortages of previous years, it noted that the highest proportion of vacancies were for posts related to South Asia. Staff in East and South Asia reported 'that vacancies in these sections had limited their capacity to engage with host government officials on important, strategic issues'.[42]

Unlike the discipline that characterised the carefully crafted discourse and prudent behaviour of the Obama government in support of its Rebalance policy in Asia, the Trump administration's initiatives have, to date, been replete with uncertainties and ambiguities. Notably, the avowed tougher US government approach to China contained caveats including ongoing negotiations with China, Trump's positive personal relationship with his Chinese counterpart, and his avoidance of the type of tough rhetoric against China seen in the National Security Strategy. Perhaps of most importance has been Trump's avowed unpredictability, which led to his two summit meetings with North Korea's Kim Jong-un in 2018 and 2019 and which could allow for top-level deal making over key differences with China that would belie the stated administration strategy.

In sum, the deliberative and moderate approach of Barack Obama's Rebalance policy has, in the first two years of the Trump administration, been put aside in favour of a still ill-defined approach of the much more flamboyant and unpredictable Donald Trump. The Trump government shows in spades its willingness to apply power against those it opposes – a perceived weakness in Obama's approach to China. It has used the wide range of economic, diplomatic and military power available to the American superpower. The consequences of the policy shift are wearing on American allies and partners. Evaluating their overall impact will need to take account of the results of the policy shift, which are only vaguely evident at present and subject to be overtaken by unexpected moves by the US President or others.

Notes

1 J. Tankersley, 'Trump's Tariffs Keep Allies and Industry Apprehensive', *New York Times* (26 March 2018), p. B1.

2 A. Panda, 'The "Pivot" to Asia Is Over', *The Diplomat* (14 March 2017), https://thediplomat.com/2017/03/straight-from-the-us-state-department-the-pivot-to-asia-is-over/, accessed 12 March 2018.

3 H. Meijer (ed.), *Origins and Evolution of the US Rebalance toward Asia: Diplomatic, Military and Economic Dimensions* (London: Palgrave Macmillan, 2015); K. Campbell, *The Pivot: The Future of American Statecraft in Asia* (New York: Twelve, 2016).

4 R. Sutter, *China–US Relations*, 3rd edition (Lanham, MD: Rowman & Littlefield, 2018), pp. 151–9.

5 See among others, L. Hadar, 'Obama's West Point Realism', *The American Conservative* (30 May 2014), www.theamericanconservative.com/articles/obamas-west-point-realism/, accessed 12 March 2019.

6 W. Lohman, 'Top Five Political-Security Priorities for the Asia Pacific in 2016', Heritage Foundation (5 February 2016), www.heritage.org/asia/report/top-five-political-security-priorities-the-asia-pacific-2016, accessed 23 October 2019.

7   R. Sutter and S. Limaye, 'America's 2016 Election Debate on Asia Policy and Asian Reactions', East-West Center (2016), pp. 6–7.

8   *Ibid.*, p. 7.

9   J. Martin and A. Burns, 'Donald Trump's Slip in Polls has GOP Worried About Congress', *New York Times* (5 October 2016), www.nytimes.com/2016/10/06/us/politics/donald-trump-campaign.html, accessed 12 March 2019.

10 Sutter and Limaye, 'America's 2016 Election Debate', pp. 7–8.

11 White House, 'National Security Strategy of the United States' (December 2017), www.whitehouse.gov/wp-content/uploads/2017/12/NSS-Final-12-18-2017-0905. pdf, accessed 12 March 2019; US Department of Defense, 'Summary of the National Defense Strategy of the United States' (January 2018), www.defense. gov/Portals/1/Documents/pubs/2018-National-Defense-Strategy-Summary.pdf, accessed 12 March 2019.

12 R. Delaney, 'China Offers Trump US$200 Billion Cut in Trade Surplus', *South China Morning Post* (18 May 2018), www.scmp.com/news/china/diplomacy-defence/article/2146660/us-president-donald-trump-meet-chinese-vice-premier-liu, accessed 12 March 2019.

13 A. Macias, 'Defense-Friendly Spending Bill', *CNBC* (22 March 2018), www.cnbc. com/2018/03/22/defense-friendly-spending-bill-big-for-military.html, accessed 12 March 2019.

14 K. Demirjian, 'Trump's Nuclear Authority Divides Senators "Alarmed" by his Volatile Behavior', *Washington Post* (14 November 2017), www.washingtonpost. com/powerpost/senators-deadlock-in-debate-over-whether-to-restrain-trumps-nuclear-launch-authority/2017/11/14/491a994a-c95b-11e7-8321-481fd63f174d_story.html, accessed 12 March 2019.

15 BBC, 'North Korea Summit' (18 May 2018), www.bbc.com/news/world-asia-44158566, accessed 12 March 2019; *New York Times*, 'Trump-Kim Summit: Leaders Have Dinner in Vietnam' (26 February 2019), www.nytimes. com/2019/02/26/world/asia/trump-kim-summit-vietnam.html, accessed 14 March 2019.

16 R. Sutter, 'The United States and Asia in 2017', *Asian Survey*, 58:1 (2018), pp. 10–20.

17 D. Steinberg, 'Trump Administration Alienates Asia Hands', *Nikkei Asian Review* (1 April 2017), https://asia.nikkei.com/Viewpoints/David-I.-Steinberg/Trump-administration-alienates-Asia-hands-at-America-s-peril, accessed 12 March 2019.

18 R. Sutter, 'Trump and China', *East Asia Forum Quarterly*, 9:2 (2017), pp. 121–8.

19 Panda, 'The "Pivot" to Asia Is Over'.

20 P. Parameswaran, 'What Mattis' Shangri-La Dialogue Speech Revealed', *The Diplomat* (6 June 2017), https://thediplomat.com/2017/06/what-mattis-shangri-la-dialogue-speech-revealed-about-trumps-asia-policy/, accessed 12 March 2019.

21 *Ibid.*

22 P. Baker and D. Sanger, 'Trump Says Tillerson is "Wasting his Time" on North Korea', *New York Times* (1 October 2017), www.nytimes.com/2017/10/01/us/politics/trump-tillerson-north-korea.html, accessed 12 March 2019.

23 Sutter and Limaye, 'America's 2016 Election Debate', p. 21.

24 Sutter, 'The United States and Asia in 2017', p. 12.

25 B. Glaser and C. Norkiewicz, 'North Korea and trade dominate the agenda', *Comparative Connections*, 19:2 (2017) pp. 21–34

26 Sutter, 'The United States and Asia in 2017', p. 13.

27 R. Sutter and C. Huang, 'Steady gains in the South China Sea', *Comparative Connections*, 19:2 (2017), pp. 53–62.

28 Y. Tatsumi, 'Trump Meets Abe: Beyond the Publicity', *The Diplomat* (8 November 2017), https://thediplomat.com/2017/11/trump-meets-abe-beyond-the-publicity/, accessed 12 March 2019.

29 L. Figueroa, 'President Trump Meet Australian PM', *Newsday* (4 May 2017), www.newsday.com/news/new-york/president-donald-trump-returns-to-ny-meets-australian-pm-1.13563086, accessed 12 March 2019.

30 Sutter, 'Trump and China'.

31 M. Landler, 'Trump Hosts Prime Minister Phuc of Vietnam', *New York Times* (31 May 2017), www.nytimes.com/2017/05/31/world/asia/vietnam-nguyen-xuan-phuc-trump.html, accessed 12 March 2019.

32 C. E. Lee, W. Mauldin and E. Stokols, 'Trump and South Korea's Moon Assert Unity Against North Korea', *Wall Street Journal* (30 June 2017), www.wsj.com/articles/trump-meets-south-koreas-moon-jae-in-calls-for-new-trade-deal-1498836731, accessed 12 March 2019.

33 H. Pant, 'Mattis Comes to India: What's on the Agenda', *The Diplomat* (26 September 2017), https://thediplomat.com/2017/09/mattis-comes-to-india-whats-on-the-agenda/, accessed 12 March 2019.

34 W. S. Wan, 'Why Najib's Washington Visit Was a Success', *New Straits Times* (17 September 2017), www.nst.com.my/opinion/columnists/2017/09/280743/why-najibs-washington-visit-was-success, accessed 12 March 2019.

35 R. Ehrlich, 'White House Meet Legitimates Thailand's Strongman Rule', *Asia Times* (1 October 2017), www.atimes.com/article/white-house-meet-legitimates-thailands-strongman-rule/, accessed 12 March 2019.

36 Xinhua, 'Good US-China Relations Benefit Region, World: Singapore PM' (24 October 2107), http://en.people.cn/n3/2017/1024/c90000-9284064.html, accessed 12 March 2019.

37 K. Phillips, 'Philippines Duterte Vows Not to Come to the US', *Washington Post* (22 July 2017), www.washingtonpost.com/news/worldviews/wp/2017/07/22/philippines-duterte-vows-to-not-come-to-the-u-s-ive-seen-america-and-its-lousy/?utm_term=.30c9ee0a66cf, accessed 12 March 2019; *New York Post*, 'Trump-Duterte Have Cordial First Meeting' (11 November 2017), https://nypost.com/2017/11/11/trump-duterte-have-cordial-first-meeting-at-apec-summit/, accessed 12 March 2019.

38 *Guardian*, 'Donald Trump Skips East Asian Summit' (14 November 2017), www.theguardian.com/us-news/2017/nov/14/donald-trump-skips-east-asia-summit-on-final-day-of-12-day-tour, accessed 12 March 2019.

39   For coverage and details on the various stops and activities during the visit, see
     relevant articles in *Comparative Connections*, 19:3 (2018).
40   See R. Sutter, 'The United States and Asia in 2018', *Asian Survey*, 59:1 (2019).
41   US Department of Defense, 'Remarks by Secretary Mattis at Plenary Session of
     the 2018 Shangri-La Dialogue' (2 June 2018), https://dod.defense.gov/News/
     Transcripts/Transcript-View/Article/1538599/remarks-by-secretary-mattis-at-
     plenary-session-of-the-2018-shangri-la-dialogue/, accessed 18 March 2019.
42   US Government Accountability Office, 'Integrated Action Plan Could Enhance
     Efforts to Reduce Persistent Overseas Foreign Service Vacancies' (March
     2019), p. 18.

10

Security policy in Asia from Obama to Trump: Autopilot, neglect or worse?

Nick Bisley

Introduction

Donald Trump's 2016 election threatened a revolution in US Asia policy. Since the early years of the Cold War, the United States has been a constant presence in the region's security setting.[1] American military power has been the pre-eminent force in the region, organised through a series of bilateral alliances and quasi-alliance guarantees. This presence was part of the larger US Cold War grand strategy in which Washington sought to ensure a favourable strategic balance in Western Europe, the Middle East and East Asia.[2] Although the Obama administration put considerable public emphasis on its "Pivot", or "Rebalance", to Asia, and there were key differences between Obama and Bush's approaches to the region, in its major elements, the approach of the forty-fourth president towards Asia was very much in keeping with longer-run US strategic policy. Given what Trump said during the election campaign, and his activity during the transition and in the early days of the presidency, a fundamental break with the past looked entirely possible. As candidate he had demeaned alliances; during the campaign he showed a worrying lack of concern about nuclear proliferation in Northeast Asia and promised a trade war with the world's second largest economy. As President, Trump looked like he might govern US foreign policy in the same norm-busting manner in which he had campaigned, with dramatic consequences for regional security.

But after two years in office, those hoping for radical change in US security policy towards the region have been disappointed. Much in the way that Obama's Pivot was more about the presentation of US strategic policy and involved much less substantive change, Trump has not yet instigated any significant shifts. Indeed, the level of continuity with his predecessor's policy is striking, particularly given his instinct to reject almost anything to do with the Obama presidency. Alliances have been reaffirmed, as has the One China policy. Indeed, much to the surprise of critics and friends alike, Trump developed a good working relationship with

China's President Xi Jinping, engaged with regional multilateralism and even participated in the Asia summit season in November 2017, albeit in a slightly chaotic fashion by opting out of the East Asia Summit at the last minute. His administration has so far been more explicit in seeing China as a long-term geopolitical rival but has not yet made substantive changes to US security policy to match this shift in declaratory tone.

In this chapter I argue that US security policy in Asia is stuck somewhere between inertia and neglect. The continuity is not the result of a carefully considered policy choice; rather it is in the main due to the heavy inertial qualities of a strategic policy that has been in place for many decades. And when the Trump administration has focused on regional security rather than taking its cues from a larger strategic plan, it views things through the narrow prism of bilateral ties, with a heavy emphasis on a mercantilist view of economic relations, and crisis management. It is also constrained by a lack of adequate resources with many key bureaucratic posts still vacant. The consequence of this negligent and a-strategic approach has been to strengthen China's relative position in the region. This approach is also prompting friends and allies to accelerate their planning for a region in which the United States plays a more diminished role.

The chapter is in four parts. The first will discuss the Asia policy that Trump inherited from Obama. It will draw attention to the longer-term trends in US policy and the subtle differences introduced into that policy by Obama's team. The second will sketch out the range of possibilities that Trump's Asia policy promised. Here a composite picture will be drawn up based both on campaign promises and action during the transition. This is necessary because as candidate there was no clear and systematic articulation of how he would approach Asia's many significant security challenges with most of his regionally oriented pronouncements focused on China and trade. The third will explain why US security policy can be described as continuity by neglect. The chapter will conclude with an assessment of the consequences of this policy and how it is accelerating a significant transformation of Asia's regional order. Ultimately, Obama sought to sustain long-term US security policy in the face of a changing region, but failed to recognise the scale of the changes it faced; the Trump administration's careless approach to the region throughout its first two years has hastened a significant shift in Asia's security setting.

Obama's Asia legacy

Unsurprisingly for a president who came to national prominence because of his objection to the Iraq War, foreign policy was a significant focus of the Obama administration. And of the many achievements which the administration claimed, such as the Iran nuclear deal, the rapprochement with Cuba and the Paris climate change accord, their most significant long-term strategic effort was the emphasis put on Asia.[3] Indeed the attempt to put the region at the centre of US international policy is described by many in the administration as their most significant long-term contribution.[4]

Obama's electoral victory in 2008 was interpreted by the incoming administration as a mandate to end the war in Iraq and to focus in the first instance on the conflict in Afghanistan. The new government's aim was not only to make good on its commitment to extricate the United States from Iraq and to resolve the security problems of radical Islam in Afghanistan, but also to reorient US policy so as to better focus on the big trends in world politics. Obama's senior officials perceived that the major conflicts in the Middle East had not only sapped blood and treasure to no obvious strategic advantage, they had also warped the government's priorities and taken its focus off the major forces that were shaping America's global interests. In particular, so claimed the administration, Bush's focus on Iraq and Afghanistan had come at the cost of America's position in Asia, the region that was fast becoming the world's most important.

The response to this perceived neglect of the Bush administration, as well as the realisation of Asia's growing significance to US interests and the world, was to craft what was first described as the Pivot to Asia but which was soon rebranded as the "Rebalance" to the region.[5] Outlined in a number of speeches, most notably Secretary of State Hillary Clinton's speech to the East-West Center, Honolulu,[6] and the President's address to the Australian parliament in 2011,[7] "rebalancing" US policy towards Asia had a number of key aims. First, it was intended to realign US strategic policy to America's primary long-term interests, moving away from the disproportionate emphasis that had been placed on Iraq and Afghanistan. Too much time, money and bureaucratic resources had been tied up in parts of the world that were out of proportion to their long-term strategic significance. Second, the administration wanted to signal internationally as well as domestically the priority of the Asian region to its strategic policy. Allies and partners in Asia who were concerned that the US focus on the Middle East had opened the door to Chinese influence were to be reassured, and Beijing was to be reminded of America's emphasis on the region. As Obama said to the Australian parliament: 'in the Asia Pacific in the twenty-first century, the United States of America is all in.'[8] The desire to retain its strategic preponderance was made very clear. It was also intended to send signals within the bureaucracy about how resources should be allocated. More was to be invested so public servants would be incentivised to focus on the region.

America's long-term strategic policy is to remain the dominant power in Western Europe, the Middle East and East Asia. The Pivot to Asia, sold publicly as an emphasis on the most important region in the world, was ultimately about ensuring that long-term goal in the face of transformations caused by the rapid rise in wealth and influence of the People's Republic of China (PRC). Whether or not one agreed with the Obama critique that Bush had neglected the region – and many did not[9] – the underlying imperative for US security policy was that China's dramatic growth was fundamentally changing the region. Even though the United States wanted to retain the basic pattern of Asia's strategic balance, it realised that it would have to adjust its policy to reflect the realities of a shifting distribution of power. To do so it would take a number of steps. The most obvious was to devote more military assets to the region. Prominently announced at the Shangri-La Dialogue in 2012, the United States committed to devoting 60 per cent of its naval assets to the Pacific theatre.[10] More broadly, it signalled that Washington intended to remain the pre-eminent regional military power in both conventional and nuclear terms.

Washington also indicated that it wanted to distribute that military force more broadly, signing agreements with Australia and Singapore, as China's rise and its expanding capacities meant that the Cold War emphasis on Northeast Asia would no longer suffice. Equally, Obama wanted US allies to do more, both individually and collectively. If the US approach to the region in the past had been a "hub and spoke" model, in which the United States was the hub and its bilateral links to allies and part-ners the spokes, under the Rebalance, Washington wanted allies to do more to sustain the existing security order. This was in part about sharing the burden of security order provision, but was also about making it more flexible and nimble, allowing it a wider geographic expanse in which to be effective. It was also about broadening the polit-ical base for the US regional role. A more integrated security order in which allies like Japan and Australia work together as well as with the United States looks a lot less like hegemonism than the asymmetries of the past.

Critics of Obama might suggest that there was nothing especially new here. Bush had been keen on allies doing more, individually and collectively. But in other respects the Rebalance was rather more novel. The United States had long been ambivalent about regional multilateralism. While not outright opposed to the various multilateral institutions and structures that had been created in the 1990s and early 2000s, it had shown neither significant leadership in any initiative nor any particular enthusiasm beyond a Clinton-era focus on APEC.[11] The criti-cism that the Bush administration had neglected the region was most on the mark in relation to regional institutions with summits regularly skipped, most notably the ASEAN Regional Forum.[12] Commitment to and participation in multilat-eralism was a key third dimension of Obama's Asia policy.[13] The United States joined the East Asia Summit, notably acceding to ASEAN's Treaty of Amity and Cooperation (albeit with some opt-out clauses), and joined the efforts to make it a "peak" regional institution. Equally, the United States ensured high level and con-sistent participation across the board such as Hillary Clinton's 100 per cent record attending ARF meetings. Also, Obama hosted the first US–ASEAN Leaders' Meeting at Sunnylands in California in 2016.

There were a number of reasons for putting such an emphasis on multilateral engagement. Most immediately, commitment to these bodies signalled very directly Asia's importance to the United States. The conventional wisdom in Washington is that one can measure the significance of an issue by the amount of time the senior leaders, and in particular the President, spends on it. By committing not only to make up for the Bush administration's perceived neglect of regional institutions, but to make ASEAN engagement a high-profile commitment, Obama could in very visible ways communicate his priority on the region. And while Asian multilateral institutions have been criticised for being little more than exercises in political theatre,[14] there was an intent to the US emphasis as well. In the first instance, the United States saw these bodies as having good potential to broaden the support for maintaining the US role in a changing region. Through regular engagement with institutions in which it is one amongst equals, Washington felt it could strengthen the political consensus around its regional role. Relatedly, the political intent was also about buttressing the underlying status quo. Whether they were right to make this judgement is a separate issue but the White House saw in regional bodies like the EAS and APEC, and ASEAN in particular, an existing set of institutional means to strengthen the existing regional order in the face of disruptions caused by China's rise and its growing power and ambition.

In the past, US policy had benefited from the alignment between the economic and security interests of most regional states; the United States was the most important market and source of foreign direct investment (FDI) as well as the predominant military power. This made the pursuit of its strategic interests much more straightforward. The Obama administration realised that China's centrality in regional production chains and the growing asymmetric economic relationship with virtually every regional economy, meant that this could no longer be relied upon. The United States would need to actively pursue an economic strategy in the region to support its security policy, and saw in the Trans-Pacific Partnership (TPP) a means through which it could yoke economic and strategic interests. The United States had not initially launched the TPP, but once it became the centre-piece of the economic side of US Asia policy it became the most important player, not surprising given that the United States remains the world's biggest developed market. And in trying to sell the agreement to a sceptical and increasingly mercantilist minded Congress, Obama made clear the true geoeconomic intent of the TPP. That is, to ensure the trading interests of Asian countries are in line with America's vision for the region, for it was those interests that appeared to be the most immediate risk to the status quo.[15]

Even though Obama had emphasised Asia and the distinctiveness of his Rebalance to the region, his approach represented more in the way of continuation than change in US regional policy. The emphases on multilateralism and geoeconomics were novel. Yet they were in the service of a status quo security policy. With the surprising election of Donald J. Trump on 8 November 2016, that all looked set to change.

Expectations of President Trump's Asia policy

The results of the US election began to come through to East Asia in the late morning of 9 November 2016. As his victory went from unlikely to certain, policy makers, analysts and scholars tried to figure out what Trump might mean for the region. Virtually all had assumed Hillary Clinton would win and that her policy would be a continuation of Obama's Pivot, perhaps with a few sharper edges.[16] But Trump's campaign had not really focused on foreign policy, beyond trade, and had made almost no mention of the region as a whole. The only regional issue that had had any prominence was his threat to ditch the TPP and start what would effectively be a trade war with China. In an interview with the *New York Times* during the campaign, he claimed that allies in the region were getting a free ride and would have to pay for their security guarantees or have them withdrawn. When his interlocutors pointed out that that might cause Japan and South Korea to acquire their own nuclear weapons, he evinced virtually no concern.[17]

Trump's unorthodoxy as a candidate and his lack of political experience meant that, prior to taking office, no one could say with any confidence whether or not these threats would be carried out. Would alliances be trashed in favour of a nativist approach to America's global role? Would the world's two biggest economies really engage in trade warfare? Or was it all campaign bluster? No one could say with any degree of certainty. As a result, analysts began to examine public comments and publications produced by figures who were going into the administration. Significant emphasis was put on a piece by Peter Navarro and Alexander Gray. Navarro was to be part of a newly created National Trade Council and who was purported to have particular sway over China policy. The piece intimated that Trump's approach to Asia would follow what was purported to be the Reagan approach to the Soviet Union of pursuing peace from a position of military strength.[18] This promised a massive ramping up of military expenditure with the intent of staring down all challengers. A trade war and an arms race looked like they might be in the offing, fundamentally changing US security policy in the region.

As the days and weeks of the transition unfolded, more disconcerting signals were sent about what Trump might mean for the region. Perhaps none more so was the telephone conversation with Taiwanese President Tsai Ing-wen. Since the cessation of diplomatic relations with Taiwan, no president or president-elect has communicated directly with the leader of the Republic of China. The call was carefully planned and communicated effusively.[19] But quite what it meant was again not at all clear. Would the United States ditch the One China policy, the anchor of its regional engagement since the 1970s? Or was this a first step in some grand bargain with the PRC in which Taiwan would be offered up as part of a neo-Kissingerian deal to carve Asia up into security spheres of influence? With the wilfully unpredictable former TV star turned president no one could say. And when Rex Tillerson said that China should be barred from access to the disputed islands in the South China Sea during his Senate confirmation hearings, the administration looked as though it were on a collision course with the region's most important resident power.[20]

President-elect Trump appeared to promise an almost complete repudiation of the Obama legacy. Certainly, in many areas of government policy he appeared to take instinctively anti-Obama positions. Signature Obama policies, like health care and immigration reform, were a particular focus of ire. As Thomas Wright of Brookings pointed out, Trump was a politician of few hard convictions, but trade policy was one exception. He has been consistently mercantilist since the 1980s and seemed particularly put out by large-scale multilateral agreements.[21] Trump's "America First" rhetoric of the campaign promised that a wounded nationalism would lead to a narrow transactionalism, and zero-sum thinking would replace the liberal internationalism that had driven Washington's global role. Asia policy seemed set for a radical transformation.

Trump's Asia policy: Continuity and neglect

After two years in office, the most striking feature of the US approach to regional security under President Trump is the extent to which it retains most of the key features of Obama's approach. There are some notable exceptions, most obviously the ramping up of rhetorical pressure on North Korea and a shift in tone towards China, but there is far more continuity than change between Obama and Trump. In many respects, Trumpian policy is effectively Obama policy with the added dimension of bellicose rhetoric and without the overarching strategic vision of his predecessor.

US security policy in Asia had been predicated on the perpetuation of military primacy and a "congagement" approach to China which attempted to bind the PRC's interests to the prevailing security order. Trump entered office evidently looking to use the former to overturn the latter. Yet in spite of flirting with Taiwan and hard-line rhetoric on the PRC, security relations with China are striking for their broad continuity.[22] Trump formally honoured the One China policy early on in his presidency,[23] and focused on building a good personal rapport with Xi Jinping in the early months of his presidency. At the Mar-a-Lago meeting in April 2017 they agreed to establish a formal process for managing inter-governmental relations that was little more than a retooling of the Obama era Strategic and Economic Dialogue.[24]

Strategic policy has taken a more stern declaratory policy – with the PRC figuring more explicitly as a geopolitical rivalry – and there has been an increase in the tempo of freedom of navigation exercises in the South China Sea,[25] a militarised contestation has not materialised and indeed Washington looks as though it has found a way to live with what Beijing has done in Southeast Asia's contested waters. And the one security domain in which Trump has made change – in relation to North Korea – requires the cultivation of Beijing. Put simply, the state of Sino-American security relations stands some way from the revolution threatened in late 2016.

Equally, allies who were concerned that Trump may be prepared to make them pay for protection were particularly worried by a difficult first phone call between Trump and the Australian Prime Minister Malcolm Turnbull.[26] If an ally as close as Australia could be treated as badly as Turnbull had been, and so publicly, then what lay in store for the others? Yet within weeks of the inauguration, key senior figures in the administration were sent on a series of "reassurance tours".[27] Vice President Mike Pence, Secretary of Defense Jim Mattis and then Secretary of State Rex Tillerson, were dispatched to the region to reassure allies and partners that the underlying purpose, structure and funding of US regional strategy were going to remain as they had been in the past.

Yet even though the initial fears that the United States was going to undercut its alliances or radically transform the financial arrangements of security guarantees have been assuaged, South Korea, Australia, Japan and others remain unsettled by Trump. During the campaign Trump indicated he wanted allies to do more for themselves, although perhaps the message was communicated in a somewhat rough fashion. The fact of his election and the uncertainties that it has prompted has led many in the region to begin to do just that. Although there has been no major change to US strategy, in form or function, as yet, Trump has still had a noticeable impact upon the region's security arrangements as Asian states begin to take steps to better look after themselves. After all, an America that elected Trump is not the country that allies had come to expect. And the issue of increasing the financial contributions of host nations remains a fixation of the administration, leaving partners jittery about the longer-term future.

It was on one of those tours that Vice President Pence announced probably the greatest surprise of Trump's Asia policy in its first twelve months: that the President would attend APEC and the gaggle of meetings that comprise the region's multilateral summit season in November 2017.[28] Not only was Trump cosying up to China that year, he was going to partake in that most quintessentially Obama move: engagement with regional institutions. Typically, it was not all smooth sailing. Prior to the trip the White House announced that Trump would not ultimately go to the EAS, but at the last minute changed tack again to say he was going, only finally skipping out at the last minute. Notwithstanding some clumsy handling, Trump did go and comported himself more effectively than when he took part in NATO meetings in May 2017.[29]

North Korea policy has been the most visible facet of US security policy in Asia under Trump and arguably where he has most visibly broken with the past. Within five months of coming to office the administration announced the era of "strategic patience" was over.[30] The US policy would now be one of "maximum pressure" in which Washington upped the ante of sanctions – pursuing not only a tighter and more closely enforced regime but also imposing secondary sanctions as well – and adopted a dangerously bellicose public diplomacy. Clearly this was a ratcheting up of pressure and a break with Obama's approach. But it also reflected the reality that the DPRK was within touching distance of achieving its long-held nuclear ambitions. Trump met with Kim in a visually powerful summit in Singapore in June 2018. The meeting delivered little but a break in the tensions that Trump had ratcheted up. The North remains a long way from denuclearisation and Trump looks increasingly to have been played by Pyongyang. But beyond North Korea policy, which in spite of its weighty nuclear dimensions remains a crisis management exercise, in its big strategic dimensions, Trump's policy maintains the direction of Obama which in turn was largely in keeping with US policy in the region over the past decades.

Trump's approach to Asia is most visibly different from his predecessors in the trade sphere. The Obama administration tried to use economic policy to sustain the old alignment of economic and security interests that was being disrupted by China's rise. In walking away from trade agreements and adopting a narrowly instrumental approach to trade and economic relations, Trump is unwittingly strengthening China's position and undermining US security policy as it is widening the gap between regional countries' economic and security interests. It also risks adding an overtly politicised dimension to regional economics. But Trump has brought about some important changes to the US approach to the region.

A further change in the US approach to Asia from Obama to Trump is the lowering in the importance of values in American priorities. For Obama, US policy was about advancing American interests in regional security, prosperity and human dignity.[31] Each component was given equal weighting and seen as mutually reinforcing. For the Trump administration the third pillar, relating to human rights, democracy and freedom, is of much lesser importance. These ideas barely figure in public remarks by the President or senior officials in relation to Asia, nor indeed do they seem to be particularly emphasised in any aspect of US foreign policy. Where in the past the US vision of the region saw peace, prosperity and the advancement of liberal values as mutually reinforcing, the Trump administration sees economic and security questions as separate from, and of greater importance than, questions of values and rights. The United States has not completely walked away from any commitment to these issues – the theme of Trump's APEC speech was a 'free and open Indo-Pacific',[32] the rhetoric of which was embellished by these ideas – but the substantive emphasis on freedom, rights and democracy is noticeably lower.

The Obama administration's approach to Asia was in keeping with the longer run trends in US regional policy. It also reflected the continuing belief that China's economic rise could be compatible with the prevailing regional order and America's place at the centre of that order. Whether informed by the idea that an increasingly wealthy China would become more liberal, or just by the notion that a China that is prosperous and economically integrated with its neighbours has no incentive to disrupt the region, up until Trump's election, the view from Washington was that China could find wealth and satisfaction in a region in which the United States maintained its current position. In 2017 it became clear, due both to the actions and activities of the PRC as well as the response of the United States, that that view no longer has the grip it once did in Washington. Indeed, Trump's administration seems to have believed that long-term geopolitical competition amongst great powers is the central feature of world politics.[33] If Obama's policy represented a broadly liberal internationalist outlook on the region and its dynamics, Trump's approach has so far been informed by a strong dose of realpolitik. This was perhaps most clearly articulated in the National Security Strategy released late in 2017 which states:

> These [great power] competitions require the United States to rethink the policies of the past two decades – policies based on the assumption that engagement with rivals and their inclusion in international institutions and global commerce would turn them into benign actors and trustworthy partners. For the most part, this premise turned out to be false.[34]

If these ideas are acted upon then Trump's approach to trade and his approach to the broader dynamics of security would mark the end of a broadly liberal American foreign policy and the start of a more realist and nationalist outlook in US policy.

It is tempting to see in the mercantilism of Trump's trade policy and the realism of his security strategy a coherent worldview and a decisive break with the past based on that philosophy. Notwithstanding the changes outlined above, the puzzle of Trump's Asia policy to date is that even though he seems to evince an outlook at odds with what has come before him, US Asia policy has not substantially changed.

The continuity with Obama policy alongside the absence of what can be described as joined-up thinking has led some to describe US policy as being on autopilot. As Aaron Connelly observes, in spite of the odd tweet and snarling press conference, US regional policy 'is charting a pre-programmed course, much of it last mapped during the Obama administration'.[35] To date there has been little evidence of an "America First" agenda in US security policy. The most notable feature of Trump's approach to the region is a strong emphasis on bilateral relationships. That is, rather than think about US security interests in the region as a whole, whether conceived as East Asia, Asia Pacific or Indo-Pacific, US interests are assessed and prosecuted on a country-by-country basis. Any issue linkage is narrow, instrumental and largely driven by crisis. There is no evidence of a big picture vision of America's regional ambitions and consequently little attempt to match statecraft and resources to drive those ambitions. Instead policy is highly reactive, driven by instincts and concerns about optics. Crucially, it is poorly resourced.

At the time of writing in early 2019, crucial posts in the machinery of US Asia policy remain unfilled. The Assistant Secretary for East Asian Affairs, Susan Thornton, remains in an acting capacity as the White House refuses to endorse her in a permanent capacity. The equivalent post in the Defense Department, Randall Schriver, was appointed on 8 January 2018. The Asia section of the National Security Council, a vital coordinating body for regional policy, remains badly understaffed. Meanwhile, ambassadorial posts to South Korea, Australia and Singapore were vacant for most of the first two years. Given the importance of the region to US security interests and to the broader international system, why has US policy been one of autopilot, at best, if not downright neglect at worst?

Even those who expected Trump to bring about significant changes to US international policy, whether in Asia or elsewhere, did not expect revolution to be achieved immediately. The US government is vast and its inertial qualities are tremendous. US policy in Asia has pursued the aims of regional primacy and the means of bilateral alliance relationships and open markets for decades. To change either the ends or the means of the country's Asia policy would take significant effort, and time. The question thus is whether Trump has a different set of policy ends in mind. Is he prepared to expend the energy to change that policy, and over what time might one reasonably expect to see change?

Since Trump's inauguration, there has been a major cleavage within the West Wing between what is effectively an orthodox Republican foreign policy posture and the nativist "America First" outlook of Peter Navarro, Steven Miller and (the now ousted) Steve Bannon, amongst others. This division and the efforts of the two sides to capture what both seem to think is the open market of the President's attention is one factor in the slow-moving nature of US Asia policy. To date, the lack of significant shifts away from the underlying pattern set by Obama and his predecessors seems to indicate that Trump's Asia policy represents the victory of the orthodox wing of the administration. What is less clear is whether the pattern so far, of US security policy as largely a continuation of the Obama period, will persist or whether this is a temporary state of affairs with more significant changes yet to come.

The other important reason for the continuity of US security policy in Asia – albeit in a somewhat bureaucratically anaemic state – is the absence of serious alternatives. While Trump's campaign was filled with overheated rhetoric and ideas at some remove from US government business as usual, as the presidency has progressed it has become increasingly clear that much of the bombast was little more than rhetoric. Trump and his team do not appear to have a well-developed view of America's global role, whether "America First", Kissingerian realpolitik, or any other. To shift US policy in the region requires a well thought through alternative and not only does none currently exist, there is little evidence that any effort is being put into new policy development. All signs thus far indicate that US policy in Asia is likely to continue to be broadly in keeping with the past, but that it will be shaped by a reactive administration fond of theatrics and bluster. Relations with China may become more fraught, particularly if trade tensions spike or if the United States decides to push back on Chinese maritime activity.

The ability of the radicals to shift policy will depend on their ability not only to generate compelling new policies in the face of well-marshalled orthodox opposition, but also to capture the imagination of the President. Trump appears to like muscularity in foreign policy and regional security policy is premised on US primacy. One of the problems US policy faces is that while Trump is clearly nativist on trade policy, he has been fairly orthodox in terms of strategic policy. This means that the current settings are likely to remain as they are, with a significant line of tension between a strategic status quo and a revisionism on trade policy. Ultimately, it seems that US Asia policy to 2020 will look much as it did between 2016 and 2018.

Conclusion

Over the past half-decade or so, Asia's security landscape has shifted decisively. From the late 1970s until around 2010 the region was notable for its geopolitical stability and its remarkable growth in economic prosperity. That has begun to change. The region's key powers all feel unsettled by the shifting power dynamics with a more prosperous and powerful China prompting increased uncertainty. The election of Donald Trump in 2016 seemed to underline a second long-term source of that shift in the region's security setting. Since 2008 the United States had cut a more cautious figure in the region. Obama's Rebalance sought to recalibrate US policy to sustain its long-term primacy in the face of a rising China while reducing its risk profile. This led to a decline in American strategic credibility as its dependability was being openly questioned.

Trump has exacerbated that trend. The United States is seen not only as in long-term relative decline in influence, but its political leadership has turned inward. Prior to 2016 few would have deemed credible that a candidate as nativist as Donald Trump would win the nomination of a major party, let alone capture the White House. And it is this double movement – China's growing power and assertiveness, and uncertainty about American influence and purpose – which has unsettled the region's security environment most of all. Trump's election has opened a door for China to increase its influence in the region, which it is plainly trying to do. Equally, US allies and partners are beginning to explore ways by which they can become less dependent on Washington.

Since the Sino-American rapprochement, the United States has sought to retain its position as the pre-eminent power in the region. After a brief period in the mid-1990s in which it looked as though it might retreat, the United States has committed to retaining its posture. In the past this kept the region stable because at the time the United States was, in the words of the late Singaporean statesman Lee Kuan Yew, the region's 'least distrusted power'. Yet as China has become more confident and capable, the likely implications of the United States seeking to retain its military position are growing rivalry and contestation. The problem the region faces is that in pursuing essentially the same strategic policy nearly two decades into the twenty-first century as it did in the late 1990s, Washington is now contributing to regional instability and not assuaging it. One of the possibilities that Trump held out in the transition period, of a grand strategic bargain with China, offered a break from this. However, as the prospects of that occurring seem to have dissipated, US policy has reverted to its long-term pattern; scholars and analysts should recognise that maintaining the same policy now has a different set of strategic implications than it did at the turn of the millennium.

The Obama legacy in Asia is something of a paradox. On the one hand his strong emphasis on the region indicated that this part of the world would be the top priority for the world's most important economic and military power. On the other, the vision for the United States in the region was one of reduced capacity and leadership. Informed by the somewhat naïve view that China and indeed all regional countries could prosper and find satisfaction in a part of the world in which the United States forever remained the dominant power, Washington acted as if nothing really had changed. Some adjustments in the disposition of its forces might be necessary; some broadening of the political base of US policy would help. Yet the underlying view was that the basic settings were fine.

Xi Jinping's China has shown us that this was a misplaced view. China sees the US role in the region – at least as it has been over the past few decades – as ultimately incompatible with it achieving its long-term interests. It has begun to take steps to provide alternative leadership, to secure its interests and to create a different international environment from that which has prevailed. Across its first two years in office, the Trump administration apparently failed to realise the scale of the challenge China presents, and until it can develop a larger-scale strategic outlook and grapple with China's ambition, then the US position in the region will continue the erosion that began under George W. Bush, and that was increased by Obama. Trump's Asia policy, in contrast to the surface appearances, is entirely in keeping with long-term trends.

Notes

1   R. Buckley, *The US in the Asia-Pacific Since 1945* (Cambridge: Cambridge University Press).

2   S. M. Walt, *Taming American Power: The Global Response to American Primacy* (New York: W. W. Norton, 2006).

3   For an insider's account see D. Chollet, *The Long Game: How Obama Defied Washington and Redefined America's Role in the World* (New York: Public Affairs, 2016).

4   K. M. Campbell, *The Pivot: The Future of American Statecraft in Asia* (New York: Twelve, 2016).

5   R. Weitz, 'Pivot Out, Rebalance In', *The Diplomat* (3 May 2012), https:// thediplomat.com/2012/05/pivot-out-rebalance-in/, accessed 13 March 2019.

6   H. Clinton, 'America's Pacific Century', *Foreign Policy* (11 October 2011), http:// foreignpolicy.com/2011/10/11/americas-pacific-century/, accessed 13 March 2019.

7   White House, 'Remarks by President Obama to the Australian Parliament' (17 November 2011), https://obamawhitehouse.archives.gov/the-press-office/2011/11/ 17/remarks-president-obama-australian-parliament, accessed 13 March 2019.

8   *Ibid.*

9   M. Green, 'The Legacy of Obama's "Pivot" to Asia', *Foreign Policy* (3 September 2016), https://foreignpolicy.com/2016/09/03/the-legacy-of-obamas-pivot-to-asia/, accessed 13 March.

10 L. Panetta, 'The US Rebalance Towards the Asia-Pacific', IISS-Shangri La Dialogue (2 June 2012), www.iiss.org/en/events/shangri-la-dialogue/archive/sld12-43d9/ first-plenary-session-2749/leon-panetta-d67b, accessed 13 March 2019.

11 M. Beeson, 'American hegemony and regionalism: The rise of East Asia and the end of the Asia-Pacific', *Geopolitics*, 11:4 (2006), pp. 541–60.

12 T. J. Pempel, 'How Bush bungled Asia: Militarism, economic indifference and unilateralism have weakened the United States across Asia', *The Pacific Review*, 21:5 (2008), pp. 547–81.

13 S. Limaye, 'Prospects of multilateral cooperation in the Asia-Pacific: To overcome the gap of security outlooks', in National Institute for Defence Studies, *Prospects of Multilateral Cooperation the Asia Pacific: To Overcome the Gap of Security Outlooks* (Tokyo: National Institute for Defence Studies, 2014), pp. 127–38.

14 D. M. Jones and M. L. R. Smith, 'Making process not progress: ASEAN and the evolving East Asian regional order', *International Security*, 32:1 (2007), pp. 148–84.

15 White House, 'Statement by the President on the Trans-Pacific Partnership' (5 October 2015), https://obamawhitehouse.archives.gov/the-press-office/2015/10/ 05/statement-president-trans-pacific-partnership, accessed 13 March 2019.

16 A. Ni, 'Clinton or Trump: Who Does China Want?', *The World Today*, www. chathamhouse.org/publications/twt/clinton-or-trump-who-does-china-want, accessed 13 March 2019.

17 *New York Times*, 'Transcript: Donald Trump Expounds his Foreign Policy Views' (26 March 2016), www.nytimes.com/2016/03/27/us/politics/donald-trump-transcript.html, accessed 13 March 2019.

18 A. Gray and P. Navarro, 'Donald Trump's Peace Through Strength Vision for the Asia-Pacific', *Foreign Policy* (7 November 2016), http://foreignpolicy.com/2016/11/07/donald-trumps-peace-through-strength-vision-for-the-asia-pacific/, accessed 13 March 2019.

19 A. Gearon, 'Trump Speaks with Taiwanese President, A Major Break with Decades of US Policy', *Washington Post* (3 December 2016), www.washingtonpost.com/world/national-security/trump-spoke-with-taiwanese-president-a-major-break-with-decades-of-us-policy-on-china/2016/12/02/b98d3a22-b8ca-11e6-959c-172c82123976_story.html, accessed 13 March 2019.

20 D. Brunnstrom and M. Spetalnick, 'Tillerson Says China Should be Barred from South China Sea Islands', Reuters (12 January 2017), www.reuters.com/article/us-congress-tillerson-china/tillerson-says-china-should-be-barred-from-south-china-sea-islands-idUSKBN14V2KZ, accessed 13 March 2019.

21 T. Wright, 'The 2016 Presidential Campaign and the Crisis of US Foreign Policy', Lowy Institute (10 October 2016), www.lowyinstitute.org/publications/2016-presidential-campaign-and-crisis-us-foreign-policy, accessed 13 March 2019.

22 W. Xinbo, 'Constructive engagement: China's handling of Trump', *Global Asia*, 12:4 (2017), pp. 38–41.

23 BBC, 'Trump Agrees to Honour "One China" Policy Despite Threats' (10 February 2017), http://www.bbc.com/news/world-asia-china-38927891, accessed 13 March 2019.

24 White House, 'Statement from the Press Secretary on the United States-China Visit' (7 April 2017), www.whitehouse.gov/briefings-statements/statement-press-secretary-united-states-china-visit/, accessed 13 March 2019.

25 A. Panda, 'South China Sea: Fourth US FONOP in Five Months Suggests a New Operational Rhythm', *The Diplomat* (12 October 2017), https://thediplomat.com/2017/10/south-china-sea-fourth-us-fonop-in-five-months-suggests-a-new-operational-rhythm/, accessed 13 March 2019.

26 J. Kehoe, 'Donald Trump Hammered Malcolm Turnbull in January Call, Transcript Shows', *Australian Financial Review* (4 August 2017), www.afr.com/news/politics/world/donald-trump-hammered-malcolm-turnbull-in-january-call-transcript-shows-20170804-gxp1b8, accessed 13 March 2019.

27 *American Interest*, 'James Mattis' Asian Reassurance Tour' (6 Feburary 2017), www.the-american-interest.com/2017/02/06/james-mattiss-asian-reassurance-tour/, accessed 13 March 2019.

28 Reuters, 'Trump to Attend Three Asian Summits in November: Pence' (20 April 2017), www.reuters.com/article/us-pence-asia-indonesia-trump/trump-to-attend-three-asian-summits-in-november-pence-idUSKBN17M1BZ, accessed 13 March 2019.

29   *LA Times*, 'Trump Didn't Win Any Friends in Europe' (26 May 2017), www.
     latimes.com/opinion/editorials/la-ed-trump-europe-20170527-story.html,
     accessed 13 March 2019.

30   J. Diamond, 'Trump: US Patience with the North Korean Regime is "Over"', CNN
     (30 June 2017), https://edition.cnn.com/2017/06/30/politics/trump-moon-jae-in-
     rose-garden/index.html, accessed 13 March 2019.

31   White House, 'Remarks to Australian Parliament'.

32   White House, 'Remarks by President Trump at APEC CEO Summit' (10 November
     2017), www.whitehouse.gov/briefings-statements/remarks-president-trump-apec-
     ceo-summit-da-nang-vietnam/, accessed 13 March 2019.

33   US Department of Defense, 'Summary of the 2018 National Defense Strategy of
     the United States of America: Sharpening the American Military's Competitive
     Edge' (January 2018), www.defense.gov/Portals/1/Documents/pubs/2018-
     National-Defense-Strategy-Summary.pdf, accessed 13 March 2019.

34   White House, 'National Security Strategy of the United States' (December 2017),
     www.whitehouse.gov/wp-content/uploads/2017/12/NSS-Final-12-18-2017-0905.
     pdf, accessed 13 March 2019.

35   A. Connelly, 'Autopilot: East Asia Policy Under Trump', Lowy Institute (31 October
     2017), www.lowyinstitute.org/publications/autopilot-east-asia-policy-under-
     trump, accessed 13 March 2019.

11

A grand strategic transition? Obama, Trump and the Asia Pacific political economy

Michael Mastanduno

Introduction

Hegemony and balancing are alternative foreign policy strategies available to powerful states in the international system. A state pursuing a hegemonic strategy seeks to create and preserve an order, regionally or globally, that reflects and reinforces its values and interests.[1] It strives to provide sufficient benefits so that other states prove willing to support that hegemonic order and the special role of the hegemonic state within it.[2] Alternatively, a state that adopts a balancing strategy acknowledges the existence of "peer competitors" with their own conceptions of regional or global order. It may compete or at times cooperate with those states but does not expect to incorporate them into its own order.

Balance of power or hegemony? For roughly seventy years, the United States has resolved this fundamental grand strategic question. During the Cold War, successive US administrations pursued a *global* balancing strategy against the Soviet Union but embedded within it *regional* hegemonic strategies in Western Europe and East Asia. The latter included the creation of durable alliances and the re-orienting of former adversaries – Germany in Europe and Japan in Asia – into partners supportive of US-inspired economic and security orders. With the collapse of the Soviet Union, post-war administrations sought to broaden and deepen the US hegemonic order. The United States cast itself as indispensable to global order and as the self-appointed regional stabiliser in Europe, Asia and the Middle East. It sought to entice Russia and China, despite not being US security allies, to follow the post-war German and Japanese examples and partner with Washington in support of an international order informed by US values and interests.[3]

The Trump administration is the first in the post-war era to question explicitly the desirability of America's hegemonic aspiration and the durability of its hegemonic role. Its "America First" rhetoric and objectives signal a preference to depart from order maintenance in favour of the more transactional politics of the balance of power. Its National Security Strategy (NSS) of 2017 explicitly casts China and Russia as competitors, rather than as potential partners in the US hegemonic project.

Strategic transitions are neither simple nor straightforward, and in its first two years the Trump administration struggled to articulate and carry out a coherent grand strategy. Whether it can develop and implement an alternative to hegemony remains to be seen. But it has taken the initial steps to reframe the US strategic debate from its post-Cold War emphasis on means – how best to pursue hegemony – to ends – whether to pursue hegemony at all.

This chapter focuses on the transition from Presidents Obama to Trump with emphasis on the political economy of the Asia Pacific. Throughout the post-war era, US foreign economic policies have been shaped significantly by broader geopolitical and security strategies. This is true for both Obama and Trump. For Obama, the pursuit of hegemony using more limited means dictated a regional shift to the Asia Pacific. His administration devised an economic strategy that complemented this geopolitical approach and simultaneously reaffirmed America's traditional role as leader of a liberalising world economy. For Trump, the overall rejection of America's hegemonic project has been accompanied by a departure from America's traditional leadership role in the world economy in favour of a more nationalist and transactional approach to foreign economic relations.

The next section reviews the Obama administration's Asia Pacific economic strategy in the context of its larger geopolitical strategy. The following sections link Trump's worldview, its implications for grand strategy, and the administration's initial approach to the Asia Pacific. A concluding section considers Trump's departure from Obama's policies and how US strategy in the Asia Pacific from early 2019 might evolve over the remainder of Trump's tenure.

The Obama administration: Hegemony's last gasp?

The 1990s were the golden age of American hegemony. George H. W. Bush ended the Cold War peacefully on Western terms, and his Defense Department outlined a strategy such that no peer competitor might challenge America's newfound pre-eminent position.[4] The Clinton administration moved the hegemonic project forward by reaffirming the US presence in the Asia Pacific and Europe through a strategy of deep engagement. Under the "Washington Consensus", US officials celebrated open trade and financial markets and the American model of deregulated capitalism.

The tragedy of 11 September 2001 shifted the means to assert US hegemony rather than the goal itself. George W. Bush's National Security Strategy of 2002 proclaimed the end of great power rivalry and that all major states stood with the

United States against global terrorism.[5] Bush turned his attention from traditional great power politics to the periphery of the international system. In the face of a new threat he overcame America's Vietnam era-inspired reluctance to intervene and engaged US forces directly in Afghanistan and Iraq.

Barack Obama embraced the hegemonic responsibility he inherited yet faced a more constrained domestic and international setting. Whereas Bush enjoyed the domestic discretion to start two conflicts, Obama faced an American public weary of what had become long, costly and inconclusive wars in the Middle East. The global financial crisis of 2007/8 and subsequent deep recession compounded the problem and reinforced Obama's instinct that US hegemonic strategy would have to make do with limited means.[6] The United States could no longer, as John F. Kennedy once proclaimed it could, 'pay any price and bear any burden' to achieve its foreign policy objectives. In Obama's own words, 'I refuse to set goals that go beyond our responsibility, our means, or our interests.'[7] Choices would have to be made.

The logic of Obama's signature geopolitical move, the so-called "Pivot", was simple.[8] US hegemony after the Cold War centred on engagement in three key regions, Europe, the Middle East, and East Asia. After 9/11, the United States had overinvested attention and resources in one region. It needed to shift attention ("Rebalance") to the Asia Pacific, which had become both the core of the global economy and the setting for the possible emergence of a peer competitor, China.

The intended central messages of the Pivot were clear and consistent with the US hegemonic project. One message was designed for friends and allies in the region, who understandably questioned America's staying power in the Asia Pacific considering its preoccupation and (over)commitment for a decade in the Middle East. The Pivot meant to convey that the United States, as a "resident power" in East Asia, had every intention of remaining in the neighbourhood to pursue its economic and security interests while also serving as a regional stabiliser, whether on the Korean Peninsula, in the South China Sea, or elsewhere.[9]

The second message, intended for China, was more nuanced. On one hand, and as Chinese leaders suspected, the Pivot suggested a US willingness to contain China, should that become necessary. The United States planned to strengthen its existing alliances with Japan, South Korea and Australia and increase its regional military presence. Obama's team resisted China's provocations in the South China Sea and emphasised freedom of navigation, or the enforcement of rules that favoured superior US naval power. As the two countries jockeyed for position in East Asia, it is not surprising that a so-called trust deficit emerged in the bilateral relationship.[10]

On the other hand, the operational vagueness of Obama's Pivot opened space for an alternative message, namely that the United States preferred, as it had for the past two decades, to continue cooperation and engagement with China. The world's two largest national economies had developed deep economic interdependence across trade, finance and investment. Particularly during the financial crisis, the Obama team encouraged the idea of joint US–China leadership in the world economy. America's market was most significant for Chinese exports, and China's willingness to purchase and hold US Treasury bonds reinforced for the United States the hegemonic privilege of enjoying low inflation and stable growth without having to raise taxes or sacrifice consumption or military spending.

The Bush administration had proposed the term "responsible stakeholder" to convey that China had benefited greatly from its integration into the American-led world economy, and in return needed to do its part to ensure global stability, defined in terms of the priorities of the US foreign policy agenda.[11] Obama's team embraced China's promise as a responsible stakeholder. The President frequently stated that the United States 'welcomed the rise of China' and characterised US–China relations as the most important bilateral relationship of our time.[12] The administration took opportunities to deepen bilateral cooperation (e.g. the US–China Economic and Strategic Dialogue) and to celebrate initiatives in which China demonstrated responsibility, such as in the Paris climate change negotiations. Although to some Obama's willingness to steer between engagement and containment seemed indecisive, to others the Pivot offered an appropriate combination of incentives and threats in the face of uncertain Chinese foreign policy intentions. "Congagement" – an awkward term coined at the end of the 1990s – captured the spirit of Obama's strategy.[13]

The economic dimension of Obama's hegemonic strategy

The Pivot was Obama's key strategic initiative and participation in the TPP (Trans-Pacific Partnership) was its main supporting economic component. At one level the TPP was simply a regional trade agreement, albeit a vast one involving twelve countries whose economies collectively accounted for 37 per cent of global GDP.[14] But for the Obama administration the TPP had intrinsic strategic significance, as a tangible sign of both US commitment to the Asia Pacific and US leadership in developing the rules of the global economy. Hegemonic states view themselves as establishing and exercising rule-making authority. President Obama was unusually explicit on this, stating in an official press release that 'we can't let countries like China write the rules of the global economy'.[15] His Trade Representative echoed this sentiment, calling the TPP an 'unprecedented opportunity to update the rules of the road'.[16] Although it was unusual for a Defense Secretary to weigh in on a trade agreement, Ashton Carter noted publicly that 'passing the TPP is as important to me as another aircraft carrier'.[17]

The rules put forth by the TPP reflected both US economic interests and America's preferred approach to trade liberalisation. Since the formation of the WTO in the early 1990s, the United States has pushed for "behind the border" liberalisation, going beyond tariffs to cover restrictions embedded in domestic political economies including in the areas of services, intellectual property, invest-ment, rules of origin, state-owned enterprises, and government procurement. The TPP, as a "high standard" trade agreement, also established strong labour and environmental regulations.[18]

As the United States turned the TPP into a strategic and economic priority, the stakes increased for others. Japan had initially been reluctant to participate but came on board under Prime Minister Shinzo Abe, who proved willing to defy Japan's powerful agricultural lobby to support the strategic initiative of his country's most important security ally. As a technologically-advanced economy, Japan also stood to benefit from stronger behind-the-border rules.[19] Australia envisioned an expansion of its agricultural exports, and Singapore anticipated gains in trans-Pacific shipping services. For Vietnam, the TPP promised market access for its exports, international pressure (that Vietnam welcomed) to accel-erate its domestic economic reforms, and the opportunity to forge closer strategic ties with Washington in the face of rising China.[20]

The geopolitical stakes were highest for China. From the perspective of the United States, the purpose of the TPP was not to exclude China but to force it into a difficult choice. In an echo of early post-war US offers to the Soviet Union to join the Bretton Woods system, the Obama administration signalled that it welcomed China's participation, but on American terms. China's dilemma was obvious. On the one hand, it did not want to sit on the side-lines if the TPP ultimately defined the economic architecture of the Asia Pacific. On the other, it could not easily sign on to rules promoted by the United States and embedded within the TPP. Those rules posed a direct challenge to China's model of state capitalism, including its support for state-owned enterprises, its penchant for industrial policy, and its laissez-faire approach to intellectual property protection.

Not surprisingly, an increasingly powerful China sought to play its own role in regional rule-making. As an alternative to the TPP it embraced the Regional Comprehensive Economic Partnership (RCEP), a "low standard" initiative that focused at the border rather than behind it and excluded the United States. China's President Xi Jinping also implemented the ambitious Belt and Road Initiative to develop the infrastructure of regional neighbours and to provide an outlet for China's excess capacity in construction materials.[21] By the end of Obama's term, a rule-making competition emerged, with China promoting a Eurasian highway friendly to state-led capitalism, and the United States pushing for behind-the-border, market-led agreements, the TPP and TTIP (Transatlantic Trade and Investment Partnership), at either end of it.

By embracing the TPP, the Obama administration assured that its regional economic strategy complemented its overall geopolitical one. Just as contain-ment of the Soviet Union had been accompanied by an economic embargo, and US alliances with Western Europe and Japan were cemented by interdependent trade and monetary ties, the TPP reinforced Obama's efforts to Pivot to Asia and preserve hegemony with more limited means. It signalled to traditional US allies like Japan, the Philippines and Australia, as well as to China, that America intended to reassert its familiar hegemonic position at the centre of global economic management and to drive forward international economic rules that reflected US ideological preferences and economic interests.

Support for the TPP was also consistent with America's preference ordering for types of international trade agreements. Global, multilateral agreements were the best option whenever possible. Regional agreements were a respectable second-best when multilateral efforts faltered. This logic led the United States to promote NAFTA in the early 1990s when the Uruguay Round stalled, and to push the TPP and TTIP when the Doha Round faltered. Bilateralism was the relatively least-favoured option, a last resort to maintain forward momentum while multilateral or regional agendas played out. Reflecting the close connection between security and economic policies, US officials often negotiated bilateral trade agreements to strengthen security ties with key US allies such as Israel, Jordan, Bahrain and South Korea.

Obama's promotion of the TPP was also in keeping with the traditional role post-war American presidents played at the intersection of domestic and international political economies. Protectionist pressures typically emanate from import-sensitive societal interests and are given political voice by members of Congress. The presidential task has been to buy off protectionist interests selectively, but more importantly to deflect broader protectionist sentiment by mobilising export interests (e.g. large transnational firms), and promising to open markets abroad.[22] Market access abroad was the hegemonic response to protectionist pressure at home. The TPP, by offering to US multinationals the promise of state-of-the-art liberalisation in the global economy's most dynamic region, did just that.

Trump: From hegemony to balancing?

Any analysis that extrapolates enduring foreign policy patterns from the early experience of a new administration must proceed with caution. In the case of President Trump, additional caveats are in order. The range of policy uncertainty is much greater since Trump is an inexperienced president with limited knowledge of foreign affairs, is prone to make and retreat from provocative threats, and is inclined to say (or tweet) one thing today and its opposite tomorrow.[23] Across the first two years of his time in office, Trump has consistently conflated his personal interests and the national interest, as suggested by his unwillingness to acknowledge Russian interference in the election he won and his efforts to derail official investigations that might implicate him or his family members. Finally, one must be careful equating President Trump and the Trump administration.

Every administration experiences some divisions between the president, political appointees and the permanent government. In Trump's first two years, those divisions were profound.[24] Nevertheless, since the president is America's top decision maker, it is important to analyse Trump's international perspective even though it may be neither fully shared by other high officials nor consistently translated into policy.

Trump's worldview

US presidents typically disavow the policies of their opposing party predecessors, and Trump is no exception. But he is an exception in disavowing central tenets of post-war America's overall approach to foreign policy. Three related departures stand out. First, Trump is an unapologetic nationalist who perceives a stark dichotomy between America's national interest and international commitments. Post-war American presidents, whether Republicans or Democrats, have typically viewed national interest and international commitments as complements rather than substitutes. For Trump it is one or the other; when he announced his intention to withdraw the United States from the Paris Climate agreement in June 2017, he stated that 'I was elected to represent the citizens of Pittsburgh, not Paris.'[25]

Second, Trump emphasises transactions rather than relationships. Post-war US foreign policy has been built on enduring relationships including long-term commitments to allies, confrontational approaches to perceived adversaries, and sustained engagement with states (e.g. China) that might be coaxed into becoming US supporters. Trump views international relations as more episodic. Foreign policy is a sequence of deals, some good ("America wins") and some bad ("foreigners win"). Bad deals, such as the US–South Korea trade agreement or the Iranian nuclear agreement, need to be abandoned or renegotiated. Trump's criticisms of Japan, South Korea and NATO allies for not paying a fair share of alliance costs reframed what American policy makers have normally depicted as long-standing commitments of mutual benefit into an undesirable situation in which one side was winning economically at the expense of the other.

Third, instead of viewing America, in the words of former Secretary of State Madeleine Albright, as the "indispensable nation" with obligations and commitments to sustain a liberal international order, Trump depicts his country as an aggrieved nation over which other states routinely take advantage. Trump does not reference American leadership, the international community, the liberal international order, or the rule of law – common phrases that high officials have long used to signal America's enduring global role and commitments.[26] His insistence on putting America first suggests that by maintaining international commitments, the United States is placing a lower priority on its own interests.

Although Trump is an outlier among post-war US presidents, some have aptly compared him to a nineteenth-century predecessor, Andrew Jackson. Like Jackson,

Trump projects himself as a populist, giving voice to groups that have been forgotten and pledging to "drain the swamp" of Washington elites. Jacksonians are tribal, distinguishing insiders from outsiders and promising to lash out disproportionately at those who would dare to provoke an America that would prefer to be left alone.[27] Trump embraces this tribal perspective at home and abroad. He views his domestic support base as left behind by globalisation and besieged by foreigners and immigrants. He views the American national tribe as victimised by non-state actors and countries, including supposed friends, who have taken advantage of America's generosity and negotiating naïvety.

Trump and grand strategy

To what extent does Trump's worldview translate into a coherent grand strategy? His rhetoric and initial foreign policy suggest some preliminary conclusions. The most obvious is the rejection of America's post-Cold War hegemonic strategy. Trump's team is not inclined to remake the world in America's image politically or economically. Democratisation and human rights have moved to the back of the foreign policy agenda, and the President frequently takes the opposite tack and praises authoritarian leaders. He views the idea of America as principal provider of international public goods, whether in trade, the environment, or regional security, with suspicion or hostility. Despite Trump's personal admiration for Vladimir Putin and Xi Jinping, his administration approaches Russia and China as geopolitical competitors rather than possible supporters of America's hegemonic project.

The grand strategy most consistent with Trump's worldview is offshore balancing which, considering America's current extensive global commitments, would involve some degree of retrenchment. The administration's 2017 National Security Strategy posits that the highest priority is to 'protect the American people, the homeland, and the American way of life'.[28] The need to rejuvenate the domestic economy, strike more advantageous trade deals, and achieve energy 'dominance' and independence are also cited. These objectives, coupled with the President's beliefs that international commitments and global engagement generate more costs than benefits, and that America's post-war allies are now wealthy enough to stand on their own, suggest the strategic desirability of pullback. The Trump administration's early foreign policy, however, neither indicates nor foreshadows significant retrenchment.[29] Under Trump, the United States has strengthened its commitment to NATO, proved unwilling to withdraw from the Middle East (despite the President's eagerness to do so), and continued engagement as a resident power in the Asia Pacific.

If neither hegemony nor retrenchment, then what? The NSS suggests a third alternative – a muscular activism that informs a strategy of *onshore balancing*, including forward military deployments, against regional threats. Iran is the target in the Middle East; Trump officials abandoned the Iranian nuclear deal, re-imposed sanctions, and tried to organise a de facto coalition against it to include Israel and America's traditional Sunni allies. In Europe, Russia is the target. The Trump administration rotated troops and equipment to Poland and the Baltics, provided arms to Ukraine, and increased sanctions in response to Russia's use of force and violation of arms control commitments. In the Asia Pacific, the target is China. The Pentagon's 2017 National Defense Strategy called out China as a revisionist power that had failed as a responsible stakeholder, and the Trump team responded by confronting China strategically and economically.[30]

Trump and the Asia Pacific: Economics and security

Three initiatives stand out in Trump's opening approach to the Asia Pacific, and each represents a departure from the Obama administration. The first is a shift in political economy from regionalism and economic liberalism to bilateralism and economic nationalism. Second, Trump shifted tactically from confrontation to personal engagement in dealing with North Korea. Third, the administration clarified China's role as a great power competitor and lined up US economic strategy to support this new strategic direction.

Bilateralism and economic nationalism

The Trump administration's explicit rejection of the TPP, after a decade of negotiations produced a final agreement, has been the most striking regional step taken thus far. Most analysts have pointed to the high costs of US withdrawal, including the missed opportunity to shape commercial rules in the world's most dynamic region, the diplomatic uncertainty created for America's regional partners, and the ceding of initiative to China. These costs are highest in the context of an American hegemonic strategy. But Trump abandoned that strategy, and thus it was plausible for him to downplay the costs of withdrawal and emphasise the narrative, popular with his political base, that multilateral trade agreements harm the economic prospects of ordinary Americans.

Abandoning the TPP created space for bilateralism, Trump's preferred alternative to regional or multilateral trade negotiations. During the 2017 APEC Summit in Vietnam, Trump offered to 'make bilateral trade agreements with any Indo-Pacific nation that wants to be our partner and that will abide by the principles of fair and reciprocal trade'. He also promised that 'we will no longer enter into large agreements that tie our hands, surrender our sovereignty, and make meaningful enforcement practically impossible'.[31] Not surprisingly, Trump's offer fell on deaf ears. Asia Pacific countries, including America's closet regional ally, Japan, preferred to move forward with the TPP without the United States rather than engage one-on-one with a powerful trading partner determined to "win" in new negotiations with them. As the remaining eleven nations announced in January 2018 that they would move forward with the TPP, the Trump administration announced restrictions on Asian imports of solar panels and washing machines.[32] In March, Trump shocked the world trading system by using the dubious pretext of national security to impose tariffs on international steel and aluminium imports.

The administration's attraction to bilateralism and economic nationalism reflects Trump's mercantilist understanding of the economics of trade. He prefers a weaker to a stronger dollar since the former advantages US exporters. He views trade as zero-sum rather than positive-sum and understands that it is easier to identify winners and losers in bilateral rather than regional or global negotiations. Bilateral deficit reduction, rather than the more traditional US objective of market access, is the administration's preferred metric to determine the success of trade negotiations and relationships. The administration created new offices, a National Trade Council and Office of Trade and Manufacturing Policy, which quickly prioritised bilateral deficit reduction negotiations with states that run trade surpluses with the United States, including Japan, Mexico, Germany, South Korea and China. Although the administration granted initial exceptions (to Mexico and Canada, because they agreed to renegotiate NAFTA) to the steel and aluminium tariffs, it waited until late in 2018 to exempt Japanese companies, once it became clear that the Japanese government would (reluctantly) engage in bilateral negotiations with the United States.

The shift to economic nationalism and bilateralism complements Trump's rejection of America's geopolitical and economic strategy of hegemony. Postwar American administrations typically espoused the aspiration of international economic leadership even if they could not always deliver. The Trump team has discarded that role so explicitly that China's Xi Jinping, notwithstanding his lack of fitness for the task, offered to step into the breach and serve as champion of free trade and globalisation. Trump has also abandoned the traditional presidential gatekeeping role; rather than deflect and turn outward protectionist pressures, his administration's initial inclination has been to encourage protectionist sentiment and initiate market restrictions itself.

Dealing with North Korea and China

In its initial two years, the Trump administration treated North Korea as an immediate strategic concern and China as a more profound long-term challenge. In each case economic strategy has lined up behind and reinforced the administration's strategic calculations.

Although by 2017 North Korea was already a nascent nuclear power, Trump, like Clinton, Bush and Obama before him, treated North Korea as a proliferation problem to be resolved rather than as a hostile nuclear power to be deterred.

Denuclearisation, however improbable, was the administration's strategic goal. Trump's departure from past administrations has been tactical, and his diplomatic approach has swung wildly. In his first year, he belittled Kim Jong-un personally and appeared willing to escalate the conflict to the brink of nuclear war. He subsequently reversed course and, in defiance of American diplomatic norm, took the unprecedented step of meeting personally with Kim in Singapore in June 2018 and Vietnam in February 2019.

Trump's personal diplomacy failed to generate meaningful progress towards denuclearisation. The first summit produced vague commitments and in the second Trump walked away without an agreement. Although clearly eager to reach one, he proved unwilling to sacrifice the considerable economic leverage the US enjoyed without a substantial North Korean commitment to denuclearisation. The long-standing US approach – maintaining punishing economic sanctions against North Korea until it capitulated on the nuclear issue – remained in place notwithstanding Trump's personal rapport with Kim.

On China, Trump's departure from Obama has been more significant. First, as noted above, Trump's administration gave up hope – however slim it was – that China would become America's responsible stakeholder and made clear that China instead is a strategic competitor that must be confronted. An important symbolic component of this approach is the Trump administration's relabelling of the Asia Pacific as the Indo-Pacific and its embrace of a Japan-led initiative – the 'free and open Indo-Pacific'.[33] To Trump officials, "free and open" means "not dominated by China". Vice President Pence and Secretary of State Pompeo asserted in 2018 that the United States would resist China's assertion of political and military influence in the region.[34] The Indo-Pacific, in other words, was not large enough to accommodate two dominant powers.

The "Indo" part refers to India as much as the Indian Ocean. By embracing the term Indo-Pacific, the Trump administration conveyed that America has regional options beyond its long-standing allies. It can draw closer to Vietnam, a former adversary. It could cultivate a special relationship with India, a rising regional power that is also a democracy and a naval power. Though at its early stages, the message to China is clear – China may have an ambitious Eurasian land strategy, the Belt and Road Initiative, but the "Quad" powers – the United States, Japan, Australia and India – are a coalition of maritime powers that could bottle up China at sea.

Second, and in a more profound departure from Obama policy, the Trump administration has pursued economic containment against China. Prior to Trump, American officials hoped that, even if US–China security competition increased, economic interdependence and cooperation would be an emergency brake that softened and held back bilateral conflict. The Trump team has released that emergency brake and has lined up a confrontational economic strategy behind its more competitive security strategy.[35]

Not surprisingly, given the President's commitment to it, most public attention has focused on the US–China tariff war. Trump has referred to himself as a "Tariff Man" who believes America can win a trade war because China starts with a sizeable bilateral surplus. During 2018, citing China's theft of intellectual property and other unfair trade practices, Trump introduced $250 billion in tariff increases on trade with China – a 25 per cent tariff on US$50 billion of Chinese goods and a 10 per cent tariff on US$200 billion of Chinese goods. He proposed to increase the latter tariffs to 25 per cent unless significant progress was made in ongoing US–China trade negotiations.

But there are two deeper US–China economic issues that are likely to persist even in the event of a tariff war truce. One is technological rivalry. As Japan learned during the 1980s, the United States does not take well to challenges at the technological frontier. Since China is a security competitor, not a security ally, the United States will be even more determined to slow China down. China is determined to do the opposite – Xi's Made in China 2025 project is designed to get China to the technological frontier by whatever means necessary – including borrowing or stealing advanced technology and pressuring foreign firms to share it as the price for access to China's market and labour force. The Trump administration responded by targeting China's model of state-led capitalism, discouraging American firms from cooperating with their Chinese counterparts – most dramatically, the Chinese technology giant Huawei – and pressuring its allies to do the same.[36]

The second deeper issue involves "decoupling". Over the last twenty-five years, US administrations encouraged the US and Chinese economies to become closely intertwined. More interdependence was better – the United States celebrated the idea of a "G-2", or "Chimerica". To the Trump administration, economic interdependence looks more dangerous than beneficial. It has enabled the Chinese challenge that worries American defence officials and has encouraged the unfair practices that worry US trade officials. Trump's Office of the US Trade Representative stated that China failed to live up to its reform promises made when it joined the WTO in 2001, and suggested that in retrospect, encouraging China to join was a strategic mistake.[37] Although a complete economic rupture with China is obviously impractical, the Trump team wishes to loosen bilateral economic ties to make America less dependent and less vulnerable.[38] It seeks to discourage Chinese investment in the United States, and it would rather American businesses invest at home rather than in China.

Obama's legacy and Trump's transformation

A central theme of this volume concerns the Obama administration's foreign policy legacy and the durability of its policy initiatives in the Asia (and wider Indo-) Pacific. The Trump administration in its initial phase has offered more change than continuity, both in grand strategy and in specific regional initiatives. Its most striking departure has been from the strategy and obligations of hegemony, which successive US administrations after the Cold War viewed as essential both to US interests and global order. Even Obama, who might be described as a reluctant or constrained hegemonic actor, was supportive of the overall strategy. While the Trump administration has maintained US international activism, it has abandoned both the rhetoric and policies of hegemony in favour of "America First" nationalism and a strategy of balancing against regional threats. Trump's international economic strategy, both generally and regionally, similarly reflects a sharp discontinuity relative to Obama. The Trump team has rejected both America's multilateral aspirations and its pursuit of ambitious, second-best regional economic agreements in favour of bilateralism, with a myopic focus on merchandise trade deficits and the routine resort to tariff increases rather than market-opening initiatives designed to inhibit behind-the-border protectionism.

Trump's North Korea policy, while certainly dramatic, reflects discontinuity in means rather than ends. His administration has embraced Obama's denuclearisation goal while experimenting, sometimes radically, with means to achieve it short of war. America's economic approach to North Korea has continued to rely on maintaining multilateral support for comprehensive economic sanctions, while pressuring China and others to comply more faithfully. The Trump administration's changes to China policy, however, have been more profound. The hopeful ambiguity of Obama's Pivot has given way to strategic competition. More strikingly, and consistent with its combative approach to international economic relations, the Trump administration has turned from economic engagement and cooperation, designed to turn China in a more accommodating direction, to economic conflict and confrontation, designed to hobble what it perceives as China's inevitable rise and challenge.

Which of the foreign policy changes introduced in Trump's first two years are likely to endure? This question must be approached with caution given the unpredictability of this president and the overall uncertainty over the extent to which his policies have altered fundamentally the character of US global engagement. Given the strength of his personal belief system and of his commitment to a narrow domestic political coalition, however, it seems plausible to infer that for as long as Trump remains President the United States will not reverse course and head back in the direction of hegemonic commitments and global leadership obligations. Similarly, America's China policy had been evolving from cooperation to competition before Trump; his policies, particularly on the economic side, have perhaps accelerated what many in the foreign policy establishment now view as an inevitable trend. That America's direction seems clear will make diplomacy more difficult for others in the region, including US allies, who prefer to cooperate with both China (in economics) and the United States (in security) rather than lining up on one side or the other.

Finally, Trump's strategy towards North Korea could plausibly change. The temptation for Trump (perhaps with the hope of a Nobel Peace Prize) to strike a dramatic deal – the easing of economic sanctions in exchange for North Korean commitments to meaningfully curtail weapons and missile testing – is a powerful one. The tacit acceptance of North Korea as a nuclear power would meet strong resistance within the US foreign policy establishment. But it would at least be viewed as preferable to a return to the escalating confrontation that marked Trump's first year.

Notes

1　On hegemonic and balance of power orders see R. Gilpin, *War and Change in World Politics* (Cambridge: Cambridge University Press, 1981); J. Ikenberry, *After Victory: Institutions, Strategic Restraint, and the Rebuilding of Order after Major Wars* (Princeton, NJ: Princeton University Press, 2001).

2　M. Mastanduno, 'System maker and privilege taker: US power and the international political economy', *World Politics*, 61:1 (2009), pp. 121–54.

3　M. Mastanduno, 'Partner politics: Russia, China, and the challenge of extending US hegemony after the Cold War', *Security Studies*, 28:3 (2019), pp. 479–504.

4　See R. Jervis, 'International primacy: Is the game worth the candle?' *International Security*, 17:4 (1993), pp. 53–4.

5　White House, 'National Security Strategy of the United States' (September 2002), www.state.gov/documents/organization/63562.pdf, accessed 13 March 2019.

6　See P. Trubowitz, *Politics and Strategy: Partisan Ambition and American Statecraft* (Princeton, NJ: Princeton University Press, 2011), pp. 145–9; David Sanger, *Confront and Conceal* (New York: Random House, 2012).

7　White House, 'Remarks by the President in Address to the Nation on the Way Forward in Afghanistan and Pakistan' (1 December 2009), https://obamawhitehouse.archives.gov/the-press-office/remarks-president-address-nation-way-forward-afghanistan-and-pakistan, accessed 13 March 2019.

8　See K. Campbell, *The Pivot: The Future of American Statecraft in Asia* (New York: Hachette, 2016).

9　See H. Clinton, 'America's Pacific Century', *Foreign Policy* (11 October 2011), https://foreignpolicy.com/2011/10/11/americas-pacific-century/, accessed 13 March 2019.

10　K. Lieberthal and W. Jisi, *Addressing US-China Strategic Distrust* (Washington, DC: Brookings Institution Press, 2012).

11　US Department of State, 'Whither China? From Membership to Responsibility' (21 September 2005), https://2001-2009.state.gov/s/d/former/zoellick/rem/53682.htm, accessed 13 March 2019.

12　C. Li, 'Assessing US-China Relations Under the Obama Administration', The Brookings Institution (30 August 2016), www.brookings.edu/opinions/assessing-u-s-china-relations-under-the-obama-administration/, accessed 13 March 2019.

13 See Z. Khalilzad *et al.*, *The United States and a Rising China: Military and Strategic Implications* (Santa Monica, CA: Rand Corporation, 1999).

14 B. Williams *et al.*, 'The Trans-Pacific Partnership: Strategic Implications', Congressional Research Service (3 February 2016), p. 6, https://fas.org/sgp/crs/row/R44361.pdf, accessed 13 March 2019.

15 White House, 'Statement by the President on the Trans-Pacific Partnership' (5 October 2015), https://obamawhitehouse.archives.gov/the-press-office/2015/10/05/statement-president-trans-pacific-partnership, accessed 13 March 2019.

16 M. Froman, 'The strategic logic of trade: New rules of the road for the global market', *Foreign Affairs* 93:6 (2014), pp. 111–18.

17 White House, 'Secretary of Defense Ashton Carter: Asia-Pacific Remarks' (6 April 2015), https://obamawhitehouse.archives.gov/sites/default/files/docs/asia-pacific_speech_asu_asdelivered.pdf, accessed 13 March 2019.

18 Froman, 'The strategic logic of trade', p. 113.

19 Y. Fukugawa, 'So many choices, so much at stake: A Japanese perspective on trade pacts in Asia', *Global Asia*, 11:4 (2016), pp. 114–18.

20 T. Hoa, 'Can Vietnam Reform without the TPP?', East Asia Forum (8 June 2017), www.eastasiaforum.org/2017/06/08/can-vietnam-reform-without-the-tpp/, accessed 13 March 2019.

21 See A. Tellis, A. Szalwinski and M. Wills (eds.), *Strategic Asia 2019: China's Expanding Strategic Ambitions* (Seattle: National Bureau of Asian Research, 2019).

22 See I. M. Destler, *American Trade Politics*, 4th edition (Washington, DC: International Institute for Economics, 2005).

23 K. Yarhi-Milo, 'After credibility: American foreign policy in the Trump era', *Foreign Affairs*, 97:1 (2018), pp. 68–77.

24 J. Michaels, 'Trump and the deep state: The government strikes back', *Foreign Affairs*, 96:5 (2017), pp. 52–6.

25 S. A. Miller, 'Trump Supporters Plan "Pittsburgh not Paris" Rally in Washington', *Washington Times* (2 June 2017), www.washingtontimes.com/news/2017/jun/2/trump-supporters-plan-pittsburgh-not-paris-rally-w/, accessed 13 March 2019.

26 J. Ikenberry, 'The plot against American foreign policy: Can the liberal order survive?', *Foreign Affairs*, 96:3 (2017), pp. 2–9.

27 See W. R. Mead, 'The Jacksonian tradition and American foreign policy', *The National Interest*, 58 (1999–2000), pp. 5–29.

28 White House, 'National Security Strategy of the United States of America' (December 2017), p. 7, www.whitehouse.gov/wp-content/uploads/2017/12/NSS-Final-12-18-2017-0905.pdf, accessed 14 March 2019.

29 E. Abrams, 'Trump the traditionalist: A surprisingly standard foreign policy', *Foreign Affairs*, 96:4 (2017), pp. 10–16.

30 US Department of Defense, 'Summary of the 2018 National Defense Strategy of the United States of America' (2018), www.defense.gov/Portals/1/Documents/pubs/2018-National-Defense-Strategy-Summary.pdf, accessed 13 March 2019.

31   J. Wagner and D. Lynch, 'Trump Said He Would Strike One-On-One Deals. That's Not Happening', *Washington Post* (14 November 2017), www.washingtonpost. com/politics/trump-said-he-would-strike-one-on-one-trade-deals-thats-not-happening/2017/11/14/eced8a4e-c949-11e7-b0cf-7689a9f2d84e_story.html, accessed 13 March 2019.

32   J. Schlesinger, 'Global Trade Tensions Rise', *Wall Street Journal* (24 January 2018), www.wsj.com/articles/trade-war-tops-global-risks-world-economic-forum-report-says-11547632801, accessed 13 March 2019.

33   N. Sonnad, 'Indo-Pacific is the Trump Administration's New Name for Asia', *Defense One* (8 November 2017), www.defenseone.com/politics/2017/11/indo-pacific-trump-administrations-new-name-asia/142380/, accessed 13 March 2019.

34   W. R. Mead, 'Mike Pence Announces Cold War II', *Wall Street Journal* (9 October 2018), www.wsj.com/articles/mike-pence-announces-cold-war-ii-1539039480, accessed 13 March 2019.

35   See A. Friedberg, 'A new US economic strategy toward China?', *Washington Quarterly*, 40:4 (2018), pp. 97–114.

36   B. Pancevski and S. Germano, 'In Rebuke to US, Germany Considers Letting Huawei In', *Wall Street Journal* (19 February 2019), www.wsj.com/articles/in-rebuke-to-u-s-germany-considers-letting-huawei-in-11550577810, accessed 13 March 2019.

37   US Trade Representative, '2017 Report to Congress on China's WTO Compliance' (January 2018).

38   R. McGregor, 'Donald Trump Begins a Conscious Uncoupling from China', *Financial Review* (16 October 2018), www.afr.com/news/economy/donald-trump-begins-a-conscious-uncoupling-from-china-20181011-h16jf4, accessed 13 March 2019.

Part III

From Obama to Trump in Asia and the Pacific: The practitioners' view

12

From Obama to Trump, and beyond: Washington's painful search for a credible China policy

Börje Ljunggren

Introduction

In 2018, one-time members of the Obama administration – Assistant Secretary of State for East Asian and Pacific Affairs, Kurt Campbell, and former Deputy National Security Advisor to Vice President Joe Biden, Ely Ratner – noted that, since the end of the Second World War '[t]he United States has always had an out-sized sense of its ability to determine China's course. Again and again, its ambitions have come up short.' Today, they argued, 'the starting point for a better approach is a new degree of humility about the United States' ability to change China ... Basing policy on a more realistic set of assumptions ... would better advance US interests and put the bilateral relationship on a more realistic footing.'[1]

At the same time, *The Economist* featured a story on 'How the West Got China Wrong'. It had, it said, 'lost its bet on China, just when its own democracies are suffering from a crisis of confidence'. China behaved as a 'regional superpower bent on driving America out of East Asia.'[2] Minxin Pei, a China commentator, declared that '[e]ngaging China may have been a noble experiment, but now is the time to go for realpolitik.'[3] Finally, and in testimony to the US Congress in February 2018, long-term neorealist critic of US China policy Aaron L. Friedberg argued that Washington's two-pronged strategy of preserving stability 'while waiting for engagement to "tame" and ultimately to transform China' had failed in its intended result.[4]

These four analyses differ significantly in a number of respects, but all ultimately agree that Washington's engagement and balancing policy towards China of the last few decades has fallen short of its objectives. The election of Donald Trump as president of the United States in late 2016 brought something of a sea change to US foreign policy. Yet it remains true that Washington needs to develop a viable policy based on today's – and tomorrow's – realities. No such policy is in sight.

From a Western perspective, it can, naturally, be tempting to dream of travelling back in time to an era when China was catching up rather than constituting an economic, military, political and even systems challenge. There have been critical moments. Notably, China's entry into the WTO in 2001 provided an added boost to its rapid economic growth. Today, China is the largest economy in the world in terms of purchasing power parity (PPP), by far the world's largest trading nation in goods, and a potential world leader in key future technologies such as artificial intelligence (AI).

In terms of alliances China may be "a lonely power", but it is pursuing an increasingly pro-active role, taking advantage of strategic opportunities and launching initiatives of its own. These include the Asian Infrastructure Investment Bank (AIIB), the Belt and Road Initiative (BRI) and the role as the world's second largest (on par with Japan) and most strategic direct foreign investor. Indeed, authoritarian China is, ironically enough, globalisation's greatest winner, with justifiably mounting US and EU demands for reciprocity. In the zero-sum worldview of President Donald Trump and his administration, China's rise, and even the United States' relationships with some of its closest Asian partners, has been at America's expense.

In his report to the nineteenth party congress, Chinese President Xi Jinping declared that 'China already stood tall in the East', and that now it is time for the nation 'to take center stage in the world and to make a greater contribution to humankind'. China's road to modernisation, he said, was 'offering a new option for other countries'.[5] In an amendment to the party constitution, it was stated that the Chinese Communist Party should 'uphold its absolute leadership over the People's Liberation Army' and 'implement Xi Jinping's thinking on strengthening the military'.[6] By the mid-twenty-first century, China's people's armed forces would be 'fully transformed into world class forces', built to fight.[7] China, to date, is still a Leninist party-state that is far from tamed. Rather than undermining the government, the Internet has become an indispensable tool of Beijing's "controlocracy".[8] China's violations of human rights have grown more brazen and the surveillance state is thriving.

Was John J. Mearsheimer, the most consistent critic of US policy of engagement, then right in saying that letting China into the WTO was a fatal mistake? Mearsheimer argues that the future Chinese threat 'might be far more powerful and dangerous than any of the potential hegemons that the United States confronted in the twentieth century', and that the United States 'has a profound interest in seeing Chinese economic growth slow considerably'. A wealthy China, he argues, would not be a status quo power, but 'an aggressive state determined to achieve regional hegemony'.[9]

How should former US President Barack Obama's China policy, and ultimately legacy, be assessed in this light? Was his sincere ambition to engage and balance China naïve? Since his inauguration in January 2017, Trump has negated much of what Obama tried to achieve, and their worldviews could hardly be more different. As president, Obama had to cope with the ongoing, seemingly inescapable US–Chinese power shift. Across the first two years of the Trump administration, to early 2019, the relationship developed more in the direction of a global rivalry, with the potential to define both his and future presidencies.

Obama's Asia Pacific vision: Engagement and Pivot

Cooperation amidst global challenges: Obama's early ambitions

Less than a year after assuming office in January 2009, Obama made a state visit to Beijing to meet China's President Hu Jintao. At the time I was in the capital, attending an EU–China conference. Rarely has Washington prepared a state visit with more care. Obama had the ambition to develop a comprehensive US China policy, based on an internationalist worldview which made it natural to aim for deeper cooperation. Still, I witnessed what would turn out to be a failed visit. The Chinese, uncertain about both how to manage their own growing role and how to assess and relate to Obama, treated him to a "state visit minus". This could later be contrasted to the boundlessly lavish "state visit plus" Trump was offered eight years later in 2017.

Still, 2009 was at a time of huge global challenges which would test the limits of the US–Chinese relationship. The visit happened in the midst of the financial crisis and just a month before the Copenhagen meeting on the global environment. The United States and China needed to cooperate to address the world's economic and financial problems, climate change, and other great challenges which demanded multilateral efforts. Pax Americana was not the answer. Obama inherently understood the importance and vast potential of the Asia Pacific broadly, and China more specifically. It was clear that he had come to Beijing with the intention of building trust and deepening the relationship.[10] He clearly wanted to create a more sustainable foundation for US–Chinese relations, channelling China's rise in as non-confrontational a direction as possible.

A very elaborate joint declaration, with a number of new concrete areas of cooperation, was adopted at the summit. To the surprise of many, Washington accepted a paragraph saying that the two countries had agreed to respect each other's "core interests". From the Chinese perspective that meant Tibet, Xinjiang, Taiwan and even the South China Sea, and suggested that Obama might be a weak president; maybe even another Jimmy Carter. Indeed, despite Obama's efforts to create a collegial climate, the visit was not a success – not in Beijing, and certainly not in Washington. Obama was only allowed to address a select public gathering in Shanghai and at home Obama was not seen to be standing up for his country's interests as the world's hegemonic power.

Soon afterwards, US China policy became more assertive. Adding to the shift was the distrust that emerged between Obama and Prime Minister Wen Jiabao shortly after the climate change summit. China's quiet response to the North Korean navy sinking of a South Korean navy ship in March 2010 contributed to the tensions, along with more forward-leaning Chinese surveillance of US activities in the South China Sea. American concerns were raised that China had begun to challenge the prevailing regional order.

The Pivot and renewed American assertion

At the beginning of 2011 the chief architects of Obama's original China policy, Deputy Secretary of State James Steinberg and Senior Director for Asian Affairs on the US National Security Council Jeffrey Bader, left office. The centre of gravity shifted to Secretary of State Hillary Clinton and her Asia manager, Kurt Campbell. From then on, the US Pivot towards Asia – by which the United States planned to devote more strategic attention and resources to the Asia Pacific – came to the fore.

A critical moment was the ASEAN Regional Forum (ARF) meeting in Hanoi in July 2010. In her speech to the Forum, Secretary Clinton – urged by a number of ASEAN countries – stressed that the United States remained neutral on which regional countries had stronger territorial claims to disputed islands in the South China Sea. Yet, she explained, Washington had an interest in preserving free shipping in the area and would facilitate talks on the issue.

Though presented as an offer to help ease tensions, the stance amounted to a sharp rebuke of Beijing. Claiming ownership of all islands within its so-called Nine Dash Line, China insisted that any disputes should be resolved bilaterally between itself and ASEAN claimants. In March 2010, senior Chinese officials had pointedly warned their American counterparts that they would brook no interference in the South China Sea, which they called part of the "core interest" of Chinese sovereignty.[11]

Washington's position was in clear alignment with implicated ASEAN members, and marked the first time it had taken sides on the dispute. China and the wider region noticed. The Chinese Foreign Minister, Yang Jiechi, lost his temper, reminding his Singaporean colleague that 'China is a big country and other countries are small countries and that is just a fact.'[12] In late 2011, Secretary Clinton stated that just as the United States once played a central role in shaping the architecture across the Atlantic, it was now doing the same across the Pacific. The twenty-first century will be America's 'Pacific Century', she insisted.[13]

At around the same time, President Obama delivered a speech to the Australian parliament in which he spoke about a broad shift in US policy to the Asia Pacific, including sending US marines to Darwin.[14] An underlying assumption, that did not materialise, was that the shift would be made possible through military disengagement in the Middle East. Inherited wars in that region, however, along with their consequences, never ceased to demand huge resources.

The Pivot was, first and foremost, a matter of reconfirming commitment to American allies and crucial forward defence lines in the Pacific. A primary objective, however, was also to enhance the United States' economic presence in the region. Initially, Obama was less committed to free trade than his immediate predecessors; George W. Bush had in 2008 begun negotiating a Trans-Pacific Partnership (TPP), though with a limited number of countries. Yet in December 2009, after his visit to China, Obama notified Congress that he planned to enter into TPP negotiations with Pacific partners. It was not until 2013 that the negotiations gained momentum, though without a crucial Trade Promotion Authority mandate from the US Congress. "Everyone but China", including communist Vietnam, was invited. It also represented a new generation of trade agreements, with labour rights as a significant new element. When all the other eleven invited countries on board stood ready to implement the agreement in 2016, it was clear that the US Congress would turn it down.

The tide had turned. In the 2016 presidential election campaign, Hillary Clinton, who once called TPP 'a gold standard trade agreement',[15] was no longer ready to defend it. Republican nominee Donald Trump pledged to cancel it on his first day in office. When visiting Washington in late 2016, the Prime Minister of Singapore called the TPP a 'litmus test' of US credibility in Asia, telling Obama that Washington had taken them all to the altar, leaving partners waiting for the bridegroom, embarrassing themselves and the United States.[16]

Human rights and a straining relationship

Human rights had a central place in the value system of the Obama administration. The way the question has evolved in China's relationship with Brussels and Washington is a stark illustration of mounting US–Chinese divergence. During my years in Beijing, human rights were a given subject on the agenda of high-level EU–China and bilateral meetings. Both the EU and the United States, along with a number of other countries, had an established human rights dialogue with China. Over time, the Chinese side became increasingly unwilling to accept such dialogues and the scrutiny they brought. Today, such dialogues have almost come to an end, no longer tolerated by today's much more assertive and nationalistic China. At the same time, China has become more vocal about human rights conditions in the United States and other countries. The Chinese Communist Party's (CCP) skin is increasingly thin.

In 1988 China signed two major UN covenants on human rights: the International Covenant on Civil and Political Rights and the International Covenant on Social, Economic and Cultural Rights. The latter was ratified after a few years, but the former never was, and today China rejects the very idea of universal human rights. In 2013 Beijing issued a central party document in which seven perils were enumerated, including Western constitutional democracy, civil society, 'universal values', and Western-inspired notions of media independence.[17] The document bore the unmistakable imprimatur of Xi Jinping. Further deteriorations happened under Obama's watch. Human rights were kept on the bilateral agenda, but not at the expense of the overall relationship.

With an ongoing shift of global power, broadly speaking from West to East, the Obama administration injected a degree of stability and predictably into US–Chinese relations, even as tensions in the South China Sea and elsewhere grew. Successful cooperation on matters of global significance was also achieved. That was true with regard to the Paris agreement on climate change, for which Obama and Xi in 2014 laid the foundations. Still, the realignment of power continued, inevitably deepening strategic competition, and making it even more important to develop stable bilateral mechanisms for managing the power rivalry.

Was an opportunity lost, given Obama's original approach to China? China's rise did indeed amount to a challenge of the predominant role of the United States in the Asia Pacific. No American administration could help but focus on the task of developing a strategy that would convincingly reconfirm long-term American commitment to the region. Such a strategy could, however, have been more or less comprehensive. Obama's first senior advisor in Asia, Jeffrey Bader, stresses that:

> at no point has US policy been based on some gauzy conception of a "benign" China that would sacrifice its own interests for ours, adopt a political system modelled on Western values, or cease to be a difficult competitor. Policy-makers have understood that the US-China relationship would be a mixture of cooperation and competition, with the hope of maximizing the former and managing the latter so that it did not escalate into conflict.[18]

In his 2016 book on the US Pivot to Asia, Kurt Campbell's primary message was that it should be made more comprehensive and more consistent in the post-Obama era.[19] That would have likely materialised if Hillary Clinton had become president. The Obama administration had the ambition to develop a more comprehensive strategic US response, both to China and the wider Asia Pacific region; it was clear by then that engagement would not produce the type of systemic convergence that President Bill Clinton in particular had hoped for when delivering China's entry into the WTO. Yet Obama fell short of striking a new viable balance between liberal internationalism and security, by underestimating the magnitude of the challenge.

In 2012, in the heat of the final debate of his second campaign for the presidency, Obama did in fact talk about China as an "adversary". Yet the main ambition of his administration was to build an effective and cooperative partnership with Beijing, through such mechanisms as the annual high level Strategic and Economic Dialogue.

The East Asian peace: Long, but fragile

China's strategic ambitions and the Trump administration

Since the end of the Vietnam War, China and the East Asian region have enjoyed what is sometimes referred to as "the long peace". The East Asian share of global battle deaths fell from around 80 per cent in 1946–79 to just 6 per cent in the 1980s, to less than 2 per cent in the 1990s, and to less than 1 per cent today.[20] "Economic Asia" prevailed, but now "security Asia" is re-emerging. East Asia, indeed, is not short of serious unresolved conflicts. Identity, sovereignty and boundaries have become key battlegrounds, in at least partial contradiction to the ideal of deeper integration. East Asia's "long peace" is increasingly fragile.

Washington's forward defence line, manifest in key alliances and a heavy regional naval presence, is a central theme in American strategic culture that for a long time has applied to the Far East.[21] The line runs near China which increasingly sees itself as the natural hegemon in a Sino-centric East Asia. In 2013, Xi Jinping suggested that the Pacific was big enough for both the United States and China. Core US policy will no doubt be tested in coming years, sharpening the focus on military strength.

Throughout his presidency, Obama incrementally reduced the US defence budget, which by the time he left office still amounted to close to one third of global defence expenditure. During his last years in office, however, additional funds were requested for ongoing operations and a military modernisation programme. US military engagements in the Middle East remained very costly in terms of resources as well as credibility.

Meanwhile, as of early 2019, China maintains its substantial military modernisation programme. China's defence budget, the second largest in the world, is estimated by the Stockholm International Peace Research Institute (SIPRI) to amount to around US$228 billion.[22] According to official Chinese figures, which are lower than SIPRI's estimates, this budget increased by 8.2 per cent in 2018 and by 7.5 per cent in 2019, a declining percentage trend but still a huge volume.[23] The Chinese budget is still just a third of the US budget, and slightly less than 2 per cent of GDP. Continued, rapid, modernisation of the People's Liberation Army (PLA), however, remains a key priority.

A salient illustration of China's vision of its own global role is the military strategy released in 2015, which states that 'the traditional mentality that land outweighs sea must be abandoned and great importance must be attached to managing the seas and oceans and protecting maritime rights and interests.'[24] Almost

600 years have passed since China was a prominent naval power. Today, China is becoming a major power in this regard, as symbolised by its ambitious air carrier programme and a fleet by some measures outsizing that of the United States.

Partly in response to this expansion of China's capabilities, after coming to office in early 2017, President Donald Trump declared that the United States is 'going to have a military like never before, because we ... just about never needed our military more than now'. In his budget proposal for 2019, he demanded US$716 billion – an increase of 6 per cent compared to his first budget.[25] Trump's then Defense Secretary James Mattis called both China and Russia 'revisionist powers' that 'seek to create a world consistent with their authoritarian models'. He warned that the US military advantage over its adversaries had eroded 'in every domain of warfare', concluding that 'Great power competition, not terrorism, is now the primary focus of US national security.'[26] The 2017 National Security Strategy echoed this view, describing China (and Russia) as a competitor, which is 'trying to erode American security and prosperity'. In this world reduced to a state of 'great-power competition', countries pursue their national interests without any commitment to creating a better world.[27]

Across its first two years, the strategic response to these challenges by the Trump administration has appeared to show little interest in the underpinning logic of Obama's Pivot to the region; to build on his predecessor's efforts would be contrary to Trump's instincts. For him, the Pivot represented another multilateral sell out. The irony now, however, is that the TPP is coming into being, renamed the Comprehensive and Progressive Agreement for Trans-Pacific Partnership (CPTPP), and to join later would now mean the United States fitting into a framework led by others.

East and Southeast Asian security challenges

The East Asian region harbours a number of unresolved conflicts which remain far from any kind of sustainable solution, and none are completely dislocated from the dynamics of US–China relations. Taiwan is the most "existential". China's One China policy is a non-negotiable feature of its national identity, and Washington's commitment to defend the island should not be underestimated. The Obama presidency was an era of relative calm here, but during his campaign for the presidency Donald Trump openly challenged the One China policy by treating Taiwan as a bargaining chip and speaking to President Tsai Ing-wen, angering Beijing.[28] For the CCP, the reunification of Taiwan with the mainland is inevitable, and Xi Jinping has expressed noticeable impatience.

North Korea's nuclear weapons programme constitutes the most serious immediate challenge, directly threatening the United States. The Obama administration chose a policy of "strategic patience", unsuccessfully trying to involve Beijing in a genuine effort to bring Pyongyang into talks, while encouraging UN sanctions.

Trump quickly made North Korea's nuclear development a test case of US–Chinese relations, in part via the threat of escalating sanctions. Military threats were used to coerce Pyongyang, but there is no military solution. For decades the international community failed to contain this poor, backward and isolated country's nuclear ambitions, allowing the current global security dilemma to emerge.

China's policy is determined by its own security concerns; Beijing wants a nuclear free peninsula, but it has attached even higher priority to stability. In 2003 China assumed a key role as convener of the Six-Party talks on North Korea's nuclear programme, a process that went on for six years but failed to deliver any lasting results. As Head of the Asia Department in the Swedish Foreign Ministry I visited North Korea a number of times. In 2001 I accompanied Prime Minister Göran Persson, then-chairperson of the European Council, to Pyongyang for an EU–North Korean summit with Kim Jong-il.

South Korean President Kim Dae-jung's Sunshine policy and the Clinton administration's advanced direct talks with Pyongyang had created a conducive climate, but when President George W. Bush entered the White House in 2001, he launched a policy reversal, choosing to discontinue dialogue and denouncing the "Axis of Evil", of which North Korea was a central element. The same year, it also became clear that North Korea was pursuing its nuclear ambitions. China, meanwhile, played a surprisingly small role and focused instead on maintaining the status quo. As ambassador to China from 2002 I observed first-hand how Beijing treated North Korea's nuclear programme as primarily an American dilemma. Ultimately, as North Korea became a de facto nuclear power, the magnitude of the challenge created a new sense of urgency, with Obama advising Trump in his final months in office to regard North Korea as an issue of the highest priority.[29]

Promising from the outset to meet North Korean threats with 'fire and fury',[30] President Trump ventured to pursue instant summit diplomacy. Yet he underestimated the magnitude of the task, with complete and verifiable denuclearisation remaining a distant goal. East Asian security has at least temporarily been enhanced as a result, but only on the provision that the diplomatic process is kept alive.

Elsewhere, the South China Sea has also recently become an arena of significant US–China tension. In 2010, following a verbal confrontation at the ASEAN Regional Forum meeting in Hanoi between Secretary of State Hillary Clinton and her Chinese counterpart Foreign Minister Yang Yiechi, a more assertive China stepped forward and expanded its presence in the region. Using gradual "salami tactics", it introduced military installations and air strips, and turned shallow reefs into islands. The United States, in response, expanded its naval presence. At a White House meeting in 2015, Xi made a commitment not to militarise artificial islands that Beijing has been building, but the process nevertheless continued.[31]

From the outset, the Trump administration declared that China's island building programme in the South China Sea had to cease. The build-up continued nonetheless, with ASEAN countries caught in the middle, forced to hedge against territorial encroachments. They did so, and continue to do so in early 2019, while uncertain about American staying power as Trump quickly showed less interest in ASEAN than Obama after taking office. On the whole, Washington has failed to strengthen key regional partnerships in the face of a rising China.

The situation in the East China Sea appears more stable, but Sino-Japanese tensions over territory, deeply rooted in history, remain. The Senkaku/Diaoyu Islands, controlled by Japan but claimed by China, are bound to remain a serious issue. Beijing will likely never give up its claims, while Tokyo does not accept the existence of a territorial issue. The United States has not taken a firm stand on the issue as such, but as tensions rose, the Obama administration in 2014 unequivocally included the islands in Washington's commitment to defend Japan. News of accelerated Chinese air and naval excursions in sensitive areas near Japan and Taiwan are also becoming increasingly common, causing concern.[32] This should come as no surprise, especially after the nineteenth party congress when Xi Jinping outlined his visions for Chinese sovereignty.[33]

Coping with strategic distrust: The emerging systems clash

The concern for authors like Graham Allison is that China and the United States are 'on a collision course for war—unless both parties take difficult and painful actions to avert it'.[34] As such, the two risk falling into a so-called "Thucydides Trap" where an ascending power challenges an established power with destabilising results. In Thucydides' analysis, it was the fear that this instilled which made war inevitable. Particularly worrying to Allison is that 'many Americans are still in denial about what China's transformation from agrarian backwater to "the biggest player in the history of the world" means for the United States',[35] and that Washington lacks a coherent strategy for dealing with a rising China. Both are major nuclear powers, now responsible for avoiding the "uncontrollable" from happening.

Key elements of a comprehensive US China strategy were developed and implemented during Obama's term in office. A key element of Obama's legacy, indeed, was reversing a systemic neglect in the White House of China's rise, which had emerged and endured during the years of George W. Bush's post-9/11 war on terror. It was inconceivable when Trump was elected in 2016 that his administration could do anything but afford China as much attention as had that of Obama, with the Pivot laying the essential foundations for Trump's 'free and open Indo-Pacific' strategy.[36] Under Obama, alliances were strengthened, the TPP was launched, and military shifts were made. The Paris Climate Accord was also proof that successful cooperative endeavours were possible. Still, all this was overshadowed by growing populism, nationalism, authoritarianism, global realignments of power, and a liberal international order in retreat. A certain shift to Asia took place but the idea of the twenty-first century becoming an "American Pacific century" in fact became more remote. By the close of Obama's tenure, US–Chinese relations seemed to have begun a drift towards a systems clash.

In its first two years in office, the Trump administration concentrated on the strategic challenges and competition in the US–China relationship, with faint signs of interest in deepening cooperation on global challenges. Trump's engagement with Obama's legacy on China is thus one of evolution rather than revolution; the ends of constraining China's influence remain consistent, while the means of multilateralism have been replaced by a preference for unilateralism. The strategy does, however, contain elements which are likely to survive the Trump presidency. A significant new element may be the idea of an Indo-Pacific strategy, bringing together US East Asian allies and India in jointly facing the geopolitical Chinese challenge.[37] (Modi's India, however, is likely to hedge its bets, rather than ally itself fully with Washington.)

The policies of the early Trump administration amounted to major shifts from that of Obama in several respects. For some time, it seemed as if the US alliance system in Asia would be an example of significant continuity, but Trump's unilateral way of handling key alliances created a new sense of unpredictability. The most significant differences between Obama and Trump lie in their basic attitudes towards international cooperation, multilateralism, and the importance of a rule- and community-based international order. Whereas Obama showed a strong commitment to global governance, that commitment was immediately questioned by Trump who not only lacked interest in strong and effective international institutions, but even seemed inclined to undermine them.

For its part, Beijing has a great interest in playing a leading role in world governance on its own terms, with less dependence on the Western-led systems that have long dominated. At the 2017 World Economic Forum in Davos, Xi Jinping came out in a rousing defence of globalisation. The contrast to Trump's strategy of "America First" was stark, but it was hardly a confirmation of the liberal economic order. Rather, it was a sermon by the prophet of the Chinese Dream of revival. China's ambition has been to continue reaping the benefits of integration into the global economy, while minimising the vulnerabilities and potential security risks associated with it.[38] Trump challenged that strategy, putting trade, intellectual property rights and technology at the forefront of his approach. The style is uniquely Trumpian, but deeper American consensus seems to have emerged around a more confrontational approach to China's emergence.

Under Trump, the relationship between China and the wider West is no longer predicated on the expectation of convergence, but of rivalry and competition. Opportunities for cooperation are not seized, and the future increasingly appears to be one of systemic dissonance. China on one side is building a party-state-driven economy based on its own distinctive vision for globalisation, while the West's adherence to a rules-based liberal order is severely weakened by the post-2017 "America First" doctrine.[39]

Trade is at the epicentre of US–Chinese competition. At the beginning of 2018, the Trump administration went as far as saying that supporting China's WTO accession was a mistake.[40] The pivotal element of Trump's protectionist confrontation with China on trade is, however, not steel or aluminium. It is over intellectual property rights and the "Made in China 2025" strategy in which China invests heavily in areas like robotics, new-energy vehicles, biotechnology and, not least, artificial intelligence. On that frontier, Trump is taking measures, far beyond trade, to contain China. Intensified confrontation around the fourth generation of industry will remain a real threat, with potentially profound global consequences.

In his first State of the Union address in January 2018, Trump reiterated his image of China as a challenge to American interests, grouping it together with 'rogue regimes and terrorist groups'. '[R]ivals like China and Russia', he explained, 'challenge our interests, our economy, and our values. In confronting these horrible dangers, we know that weakness is the surest path to conflict, and unmatched power is the surest means to our true and great defense.'[41]

Strategic distrust seems bound to define an increasingly complex US–China relationship. At no time therefore has the United States appeared to be in more urgent need of a comprehensive and viable China policy, beyond transactional improvisations and power projections. It would have been natural for Trump to build on Obama's policy, by broadening and deepening the political-economic-security agenda, and strengthening Washington's institutional capacity to manage mounting challenges. Across Trump's first two years in charge, essentially the opposite happened.

There remains ample scope for joint efforts and we can only hope for such an era, but the ongoing global power shift will cast an increasingly long shadow, challenging the status quo. US China policy seems set to progress along a slippery slope. Still, containing China is hardly a possibility for the United States. It remains, to rephrase Campbell and Ratner, an outsized ambition. The only option for Washington remains to develop a more ambitious and long-term policy, where engagement and even accommodation, must be central elements.

A major US–China war is hardly inevitable, but confrontations and miscalculations are ever-present risks. Confrontations at sea, with assumed constraints on escalation, appear alarmingly probable. Institutional mechanisms are critical, but so is sufficient trust to enable them to function effectively.[42]

Notes

1   K. Campbell and E. Ratner, 'The China reckoning: How Beijing defied American expectations', *Foreign Affairs*, 97:2 (2018), pp. 60–70.

2   *The Economist*, 'How the West Got China Wrong' (1 March 2018), www.economist.com/leaders/2018/03/01/how-the-west-got-china-wrong, accessed 14 March 2019.

3   M. Pei, 'Minxin Pei: The US Needs To Be Real About China's Ambitions', *Nikkei Asian Review* (22 February 2018), https://asia.nikkei.com/Politics/Minxin-Pei-The-US-needs-to-be-real-about-China-s-ambitions, accessed 14 March 2019.

4   A. L. Friedberg, 'Testimony Before the House Armed Services Committee Hearing on Strategic Competition with China' (15 February 2018), https://docs.house.gov/meetings/AS/AS00/20180215/106848/HHRG-115-AS00-Wstate-FriedbergA-20180215.pdf, accessed 14 March 2019.

5   Xinhua, 'Full Text of Xi Jinping's Report at 19th CPC National Congress' (18 October 2017), www.xinhuanet.com/english/special/2017-11/03/c_136725942.htm, accessed 14 March 2019.

6   Xinhua, 'Full Text of the Constitution of the Communist Party of China' (3 November 2017), http://www.xinhuanet.com/english/special/2017-11/03/c_136725945.htm, accessed 14 March 2019.

7   Xinhua, 'Full Text of Xi Jinping's Report'.

8   S. Ringen, *The Perfect Dictatorship: China in the 21st Century* (Hong Kong: Hong Kong University Press, 2016).

9   J. Mearsheimer, *The Tragedy of Great Power Politics* (New York: W. W. Norton and Company, 2001), pp. 401–2. The idea that the constraints of the international system are the primary or overriding driver of US–China antagonisms is also challenged in the literature. See for example O. Turner, '"Threatening" China and US security: The international politics of identity', *Review of International Studies*, 39:4 (2013), pp. 903–24.

10 J. A. Bader, *Obama and China's Rise: An Insider's Account of America's Asia Strategy* (Washington, DC: Brookings Institution Press, 2012).

11 M. Landler, 'Offering to Aid Talks, US Challenges China on Disputed Islands', *New York Times* (23 July 2010), www.nytimes.com/2010/07/24/world/asia/24diplo.html, accessed 14 March 2019.

12 I. Storey, 'China's Missteps in Southeast Asia: Less Charm, More Offensive', The Jamestown Foundation, China Brief (17 December 2010), https://jamestown.org/programme/chinas-missteps-in-southeast-asia-less-charm-more-offensive/, accessed 14 March 2019.

13 H. Clinton, 'America's Pacific Century', *Foreign Policy* (11 October 2011), https://foreignpolicy.com/2011/10/11/americas-pacific-century/, accessed 14 March 2019.

14 White House, 'Remarks by President Obama to the Australian Parliament' (17 November 2011), https://obamawhitehouse.archives.gov/the-press-office/2011/11/17/remarks-president-obama-australian-parliament, accessed 14 March 2019.

15 M. Memoli, 'Hillary Clinton Once Called the TPP The "Gold Standard". Here's Why, and What She Says About the Trade Deal Now', *LA Times* (26 September 2016), www.latimes.com/politics/la-na-pol-trade-tpp-20160926-snap-story.html, accessed 17 March 2019.

16 S. Donnan, 'Obama Vows to Make the Case for Pacific Trade Deal', *Financial Times* (2 August 2016), www.ft.com/content/4a020e58-58cb-11e6-9f70-badea1b336d4, accessed 14 March 2019.

17   ChinaFile, 'Document 9: A ChinaFile translation' (8 November 2013), www.
     chinafile.com/document-9-chinafile-translation, accessed 14 March 2019.

18   J. Bader and R. Hass, 'Was Pre-Trump US Policy towards China Based on "False"
     Premises? China in Trump's National Security Strategy', Brookings Institution
     (22 December 2017), www.brookings.edu/blog/order-from-chaos/2017/12/22/
     was-pre-trump-u-s-policy-towards-china-based-on-false-premises/, accessed
     14 March 2019.

19   K. Campbell, *The Pivot: The Future of American Statecraft in Asia*
     (New York: Twelve, 2016); R. D. Blackwill and K. Campbell, 'Xi Jinping on the
     Global Stage', Council on Foreign Relations (February 2016), https://cfrd8-files.cfr.
     org/sites/default/files/pdf/2016/02/CSR74_Blackwill_Campbell_Xi_Jinping.pdf,
     accessed 14 March 2019.

20   S. Tönnesson, *Explaining the East Asian Peace: A Research Story* (Copenhagen: NIAS
     Press, 2017).

21   M. Green, *By More than Providence: Grand Strategy and American Power in the
     Asia Pacific since 1783* (New York: Columbia University Press, 2017).

22   See Stockholm Internal Peace Research Institute, 'Military Expenditure by
     Country, in Constant US$ m' (2018), www.sipri.org/databases/milex, accessed
     14 March 2019.

23   Xinhua, 'China to Lower Defense Budget Growth to 7.5%' (5 March 2019),
     www.xinhuanet.com/english/2019-03/05/c_137871426.htm.

24   State Council of the PRC, 'China's Military Strategy (Full Text)' (27 May 2015),
     http://english.gov.cn/archive/white_paper/2015/05/27/content_281475115610833.
     htm, accessed 14 March 2019.

25   A. Capaccio and E. Wasson, 'Pentagon Wins as Trump Readies a $716 Billion
     Budget Request', *Bloomberg* (26 January 2018), www.bloomberg.com/news/
     articles/2018-01-26/trump-is-said-to-seek-716-billion-for-defense-in-2019-
     budget, accessed 14 March 2019.

26   K. Manson, 'Mattis Warns US Losing Edge in Rivalry with Great Powers', *Financial
     Times* (19 January 2018), www.ft.com/content/72eb74ea-fd24-11e7-9b32-
     d7d59aace167, accessed 14 March 2019; Mercator Institute for China Studies,
     'United States Takes Hard Line Against China in Defense Strategy and On Trade'
     (25 January 2018), www.merics.org/en/newsletter/china-update-2-2018, accessed
     14 March 2019.

27   White House, 'National Security Strategy of the United States of America
     (December 2017), www.whitehouse.gov/wp-content/uploads/2017/12/NSS-Final-
     12-18-2017-0905.pdf, accessed 14 March 2019.

28   M. Landler and J. Perlez, 'Trump's Call with Taiwan: A Diplomatic Gaffe or a New
     Start?', *New York Times* (3 December 2016), www.nytimes.com/2016/12/05/world/
     asia/china-donald-trump-taiwan-twitter.html, accessed 14 March 2019.

29   G. Seib, J. Solomon and C. Lee, 'Barack Obama Warns Donald Trump on North
     Korean Threat', *Wall Street Journal* (22 November 2016), www.wsj.com/articles/
     trump-faces-north-korean-challenge-1479855286, accessed 14 March 2019.

30 J. Pramuk, 'Trump Warns North Korea Threats "Will Be Met with Fire and Fury"', *CNBC* (8 August 2017), www.cnbc.com/2017/08/08/trump-warns-north-korea-threats-will-be-met-with-fire-and-fury.html, accessed 12 March 2019.

31 J. Page, C. Lee and G. Lubold, 'China's President Pledges No Militarization in Disputed Islands', *Wall Street Journal* (25 September 2015), www.wsj.com/articles/china-completes-runway-on-artificial-island-in-south-china-sea-1443184818, accessed 14 March 2019.

32 T. Shi and I. Reynolds, 'China's Push into Western Pacific Alarms US Allies in Asia', *Bloomberg* (21 January 2018), www.bloomberg.com/news/articles/2018-01-21/as-trump-focuses-on-north-korea-china-pushes-into-west-pacific, accessed 14 March 2019.

33 Xinhua, 'Full Text of Xi Jinping's Report'.

34 G. Allison, *Destined for War: Can the United States and China Escape Thucydides' Trap?* (Boston: Houghton Mifflin); B. Ljunggren, 'Can the United States and a Rising China Avoid Thucydides' Trap?', YaleGlobal Online (27 July 2017), https://yaleglobal.yale.edu/content/can-united-states-and-rising-china-avoid-thucydidess-trap, accessed 14 March 2019.

35 Allison, *Destined for War*, p. vii.

36 US State Department, 'Advancing a Free and Open Indo-Pacific Region' (18 November 2018), www.state.gov/r/pa/prs/ps/2018/11/287433.htm, accessed 18 March 2019.

37 D. Sevastopulo, 'Trump Gives Glimpse of "Indo-Pacific" Strategy to Counter China', *Financial Times* (10 November 2017), www.ft.com/content/e6d17fd6-c623-11e7-a1d2-6786f39ef675, accessed 14 March 2019.

38 A. Friedberg, 'Globalisation and Chinese grand strategy', *Survival*, 60:1 (2018), pp. 7–40.

39 J. Kynge, 'Davos 2018: China and the West Head for a Clash of Systems', *Financial Times* (21 January 2018), www.ft.com/content/6aae4a1c-e0f2-11e7-a0d4-0944c5f49e46, accessed 14 March 2019.

40 S. Donnan, 'US Says China WTO Membership Was a Mistake', *Financial Times* (19 January 2018), www.ft.com/content/edb346ec-fd3a-11e7-9b32-d7d59aace167, accessed 14 March 2019.

41 White House, 'President Donald J. Trump's State of the Union Address' (30 January 2018), www.whitehouse.gov/briefings-statements/president-donald-j-trumps-state-union-address-2/, accessed 14 March 2019.

42 Special thanks to Nayan Chanda, Robert Ross and Stein Tönnesson for indispensable advice.

13

Multilateralism to transactionalism: America and Trump in the Asia Pacific

Ketan Patel and Christian Hansmeyer

Introduction

The United States under Donald Trump has been charting a radically new course in Asia, a region that has long relied on America for stability and maintaining the balance of power. In the first half of his presidential term of 2017–21, the forty-fifth president reversed or sought to reverse many of the long-standing policies and initiatives pursued by Barack Obama and his predecessors, with potential long-term implications. A multilateral and multifaceted engagement strategy in the region is being replaced by a transactional approach to security, trade and governance that seeks to maximise gains while shifting risk to counterparties, and thereby risking eroding a strategic leadership position that has been decades in the making. Donald Trump's "America First" potentially represents an abandonment of leadership in the setting of international norms for trade, investment and security in favour of "big wins". However, it is worth noting that big wins, if they are big enough, can be game changing and provide the basis of a renewal of power and influence too. This chapter, in part, examines the potential risks and rewards inherent in such an approach.

While American abandonment of multilateralism may allow striking favourable new bilateral deals in the region – China, North Korea and Japan seem to be high on the list – the riskiness of the approach poses potentially catastrophic risk for Asia as a whole, if not the world. Win or lose, it risks changing for the worse the perceived character of the United States in the eyes of its allies and confirms the claims of its enemies and adversaries that America is a predatory force. This approach – coming at a time and in a region which hosts two emerging superpowers – has the potential to mark the turning point of America's own trajectory as a superpower. China has long pursued a "China First" policy of its own, and more recently begun to transition from a rule-taker to a rule-maker in the region, establishing its own institutions and transregional initiatives, like the Belt and Road Initiative (BRI), to pull countries formerly tied to America more closely into its orbit. Asia's other rising power, and the fastest growing major economy in the world, India, will need to reassess its strategic options in the face of US repositioning and China's increasing economic, political and military activity (as indeed will other countries in the region).

What makes this current transition particularly risky is what can be called an overt "Extreme Asymmetric Risk" approach, which passes economic and security risks to America's counterparties and allies while capturing disproportionate benefits for incurring neutral to low risk to the US homeland. Of course, maximising benefits and minimising risk is the goal of nearly every sensible foreign policy, it is the one-sidedness of their distribution and how they are applied that makes it significant for the region and the world at large. The extreme asymmetric nature of risk distribution creates win-lose outcomes on a scale unprecedented in modern times. The current pattern of engagement suggests that this is the cornerstone of Trump's approach to engagement.

The transition from Obama to Trump

Over recent decades Asia has become an increasingly important region for American foreign policy, and the United States has become an ally (or partner) of the majority of countries in Asia. So too has it become China's biggest trading partner, and as of 2015 the host to *circa* twenty million immigrants from the region (an increase of around 70 per cent since 2000).[1] The United States has become the outside country on which the Asian region has most depended, politically, economically and in terms of aspirations.

Within a generation, Asia is expected to be home to over five billion people, or more than half the world's population.[2] It is also projected to boast over 40 per cent of world GDP.[3] Obama recognised the importance of Asia for the future of America and the world, and it formed one of the core pillars of his foreign policy, albeit slowly, initially, given the wars his administration inherited. The "Pivot" to Asia redeployed political, security and economic resources to the region across a wide range of initiatives,[4] including driving regional economic integration, checking Chinese territorial expansion with naval freedom of navigation operations,[5] and engaging with India (including massive arms sales) to build a real counter-weight to China. Obama billed himself as America's first "Pacific President" to signal his commitment to the region.[6]

The Asia Pivot consisted of a wide array of initiatives: many of its key elements, such as the Trans-Pacific Partnership (TPP) and the strategic outreach to India, predated Obama's administration but were accelerated and deepened. Other elements such as the strategic engagement with ASEAN were newly conceived. While critics commented that the Asia Pivot was therefore somehow less than a strategy,[7] it undeniably recognised the ongoing global rebalancing underway in Asia's favour. The overarching goal of the Pivot therefore was to ensure continued US strategic relevance in the region and to balance a growing and more assertive China in 'an effort that harnesses all elements of US power – military, political, trade and investment, development and our values.'[8] A clearly critical part of the Pivot was the importance of multilateralism as the basis for any American initiatives, embedding US actions into partnerships and alliance. Importantly, the Pivot was not conceived to be a discrete initiative, but an encapsulation of a longer term refocusing of American military, political and economic resources to continue after Obama.

Donald Trump's approach to foreign policy in Asia, between his election in late 2016 to early 2019, was very different. The overarching philosophy of "America First" prioritises domestic over international affairs, making an implicit assumption that the two are somehow disconnected.[9] Trump, a self-confessed "deal-maker", is focused on getter a "better deal" for America, through transactional and bilateral engagements on trade, security and investment, where its superior scale provides negotiating leverage. Within this context, the Trump administration formulated only a limited vision for the Asia Pacific. Where Obama sought to both engage and contain China, at least until it learned to abide by the rules of the world order and recognise the values underpinning it, Trump's approach appears to favour confrontation, raising the stakes and threatening a unilateral trade war. The rhetoric aside and not speculating on motivations, both represent the continuation of a multi-decade, multi-presidency effort to maintain US primacy in Asia, countering China's rapid rise to achieve a more balanced sharing of power. The question remains of whether the current approach raises unacceptable risks and thereby undermines these longer-term goals.

How US policy under Trump in Asia is playing out

After approximately two years of Trump's presidency, the full ramifications of "America First" on the United States and the world are still playing out. Yet it is already clear that its impact on Asia will be significant. There is little doubt now that "America First" has profound implications for US engagement across security, trade, investment and society and values in the region, with China's reactions potentially exacerbating the consequences for America and the world along all of these dimensions.

Security engagement

The North Korean nuclear crisis has become among the most visible and immediate security challenges in Asia facing America and the region. After assuming office, the Trump administration adopted a highly inconsistent approach to Korea, threatening the use of overwhelming force against Pyongyang before attending the first summit between a North Korean leader and US president in June 2018. Two opposing interpretations of the President's approach see him as either successfully employing Nixon's "madman" theory to encourage North Korea to negotiate, or simply acting irresponsibly towards the safety of billions of people because they are far away from America. While the Trump administration throughout 2018 in particular adopted a more conciliatory approach to North Korea, the second summit between the leaders in Hanoi in February 2019 which produced no meaningful outcomes highlighted the limitations of the President's personal ability to strike a deal, and may in time lead to the pendulum swinging back to escalation.

Either way, Trump's North Korea "strategy" is a good example of Extreme Asymmetric Risk. A high stakes game in which risks are borne by America's Asian allies and the upside is shared more broadly; a North Korean military strike would probably target Japan or Seoul with little direct risk to the US homeland, while any lasting negotiated de-escalation would see the President hailed a hero. This Extreme Asymmetric Risk approach, which provides binary outcomes in which the United States comes out ahead or neutral, is a key element of the President's "America First" strategy, delivering high gains for America at the rest of the world's expense.

Meanwhile, China is demonstrating the will to actively displace America in regional power projection; building and militarising reclaimed islands; acquiring regional ports in a "String of Pearls"; opening its first overseas military base, in Djibouti; and extending its BRI mega-project to the ends of Asia. The Trump administration appears to have deprioritised these issues while proposing the notion of a "Quad" framework focusing on maritime security between the United States, India, Australia and Japan.

Trade engagements

The importance of trade for US foreign policy also shifted dramatically under President Trump. Under previous US administrations, trade was not just about economic gains but also a source of stability underpinning international relationships and economic integration, secured by a set of international rules. And while these rules may have initially favoured American interests, other countries too have created surpluses and, more importantly, developed interdependencies that have disincentivised conflict. This post-war liberal trade order enabled the greatest explosion of wealth the world has ever seen, with global GDP increasing six-fold and global trade twenty-fold between 1950 and the turn of the twenty-first century.[10] The percentage of the world's population living in poverty declined from 75 per cent to under 10 per cent.[11] Average household wages and incomes expanded almost continually across the same period, before beginning to stagnate.[12]

Under Trump, trade's role refocused to being about US wealth and jobs, with America's trade deficit seen as a drain on both. US objectives have refocused from maintaining a global trade order to reviving American manufacturing in the heartland. Importantly, the President's "America First" trade policy espouses hard-line economic nationalism focused on bilateral agreements and rejects multilateral trade deals. When Trump pulled the United States out of the TPP, he took with it an opportunity to lead new rules that could define trade in the region for a generation or longer.

This lack of US multilateral trade engagement represents a major opportunity for China. Its home-grown alternative to the TPP, the Regional Comprehensive Economic Partnership (RCEP), covers an area accounting for half of the world's population and almost one third of global GDP. The position at the centre of the global "system" of trade that Trump is abandoning has been a source of considerable power for the United States. Given that the United States remains the largest market in the world, it retains the clout to negotiate favourable deals and is likely to do so when negotiating with smaller nations, further accelerating the Trump administration's effective withdrawal from the global and regional trade systems. China, on the other hand, has begun to establish an alternative system with itself at the centre as a rule-setter. With the United States ceding leadership, China might also choose to play a more active role at the centre of the existing global and regional trade system, replacing America, rather than creating competing alternatives.

Investment engagement

Under US leadership, multilateral institutions such as the UN, World Bank, and IMF, have built-out the infrastructure of developing nations, financed trade to open new markets, ensured that sea, road and airways remain open and attempted to deal with "rogue" nations. This has not been an altruistic endeavour; in doing so, Washington has reinforced its position in the global financial system. Withdrawal from these governing institutions, not to mention US threats to defund some of them for political reasons,[13] risks weakening a system that has managed international development funding for decades and placed America in the driving seat of rule-setting and provided it with an important source of soft power globally.

In parallel, China is seeking to establish itself as the world's premier investor, both by way of establishing China-led initiatives to compete with established international financial institutions, and by way of ambitious direct investing. The Asian Infrastructure Investment Bank (AIIB) is a good example of the former. With eighty members and US$100 billion in capital, it now competes with the World Bank and Asian Development Bank as a financier of infrastructure in Eurasia with fewer transparency and governance requirements. The BRI is perhaps the most ambitious example of the latter. Covering countries inhabited by over 4.4 billion people and generating over US$21 trillion USD in annual GDP, the BRI aims to build logistics and infrastructure links connecting China and the rest of Asia and Europe, facilitating the flow of goods, services, resources and information between these regions.[14] According to one estimate, China could invest over US$500 billion in sixty-two BRI projects over the next five years,[15] breathing new life into its flagging economic growth model by compensating for construction overcapacity and lack of demand at home.

China also derives strategic benefits from its international lending, with its loans collateralised by strategically important natural assets, which can be seized in cases of default. China in 2018 was granted a ninety-nine year lease on Hambantota port in Sri Lanka to restructure US$8 billion of outstanding debt owed to Beijing. China's plan comes at a time when America has decided that control over the international development finance system is a burden rather than a source of power, which should expedite China's rise. China with US$3.1 trillion in reserves is well placed to exploit the opportunity.[16]

Yet the United States today remains the world's premier investor. American domination of the global financial system is as much a function of US-style capitalism as a cultural phenomenon and the structure of its financial markets as it is of leadership and participation in multilateral institutions. US investment and fund managers control over half of the world's investible assets.[17] Further, America remains by far the world's largest single source of foreign direct investment.[18] However, while previous administrations have believed that ongoing leadership of major institutions is a guarantor of America's position as the world's leading investor, Trump appears to believe that capitalism alone can sustain American pre-eminence.

Society and values engagement

Since the end of the Second World War, America had defined its leadership values in terms of championing freedom and opportunity, and, during the Cold War, in terms of the perceived superiority of its system over communism, promoting democracy, globalisation, capitalism, free trade and human rights. In contrast to his predecessors, President Trump espoused virtually no policies in areas like international human rights, global health, income inequality, environmental protection or climate change, endangering American soft power as a result (as evidenced by deteriorating global views of the United States[19]). This lack of leadership is partly the result of deep divisions within American society on matters of politics, ideology, race, and ultimately values, with Americans asking whether their country should continue to play the role of the world's "policeman" or withdraw to focus on domestic matters.

Despite various adventures abroad, it was clear throughout his first two years in office that Trump's "America First" platform traded the moral authority of past administrations for a transactional bargaining chip. Trump's refusal to take reporters' questions at a joint press conference with Chinese President Xi Jinping during a trip to Beijing, at 'Chinese insistence',[20] was widely perceived as a capitulation on a long-standing tradition of supporting press freedom and freedom of speech generally. His willingness to endorse authoritarian strongmen also undermines America's moral legitimacy; while Obama distanced himself from Philippines President Rodrigo Duterte, who boasted of once pushing a man out of a helicopter, Trump invited him to the White House.

The direction of travel is clear: America is now promoting a new set of values based on transactions, superseding older values that were based, at least in part, on principles. China, on the other hand, has a long-standing transactional approach to foreign relations, and its policy of non-interference is core to its attractiveness in parts of the developing world. Should America try to compete head-on with China (and its US$3 trillion of foreign reserves) in this regard, the two countries will quickly find themselves in a race to the moral bottom in terms of dealing with failing and rogue states. Importantly, it is highly unlikely that America will have the stomach to do the things that China might be willing to do.

Who wins and who loses

What are the implications of America's withdrawal from, and China's expanding engagement within, Asia? The realignment of power and interests in the region can be expected to create a series of winners and losers.

America as a traditional superpower: The biggest loser

America's withdrawal from Asia and its shift to transactional engagements is both a symptom and a driver of its decline as a superpower. Powers in history consistently go through a cycle of growth, plateau and decline, and the (twentieth) American century, which succeeded the (nineteenth) British century, is sure to be replaced itself in the future.[21] While the United States refocuses priorities under "America First", it also effectively cedes ground to a new generation of competitors such as China and India, who are both rising to world power status. Striking bilateral trade deals in Asia will of course have a positive impact on the US economy and more importantly its financial markets; other markets may stabilise and rise too given the certainty they expect. However, this would be a false victory given the likely longer-term shift in the relationship between the United States and China. In addition, if these deals are accompanied by a longer-term withdrawal of US leadership in the region, the net benefits of such deals are a strong negative for the United States and the region.

American withdrawal does not of course equate to a loss of primacy, at least for the time being. The United States still accounts for roughly a third of global defence spending.[22] However, an increasingly inward-looking America may find itself militarily powerful, but increasingly less relevant in the global scheme of things. Importantly though, US withdrawal is also weakening the Western-led multilateral liberal order it has traditionally underwritten which in turn has driven America's global influence and financial, security and political success. This order is already under attack from multiple sources: domestic populism, anti-globalisation, the rise of authoritarian states, and income inequality, among others. A United States which does not proactively engage in the process of managing this transition may find itself on the wrong side of change with the cards stacked against it when the dust settles.

China: The biggest winner

Xi Jinping has made it clear that China aspires to its share of global leadership, pledging the 'renewal of the Chinese nation' and ensuring what he sees as China's rightful return to a place on the world stage. (It remains unclear, however, when, if ever, China will surpass the United States in terms of nominal GDP.[23])

The BRI – pulling together past, current and future bilateral trade, investment and security initiatives into a geopolitical whole – is a strategic cornerstone of Chinese ambition, increasing both regional integration and Chinese influence therein. Other China-led initiatives and institutions such as the RCEP, the AIIB and the New Development Bank, further augment China's ability to chip away at the relevance and influence of existing multilateral institutions. At the same time, the United States' loss of prestige under Trump has provided soft power opportunities for China. President Xi's reaffirmation of China's commitment to globalisation and the Paris Climate Accord after Washington's withdrawal advertises a maturing China in contrast to a United States which has lost its way. And while China's execution on globalisation and trade issues may continue to fall short of international expectations, in the absence of credible alternatives it may end up being the only game in town. The United States demonstrated during the Cold War that it has the will, stamina, resourcefulness and might to destabilise and bring its rivals to overwhelming losses. However, even with sufficient motivation and determination such a policy would not be easy, given that China is learning how to use the same international institutions that America has to protect its interests.[24]

India: A potential winner

Following decades of neglect, US–India relations have deepened steadily in recent years. Obama's profession of India as an 'enduring strategic partner in the 21st century' led to the US–India nuclear deal in 2007, and support during India's various border conflicts with China.

For India, a closer relationship with Washington is partly being driven by China's growing power-positioning in the region – in Pakistan (China's biggest arms customer), the Indian Ocean (by way of a "string of pearls" of Chinese built ports) and in neighbouring Nepal and Bangladesh. As the only country in the region not signed up to the BRI, India finds itself encircled by a web of Chinese-led and financed infrastructure. However, its need for foreign investment and its increasing participation in international forums means India's requirements today have expanded well beyond security, providing the United States with many levers with which to deepen the strategic relationship. A more transactional approach by the United States under Trump, however, risks limiting engagement to a series of tactical alliances and even using India as a weapon in conflicts with China.

Despite this risk, India may yet emerge as a winner: the country's long-standing multilateralist approach has strengthened under Prime Minister Narendra Modi, who has worked hard to promote India as an investment destination. As the world's fastest growing major economy, India has already surpassed China in attracting foreign direct investment (FDI), creating a strong consumer base,[25] encouraging its major corporations to grow internationally and restructuring its finances through wide-ranging reforms. Unlike China, India is also enhancing the rule of law, reducing FDI restrictions, and maintaining open access to information and the Internet, thereby becoming an increasingly attractive partner for a wide range of developed regions and nations including Japan, Australia, Canada and the EU. India's democracy and multilateral approach makes it a natural long-term strategic partner to others including future US administrations.

Japan: A potential loser

Japan risks becoming one of the biggest losers in the reshuffling of Asian power. The country remains almost entirely dependent on the United States for security, and while Washington is unlikely to fully withdraw from its long-standing commitment, it is now more likely to charge heavily for it. A more transactional mode of accommodation between the United States and China may also encourage a more aggressive stance in Beijing across a range of regional security issues (e.g. the Senkaku/Diaoyu Islands sovereignty dispute). Japan's current interest in defence ties to other countries in the region stem from this fear, further driven by the continued American insistence that Japan shoulder more of the costs of its security.

Economically though, Japan is very much tied to its biggest trading partner China, partly to the RCEP (by necessity) while continuing to push the TPP as a hedge, albeit not a very strong one without the United States.[26] However, Japan is no longer core to China's economic growth. While Japan was critical in building China's economy in the first wave of liberalisation, China has leveraged Japanese investments, trade and intellectual property, to build scaled industries of its own, displacing former Japanese partners domestically and increasingly internationally too.[27] While Japan has an opportunity to partner with India to aid its development, cultural differences make this a slow and difficult process, despite the strategic imperative to do so and the strong personal efforts of the country's leaders.

Ultimately, while the United States' Asian withdrawal provides a strong impetus to Japan remilitarising and building stronger alliances with regional allies, these actions cannot compensate for the loss of America's sponsorship in the short term and perhaps not in the longer term, either. Japan will face the challenge of keeping the quality of its culture and values intact while leveraging its massive intellectual property and highly educated population to create value in a much rougher and mercenary world order.

America as an information age power: A potential winner

No power in history has successfully reversed a period of decline to re-attain leadership once ceded. However, the end of the "American century" is occurring during a broader transition, from the industrial to the information age, and the United States remains the undisputed global leader in technology. The United States leads global research and development in nearly every field of new technology – computer sciences, biotech, nanotech and alternative energy – and has the culture of entrepreneurship to commercialise innovation, and the financial systems of risk capital to rapidly scale it. While American industrial power may be on the decline, America as an innovator remains well positioned for the information age, leveraging technology to build and sustain its power across diverse areas such as energy, where shale and alternatives are leading to potential energy independence, and security, where advanced computing capabilities are positioning America as a leader in tomorrow's cyber warfare.

Importantly, freedom of information will be a key prerequisite for success in the coming era, and it bodes well for the United States that China is increasingly restricting information flows, reducing its ability to compete in the long-term transition underway. The United States "winning", however, will also require its own society to embrace the changes the information age brings. The 2016 presidential election has highlighted parts of the country's desire to cling to the industrial age at whatever cost necessary. Without resolving this internal tension, the United States will not be able to fully leverage its advantages and risks not having a new platform to replace its old one.

Two futures: Spheres of influence vs. an orderly transition

Obama was the custodian of America's post-war strategy built on the premise that its power rested on free trade, capitalism, globalisation, democracy, multilateralism, non-proliferation and human rights, with these values enshrined in a series of international institutions to facilitate orderly and peaceful conduct among nations. While this system clearly benefited the United States as the source of much of its power, the inclusive values upon which it was based imbued it and its allies with a sense of noble or moral purpose that was almost universally accepted. Therefore, while critics at times accused Washington of abusing the system to its own ends, and many examples exist, the wider benefits of the system were sufficient to fend off challenges to it. Leveraging this system, Obama recouped the losses to American prestige caused by the global financial crisis and two foreign wars,[28] and left behind one of the strongest economies in modern times.[29] In Asia, Obama acted to contain China through a combination of both trade and confrontation, much like his own predecessor George W. Bush had done.

The Trump presidency, by contrast, arrived at a time when many Americans felt that the major benefits of the system have already been realised unevenly distributed. With a large domestic population experiencing income and opportunity inequalities, blame was, and still is, placed on America's political class and the global system it built. Trump's own solution to the problem was to advocate exactly what his predecessors had sought to prevent others pursuing: a nationalist economic agenda that appears at core to be predatory, eschewing noble, moral or universal purpose and therefore without broader appeal internationally.

"America First" placed the United States in competition with the likes of Russia and China, who have traditionally played by more self-interested rules. China is open about its domestic priorities over promoting the values America once espoused. Russia understands how to use its military strength to extend its territory and fight ruthless wars in Syria, Ukraine and elsewhere. While the United States has so often behaved in highly questionable and immoral ways, it also established sets of international checks and balances to leave it open to being held account by others, at least some of the time. As President Trump further weakens these checks and balances, he risks finding that the Hobbesian world he sees suits China and Russia far better than that of the United States.

The United States today stands at a crossroads. The path it takes from here will help shape the contours and character of the United States itself, along with those of Asia and the wider world. The two approaches open to US foreign policy and values – continuity of global stewardship versus predatory nationalism – bring the potential for very different outcomes.

Outcome 1: The domestication of America – declining world power by design

In a world shaped by "America First", a domestically focused United States will spend less time, money and effort on foreign issues generally and assess any remaining engagements based on their domestic impact: short-term jobs creation, the US trade balance and electoral popularity. This shifting of interests is already leading to a United States that is willing to compromise on its own values, the interests of long-held allies, and the continuity of institutions that have under-written global security and prosperity. This approach makes it more likely that the United States will withdraw into a geographically defined sphere of interest, and aggressively pursue a narrowly defined set of non-negotiable goals outside of which nearly everything can be ceded given the right deal. The unfolding of this scen-ario would provide an opportunity for China to establish its own growing sphere of influence across East Asia, Southeast Asia and Central Asia. Moreover, with the United States relinquishing leadership of and even undermining key multilat-eral institutions, China can become the unimpeded "rule-setter" in the region and increasingly the rest of the world. Just as the United Kingdom, exhausted by war and the cost of its colonial empire, handed over the reins of power to a brash and energetic upstart America, so would the United States, exhausted by its leadership of the "free world", pass the reins to a brash and energetic successor.

Outcome 2: Primacy and power sharing – orderly transition to multilateralism

The alternative to decline is continued American leadership, providing an orderly transition to a new world order. The President and his policies do not enjoy the support of a majority of Americans,[30] and the repeated cases of misalignment between the President and nearly every branch of government point to a wish among key parts of the US government to pursue a continuity of policy and to lead.

Under this scenario, "America First" would be undone and America would draw on its deep resources to re-establish its influence in Asia: its military expenditure is three times the size of China's; the World Bank is twice the size of the AIIB; the United States remains the largest trading partner of North Asia and the third lar-gest of ASEAN; and the TPP is still alive and ready for US re-engagement; to name a few. Additionally, the United States would draw on friends, allies and institutions to counterbalance China within an established rules-based system. This would provide the time to reform the current world order to reflect major changing real-ities, including the decline of the West and rise of emerging nations, as well as soci-etal changes wrought by technology. America would be a constructive shaper of this reform, rather than a nation seeking to place itself outside of inevitable change by clinging to its industrial era hegemony.

Of course, the real world is not binary, and the path America takes will no doubt veer somewhere between these extremes, shaped by unforeseen events regardless of who happens to be president. Two "certainties" remain: the first is that Asia is home to two giants representing 36 per cent of the world's population who, barring a major world event, will continue to rise. The second certainty is that few countries are better placed than America to rise to whatever future challenges may present themselves. Given these "certainties" it is most likely that the United States,

China and India will share economic and political power over the long term. The nature of America's relationships with these countries is currently being recast by the Trump administration.

"America First" seems to deny that American power is based on its leadership of a multilateral world order in favour of the view of a world governed by authoritarian muscle, and is placing uneven and sometimes catastrophic risk on US allies the world over. If it succeeds, a new, aggressive and overtly predatory America may emerge, without the moral compulsions to balance its primacy with multilateralism. Given that its success involves undermining allies (and potentially strengthening China), "America First" lacks a unifying moral purpose for others to rally behind. Its failure clearly leads to a loss of trust in American leadership given that it risks both military and trade wars associated with its gambles with North Korea, China and the Middle East.

The transactional approach preferred by the President seems to suit China well. However, China has long had its own China First policy, and countries that have experienced its approach in resource trading, intellectual property and FDI, among others, will likely reject China's leadership given a reasonable alternative. More fundamentally, China recognises that "America First" offers the best chance for it to succeed America as the next great power, consummating deals with the United States that give the Trump administration a short-term victory while hurting America's long-term interests. With Xi having secured a potentially indefinite term as China's leader, these types of deals will be at the forefront of his agenda.

For it to succeed in recovering its authority, not least in the realm of ideas and the challenge to them seemingly brought by China, the United States will need to re-embrace multilateralism. This development is being facilitated by voices both in America[31] and abroad,[32] which increasingly perceive China as both a strategic competitor and geopolitical threat. The implication is clearly that, at this critical juncture, with China on the brink of great economic power presaging great political power, the multi-decade endeavour to integrate China into the world order of shared values is believed to have failed. If what began as a transactional approach to China results ultimately in a resetting of the rules of engagement and inducing of China to re-join the world order, President Trump may in the end have found his "noble" purpose.

Whatever the eventual outcomes of the Trump administration's foreign policy, democracy offers a potential respite from any negative consequences. Taking a larger view of the sweep of history, in the wings of the industrial power that is the United States today, stands an information age America establishing its position and getting ready to take over. This new energy rising in America is certainly a match for a rising China and may yet lead to the United States being the world's next great power too. What is certain is that Asia is the key theatre of twenty-first-century geopolitics and America will therefore face its most important challenges there.

Notes

1   G. Lopez, N. Ruiz and E. Patten, 'Key Facts About Asian Americans, a Diverse and Growing Population', Pew Research Center (8 September 2017), www.pewresearch.org/fact-tank/2017/09/08/key-facts-about-asian-americans/, accessed 18 March 2019.

2   United Nations, 'World Population Prospects: The 2017 Revision' (21 June 2017), www.un.org/development/desa/publications/world-population-prospects-the-2017-revision.html, accessed 17 March 2019.

3   E. Waelbroeck Rocha, P. Huet and G. Mustafa Mohatarem, 'The 2040 Economy: Long-Term Growth Determinants', IHS Markit (12 November 2014), www.ihsglobalinsight.com/gcpath/The_2040_Economy_slides.pdf, accessed 16 March 2019.

4   H. Clinton, 'America's Pacific Century', *Foreign Policy* (11 October 2011), http://foreignpolicy.com/2011/10/11/americas-pacific-century/, accessed 6 March 2019.

5   L. Kouk, 'The US FON Program in the South China Sea', Brookings Institution, East Asia Policy Paper 9 (June 2016).

6   White House, 'Remarks by President Barack Obama at Suntory Hall' (14 November 2009), https://obamawhitehouse.archives.gov/realitycheck/the-press-office/remarks-president-barack-obama-suntory-hall, accessed 17 March 2019.

7   For example, B. Friedman, 'What Asian Pivot?', China-US Focus (13 November 2013), www.chinausfocus.com/foreign-policy/what-asian-pivot, accessed 15 March 2019.

8   White House, 'Remarks by Tom Donilon, National Security Advisor to the President: "The United States and the Asia Pacific in 2013"' (11 March 2013), https://obamawhitehouse.archives.gov/the-press-office/2013/03/11/remarks-tom-donilon-national-security-advisor-president-united-states-an), accessed 14 March 2019.

9   See White House, 'A New National Security Strategy for a New Era' (18 December 2017), www.whitehouse.gov/articles/new-national-security-strategy-new-era/, accessed 16 March 2019.

10   H. Van den Berg and J. Lewer, *International Trade and Economic Growth* (London: M. E. Sharpe, 2007), p. 26.

11   F. Bourguignon and C. Morrison, 'Inequality among world citizens: 1820–1992', *American Economic Review*, 92:4 (2002), pp. 727–44.

12   D. Mason, *The End of the American Century* (New York: Rowman & Littlefield, 2009), p. 33.

13   United States Mission to the United Nations, 'Remarks Before a UN General Assembly Vote on Jerusalem' (21 December 2017), https://usun.state.gov/remarks/8232, accessed 17 March 2019.

14   H. Lu, C. Rohr, M. Hafner and A. Knack, 'China Belt and Road Initiative', RAND Europe (2018), www.rand.org/content/dam/rand/pubs/research_reports/RR2600/RR2625/RAND_RR2625.pdf, accessed 14 March 2019.

15　Credit Suisse, 'China's Belt and Road Initiative. Big Hopes, Big Fears' (17 December 2018), www.credit-suisse.com/corporate/en/articles/news-and-expertise/china-s-belt-and-road-initiative-big-hopes-big-fears-201812.html, accessed 14 March 2019.

16　C. Neely, 'Chinese foreign exchange reserves, policy choices, and the US economy', *Federal Reserve Bank of St. Louis Review*, 99:2 (2017), pp. 207–32.

17　Boston Consulting Group, 'Global Asset Management 2016: Doubling Down on Data' (July 2016).

18　OECD, 'FDI in Figures' (April 2018), www.oecd.org/daf/inv/investment-policy/FDI-in-Figures-April-2018.pdf, accessed 12 March 2019.

19　Pew Research Center, 'US Image Suffers as Publics Around World Question Trump's Leadership' (26 June 2017), www.pewglobal.org/2017/06/26/u-s-image-suffers-as-publics-around-world-question-trumps-leadership/, accessed 13 March 2019.

20　J. Walters, 'Trump's "No Questions" Press Conference in China Slammed by Former Media Staff', *Guardian* (9 November 2017), www.theguardian.com/media/2017/nov/09/trump-no-questions-press-conference-china-slammed-by-former-media-staff, accessed 13 March 2019.

21　K. Patel and C. Hansmeyer, 'American power: Patterns of rise and decline', in I. Parmar, L. Miller and M. Ledwidge (eds.), *Obama and the World: New Directions in Foreign Policy*, 2nd edition (London: Routledge, 2014), pp. 275–88.

22　Stockholm International Peace Research Institute, 'SIPRI Yearbook 2018: Armaments, Disarmament and International Security, Summary' (2018), www.sipri.org/sites/default/files/2018-06/yb_18_summary_en_0.pdf, accessed 15 March 2019.

23　D. Fickling, 'China Could Outrun the US Next Year. Or Never', *Bloomberg* (8 March 2019), www.bloomberg.com/opinion/articles/2019-03-08/will-china-overtake-u-s-gdp-depends-how-you-count, accessed 12 March 2019.

24　As evidenced by the US–China trade conflicts of 2018, where China's response to US steel tariffs included both a WTO complaint, as well as its own tariffs on US agricultural exports from predominantly Trump-voting states.

25　Robust economic growth and rising household incomes are expected to increase consumer spending to US$4 trillion by 2025. See India Brand Equity Foundation, 'Indian Consumer Market' (February 2018), www.ibef.org/archives/detail/b3ZlcnZpZXcmMzc3MzEmNDQ0, accessed 16 March 2019.

26　M. Swaine, *Creating A Stable Asia: An Agenda for US-China Balance of Power* (Washington, DC: Carnegie Endowment for International Peace, 2016).

27　Japan already imports twice the value of electronic goods from China as it exports.

28　Pew Research Center, 'As Obama Years Draw to Close, President and US Seen Favourably in Europe and Asia' (29 June 2016), http://assets.pewresearch.org/wp-content/uploads/sites/2/2016/06/14095546/Pew-Research-Center-Balance-of-Power-Report-FINAL-June-29-2016.pdf, accessed 14 March 2019.

29 L. Leatherby, 'Donald Trump's Economic Inheritance in 7 Charts', *Financial Times* (28 December 2017), www.ft.com/content/4e5af7e4-c88d-11e6-8f29-9445cac8966f, accessed 13 March 2019.

30 Pew Research Center, 'Trump's Approval Ratings So Far Are Unusually Stable – and Deeply Partisan' (1 August 2018), www.pewresearch.org/fact-tank/2018/08/01/trumps-approval-ratings-so-far-are-unusually-stable-and-deeply-partisan/, accessed 13 March 2019.

31 According to the Pew 2016 Global Attitudes Study, a majority (55 per cent) of Americans hold an unfavourable opinion of China.

32 For example, the Asian Research Network's 'Survey on America's Role in the Indo-Pacific 2017' found that only 21 per cent, 13 per cent and 9 per cent of Australians, South Koreans and Japanese respectively believed that China was having a positive impact on the Asia Pacific region.

14

Obama and Trump's marine machismo in the Indo-Pacific

Atul Bhardwaj

Introduction

The return of the United States to the Indo-Pacific is one of the most significant elements of former President Barack Obama's foreign policy legacy. He ordered a bold alteration of course, in the midst of an economic storm, to save the crumbling maritime empire against continental China's advancing influence. As will be shown, this occurred as part of Obama's efforts to rejuvenate the United States' Asia Pacific presence, a strategy his successor Donald Trump built on throughout the relabelled Indo-Pacific. Even so, the United States has long recognised itself as the dominant regional power; as far back as the 1950s, Washington's strategic community identified the Pacific as an "American Lake". At that time the United States was consumed by the war in Korea and throughout the 1960s it fought in Vietnam. US troop numbers in East Asia peaked around this time, at around 800,000 by the late 1960s.[1] It was only in the 1970s, after the Sino-Soviet split, that it temporarily retreated from the region.

In 1963 President John F. Kennedy announced the establishment of an "Atlantic community" by which the United States would focus on strengthening its economic and security relations with Europe, while remaining conscious of the threat of Chinese communism to 'Vietnam, Free China, Korea, India, Pakistan, Thailand, Greece, Turkey, and Iran'. His last speech that remained undelivered due to his assassination that year contained proposals to use these countries on the 'periphery of the Communist world' to contain China, 'infusing 3.5 million allied troops along the Communist frontier at one-tenth the cost of maintaining a comparable number of American soldiers'.[2] Immediately after Kennedy's death, Roger Hillman, Assistant Secretary of State for Far Eastern Affairs, spearheaded an "Open Door" policy with China. Hillman wanted to restart trade with China both for the economic health of the US west coast and in order to see a 'fatter China', because he believed that 'a fat country is less a threat to peace than a lean one'.[3]

China has always been a key US focus in the region, and today, from the realms of currency and cyberspace to trade and future technologies, China is challenging American power in almost every conceivable sphere. A recent decline in US authority over global affairs has gradually led twenty-first-century American presidents to once again move from courting China to confronting and containing it. This increasingly demands the direct application of US hard power. In the 1950s and 1960s, US presidents depended largely on the army to implement their Pacific policies. From 2009 Obama made the US Navy the linchpin in his Asia Pacific strategy, a policy choice to which President Donald Trump from 2017 added more marine machismo.

This chapter argues that, as more than a foreign policy shift, Obama's "Pivot" to Asia from around 2011 represented a fundamental reorientation of the US Navy from the Atlantic to the Pacific. This charting of a new course by the US Navy was not only aimed at revitalising US foreign policy but also stemming its own decline.[4] The chapter explores Obama's and Trump's maritime approaches in the Indo-Pacific against the backdrop of the continual rise of China's Navy. The chapter also asks whether a continued reliance on Mahanian tenets – in particular, fleet engagements and securing overseas bases to control maritime domains – is sufficient for Washington to protect its empire from continental China.

Will history remember Obama's "Rebalance" to Asia as a masterstroke, or condemn him – perhaps along with Trump – for restricting American strategic choices in the maritime domain by failing to anticipate the technological revolution in land logistics, and neglecting Halford Mackinder's predictions of the rise of Eurasia? It is argued that while China is fashioning the future world order with bricks and mortar across the Eurasian landmass, America is busy hoisting flags and bunting throughout the maritime "marginals".

A bold alteration of course

After defeating the Soviet Union in the Cold War the United States shifted its gaze towards the Middle East, launching regional wars at will. As Monteiro observes, 'the US has been at war for 13 of the 22 years since the end of the Cold War. The first two decades of unipolarity, which make up less than 10% of US history account for more than 25% of the nation's total time at war.'[5]

The economic and financial crisis of 2008, North Korean nuclear posturing, and the rise of China led maritime America to rethink its involvement in the Middle East and Afghanistan as the primary arenas of its post-2001 "war on terror". In November 2009, President Barack Obama proclaimed himself 'America's first Pacific President' and declared the United States an 'Asia-Pacific nation'.[6] This self-labelling exercise in Tokyo was aimed at announcing to Asian nations that the United States was refocusing on the region after some years of perceived neglect.

In 2011, the Obama administration articulated this reorientation of US foreign policy as its "Pivot" to Asia. This was a shift away from the 'Middle East-centric legacy of the Bush era'[7] and one with roots in history; Senator Gale W. McGee predicted in 1959, that

> in the time of those who listen to me today, our real concern in the world may not be Moscow, but possibly Peiping [Beijing] or New Delhi; indeed, what was once the Atlantic age of history will be swept away, or at least supplemented, by the new Pacific age of history.[8]

Writing in *Foreign Policy*, US Secretary of State Hillary Clinton insisted on directing US resources in a 'smart and systematic' manner to the Asia Pacific region.[9] Relatedly, Clinton assured APEC members of the American commitment to establish an elaborate trans-Pacific network of institutions and relationships in 2011.[10]

Despite maintaining a conciliatory tone towards China, Obama spoke about building multilateral alliances and strengthening existing and new bilateral relations in the region, which signalled a clear intention to try to limit China's increasing influence. Yet the Obama administration refrained from taking firm action to halt Chinese base-building projects in the South China Sea. It was careful to avoid antagonising Beijing because the American economy, in its recovery phase after the crash of 2008, relied heavily on China as its biggest trading partner. Furthermore, the pace and scale of Washington's planned "Pivot" away from the Middle East and Europe was held up due to the Russian moves into Crimea and Ukraine.

The most crucial element in Obama's policy realignment was the placement of maritime geography at the centre of international security discourse. It reinvigorated the US sea services trio of Navy, Marine Corps and Coast Guard, giving them a fresh raison d'être to secure maritime commons and reassert American hegemony. In 2012, Admiral Jonathan Greenert, the US Navy Chief of Naval Operations argued that the Asia Pacific was a maritime region and that sea power underwrote America's rebalancing to the region.[11] The Navy got the green light to curtail the growing maritime ambitions of China's People's Liberation Army-Navy (PLAN) in particular, and effectively counter its anti-access/area-denial (A2/AD) strategies. Plans were soon afoot to position 60 per cent of US naval assets, including the Carrier Strike Group and Amphibious Ready Group, in the Asia Pacific theatre by 2020.

Towards the very end of Obama's time in office, in 2015, the US Navy revised its 2007 report, 'A Cooperative Strategy for 21st Century Seapower', to incorporate the economic and political changes underway in the world.[12] The 2007 report posited a liberal international order in which the global maritime commons was policed by a coalition of US-led partners. The revised strategy was more explicit about the capacity of the US Navy to 'wage war and prevail'.[13] Obama's trust in the

Navy and the push to pool the resources of regional partners inspired medium and small maritime powers in the region to increase their naval spending. As a result, submarines became the most sought-after vessel in the region. As of 2019 it is estimated that 228 full-sized submarines operate in the East and South China Seas, and that within a decade this number will rise to 300.[14]

The introduction of modern, quiet vessels has changed the operational picture in the region with Australia, India, Pakistan, Japan, South Korea and Indonesia expanding and modernising their fleets. In February 2019, Australia signed a deal worth US$30 billion to build twelve attack submarines with a French shipbuilding firm. India ordered six advanced submarines at a cost of over US$5 billion.[15] China has more than seventy submarines which are likely to grow to eighty by 2030. The United States is also deploying in the region its nuclear attack submarine armed with sub-launched torpedoes and anti-ship missiles. Another important outcome of Obama's Asia Pacific policy was the gradual emergence of the Indo-Pacific as the centre of gravity in the international geostrategic discourse.

The Indo-Pacific as an economic concept has existed for centuries. The south-ernmost region of Vietnam under French colonial rule, for example, was known as Cochin-China to signify the connectivity between the Indian Ocean and South China Sea. During the Cold War, the United States kept India out of the Asia Pacific matrix and after the Sino-Indian war of 1962, which helped to widen the Sino-Soviet wedge, American strategy did not envisage any significant role for India. Washington rarely did much to oppose India's demand for the Indian Ocean as a "zone of peace" and neutrality. However, as the region's perceived geostrategic relevance to the United States increased, not least during the years of the Obama administration, the need to expand the imagined boundaries of the Asia Pacific correspondingly increased to accommodate India, a formidable naval power. This new Indo-Pacific was to be a geostrategic entity stretching from East Africa in the Indian Ocean, to the western and central Pacific, including Japan and Australia, to the west coast of the United States.

Officially, the term Indo-Pacific was first articulated by US Secretary of State Hillary Clinton at Honolulu in October 2010. Clinton referred to an integrated theatre where maritime activities could be coordinated between the United States and its allies.[16] The Australian Defence White Paper of 2013 consolidated the idea by stressing India's trade and strategic connectivity with the Pacific.[17] The US Pacific Command, up until 2017, used the term "Indo-Asia-Pacific". However, as the term Indo-Pacific continued to gather legitimacy scholarly and media articles started using it liberally.[18] Since its entry into the White House in 2017 the admin-istration of President Donald Trump has furthered the use of the term "Indo-Pacific" in official policy discourse.

The Indo-Pacific is an important concept to the United States, not least within the context of what were identified by the Pentagon in 2018 as the five main threats to national security: China, Russia, North Korea, Iran, and violent extremist organisations. Four of these are located in the Indo-Pacific.[19] As such, a key part of the strategic logic behind the creation of the Indo-Pacific is to counter the growing Chinese vision of Eurasia, bound by the so-called "Silk Road Spirit", a notion designed to encapsulate Beijing's visions to bind together a vast and disparate economic-political-cultural landscape.[20] With Europe in recent years demonstrating some preference (though cautiously at times) for conjoining with this continental landmass rather than limiting itself to the transatlantic connect, it has recently become imperative for the United States to utilise the Indian Ocean region to ward off isolation and return that maritime realm back to global discourse.

Another key reason for Washington to prioritise the Indo, over the Asia, Pacific is to better reflect the United States' deep entrenchment throughout the former. The US Indo-Pacific Command (renamed in 2018) is based at Hawaii. In the Western Pacific the United States has a large naval base in Guam which can berth aircraft carriers, as well as the Andersen airbase from where strategic B-52 bombers operate. In June 2018, Guam hosted the 'Malabar' series of exercises in which the naval forces of the United States, India and Japan participated. The US Marine expeditionary forces are based at Okinawa and the US Navy operates a base at Yokosuka, both in Japan. These forces also enjoy basing facilities at Palawan in the Philippines and Singapore. In addition, the United States occupies Diego Garcia, a base in the middle of the Indian Ocean equipped to operate bombers. In 2016 the United States signed the Logistics Exchange Memorandum of Agreement with India, to provide its units refuelling and replenishment facilities in India.

Freedom of navigation in the Indo-Pacific

On becoming President in January 2017, Donald Trump withdrew the United States from the vast, twelve-member Trans-Pacific Partnership (TPP) without presenting an alternative economic roadmap capable of competing for influence with new Chinese-led regional multilateral frameworks, notably the Belt and Road Initiative and the Regional Comprehensive Economic Partnership. This singular move generated concerns within an American foreign policy establishment and strategic community increasingly committed to treating China as a peer competitor.

This early apparent disengagement by Washington from the Indo-Pacific equally worried Asian partners who hoped to see a reinforced US naval presence in regional waters, especially the South China Sea where Beijing had begun an extensive island-building programme. The Trump administration's 2017 National Security Strategy (NSS), however, openly outlined the need to respond more assertively to a 'revisionist' China. While raising some concerns about the future direction of the US–China relationship, the NSS also helped allay fears that Washington planned to disengage from the region.

Importantly, and much like that of Obama which ordered six freedom of navigation operations (FNOs) from August 2013 to January 2017, the Trump administration in its first two years in office relied on American sea power to signal intent in the Indo-Pacific. It sanctioned enhanced FNOs by the US Navy in the disputed South China Sea, where claims and counter-claims over island sovereignty and maritime delimitation, involving China, Brunei, Vietnam, the Philippines and others, constitute among the most complex political-legal territorial disputes in the world. The escalation of these disputes has the potential to generate serious disruptions in the free flow of trade and the safety of maritime navigation.

For instance, in September 2018, while the United States and China were engaged in talks to resolve their ongoing trade dispute, the USS *Decatur* sailed into the Gaven and Johnson reefs in the Sparkly Islands. In response, China's People's Liberation Army Navy dispatched its destroyer *Luyang* to warn the US warship. The two vessels came within tens of metres of one another, endangering the prospects for the Cold Peace which exists between the two powers.[21] In January and February 2019, the US Navy completed two FNOs near Mischief Reef on which China has installed significant military structures and resources, provoking further Chinese indignation against perceived infringement of its sovereignty.

Like most coastal states, in accordance with the 1982 UN Convention on the Law of the Sea (UNCLOS), China retaliates against the warships of other nations which engage in naval exercises and surveillance activities within its 200-nautical-mile exclusive economic zones (EEZs), including those of the United States. Washington, as a non-signatory to UNCLOS, maintains that its navy has a right to conduct military activities in EEZs without informing or seeking the coastal state's consent.[22] Despite its close security partnership with the United States, India also fails to agree with the US interpretation of UNCLOS and the movement of foreign warships within national EEZs.[23] To some degree at least, the "unsafe interactions" – bullying and counter bullying at sea – raise the probability of war between the two, especially from incidents in what we might call security "grey zones". These include incidents involving China's coast guard, or its so-called "maritime militia" or "third navy" which is constituted primarily of Chinese fishing boats widely considered to be acting under orders from Beijing to provide a seemingly benign but highly visible naval presence in the region to help advance Beijing's security interests. Categorising the Chinese fishing vessels as combatants is fraught with danger as it puts severe restrictions on legitimate economic activity by Chinese fishermen in their own waters, and is likely to exacerbate anti-Americanism in China.

US actions in the Indo-Pacific are also testing the professionalism of its naval personnel who are now patrolling in a more challenging environment than they are used to. Increased stresses on naval crews were evident in 2017 when two US Navy destroyers, USS *Fitzgerald* and USS *McCain*, were involved in separate collisions with civilian vessels in the waters around Japan and Singapore respectively, resulting in the deaths of seventeen American sailors and significant damage to the image and reputation of US Navy professionalism. According to the *Stars and Stripes* military newspaper, 'The Japan-based 7th Fleet – which included both destroyers – was undermanned. Sailors were working 100-hour weeks, cutting corners on training and repairs just to keep pace with their tasking.'[24] Commenting on the incident, Seth Cropsey argued that '[t]he deployable battle force, at 276, is far smaller than what is needed to meet the demand. And it isn't growing. So, the navy has looked for other ways to answer the call.'[25]

One way to strengthen the United States' presence throughout the Indo-Pacific is to extend the periods of patrol for ships deployed in the region and the other is involving friendly navies to share the burden. While the former option is an internal matter for the United States' Department of the Navy, the latter is more complex as it involves weaving together an integrated maritime security architecture. It could, however, enable the navies of the United States, India, Japan and Australia – the members of the Quadrilateral Security Dialogue (or Quad) – to operate in an interoperable environment.

The Quad, composed of four democracies, remains fragile because all of its members are intricately tied to the Chinese economy making their oppositions to China inherently timid. India is a founder-member of the Asian Infrastructure Investment Bank (AIIB) which funds BRI projects, and yet New Delhi opposes the BRI. India is an important member of Quad, designed to contain maritime China, but is also a member of Shanghai Cooperation Organisation (SCO) that supports continental China's Eurasian connectivity. Similar contradictions are evident in Japan and Australia.

Over the years, the United States has capitalised on growing regional dissent against China's increasing power, in an attempt to build a credible trans-Indo-Pacific security and economic architecture that might prevent Beijing from bringing US allies and partners into mega infrastructure projects such as those included within the BRI and funded by Beijing's AIIB. In its first two years in office, the Trump administration has sought to rejuvenate American commitment to Indo-Pacific allies by launching the Asia Reassurance Initiative Act (ARIA), promising an additional US$1.5 billion to the region.[26] Under Trump in 2018, the annual Malabar naval exercises between Japan, India and the United States were hosted for the first time by the US naval base at Guam, where Nimitz-class, nuclear-powered super-carriers participated. The Malabar series started as a bilateral exercise between the US and Indian navies in 1992, with the Japanese navy added in 2007. The next US president may invite Australia in to make the series an annual event of the Quad. Regardless, these continuities show that successive American presidents have contributed to a long-term US naval strategy which envisages controlling the Indo-Pacific sea space with the help of friends and allies. To fully appreciate Washington's need to gather regional allies, one always has to assess China's naval growth of the past decade.

Continental China's maritime power

As of early 2019, China's PLAN is the second largest navy in the world. The US Navy continues to enjoy an asymmetric advantage over China's in military maritime capabilities, including in aircraft carriers, nuclear submarines, anti-submarine warfare and amphibious capabilities. But with the speed at which the PLAN is constructing state-of the-art ships, Chinese naval power is likely to inch closer to that of the US Navy before 2050. Between 1990 and 2010, ten destroyers were launched from Chinese shipyards. Between 2010 and 2018, by contrast, China produced twenty-four.[27] China has also built an indigenous aircraft carrier and by 2030 the Chinese navy is expected to possess three more aircraft carriers;100–110 destroyers and frigates ranging from 5,000 to 12,000 tons; around eighty submarines, including sixteen SSNs and eight or more SSBNs; and eight or more large landing ships in the amphibious category.[28]

In April 2019 China celebrated the seventieth anniversary of the founding of the PLAN, with the main attraction of the naval parade being the Nanchang (101), 10,000 ton destroyer with the capacity to become equipped with a railgun. The Chinese navy's modernisation is aimed at protecting China's trade and coastline and for expeditionary roles. At the moment, China's naval force is incapable of defeating the US Navy but it is already puncturing its vanity and signalling to the world that American sea power is no longer invincible.

Washington's strategy, meanwhile, centres on neutralising the Chinese navy's anti-access and area-denial capabilities (precision strike capabilities that restrict the movement of US naval platforms) with its own naval assets. Washington also seeks to encourage allies to develop area-denial "bubbles" of their own in various choke points. Ashley Tellis argues that Japan and South Korea are capable of restricting Chinese naval movements in the Korea Straits, and that the Philippines/Taiwan and Indonesia could similarly constrain its activities through the Luzon Straits and its access to the Sulu and Celebes Seas, respectively.[29]

The Chinese navy may be gaining in numbers, but its experience at sea is for the moment relatively limited. Chinese sailors have no experience of naval battle and are completely new to carrier-borne air operations. However, the American navy's continuous presence in the South China Sea is providing them with valuable experience of regional operations, and an opportunity to test their latest weapons. In December 2016 for example, a Chinese naval vessel picked up an underwater US spy drone which they refused to return.[30] The fear is now that the Indo-Pacific is soon to become an arena in which live artificial-intelligence weapons will be tested. Equally, however, often forgotten is that in the post-Cold War world the United States has enjoyed absolute sea control, operating largely without fear of significant challenges to its dominance in all theatres of operations. This situation is likely to change as China's naval strength expands.

Beijing's more aggressive, or at least more assertive, behaviours in the South China Sea and Indian Ocean are in fact in some respects benefiting the United States, leaving the likelihood of a large-scale Sino-US confrontation at sea more remote. Indeed, much like New Delhi's recent naval investments, Chinese developments are also helping preserve the current maritime order. Chinese construction activities in the South China Sea and its corresponding naval build-up, for example, have given the United States an opportunity and justification to reinforce its maritime capabilities. Without a real or perceived threat of China's naval build-up, Washington would also find it difficult to mobilise regional actors and encourage arms purchases. In short, then, the still-gargantuan US Navy needs a worthy enemy and at the moment China is a very useful candidate. An overstretched United States across the maritime commons is also conducive for China, as it allows relatively tension-free involvement in building Eurasian land routes.

However, a limited naval battle between China and a regional actor would add to ongoing nautical neurosis in the Indo-Pacific, and this possibility cannot be ruled out. Navalists in some European countries as well as the United States are using Chinese aggression as a pretext to demand more from their governments, notably in Paris and London. 'The dormant overseas territories held by France in the Indian Ocean and the South Pacific have suddenly come alive. The [British] Royal Navy has woken up from its imperial grave to open its new military base in Bahrain.'[31]

Transcontinental trade corridors and maritime order

In terms of commercial maritime capabilities, China is the world's largest shipbuilder, boasts the third-largest merchant marine and the largest number of vessels; and claims almost 700,000 fishing vessels. In addition, China accounts for around a quarter of the world's container trade. Indeed, 'almost all the steel boxes shipped on the world's oceans are made in China'.[32] It is widely argued that China owes its post-1970s industrial success to the open trading regime and transport channels provided and protected by the United States. China, indeed, is often blamed for being a "free rider". 'Much of the security of that trade across the Pacific is the gift of America. China "free-rides" on the protection provided by the United States Pacific Fleet [and] America's enforcement of the rules of sea-based activity.'[33]

Yet this argument overlooks the fact that "rising" China itself, by taking on the burden of global manufacturing and shipbuilding, has played a large role in ensuring that the world's oceans continue to be the mainstay of global trade and commerce. By erecting modern shipyards and ports, China has aided the sustainability of the maritime order.[34] It is estimated that the Atlantic Ocean's share of global traffic dropped from nearly 40 per cent in 1992, to 32 per cent in 2012. Over the same time period, the share accounted for by the Pacific Ocean rose from 35 per cent to 39 per cent. 'Meanwhile, ship traffic on the Indian Ocean and China Sea now make up 25 to 30 percent of global traffic, up from 17 percent in 1992.'[35]

China is also the biggest importer of dry bulk commodities and crude oil from the Gulf, as well as the largest exporter of finished products. It is flawed to label China (or any other maritime actor) in such an interlinked global trading network as a "free rider", then, because increased traffic at sea means more revenue for Western, including American and British, firms that control the insurance and reinsurance of sea trade. Control of the marine service industry also gives the United States the power to unilaterally impose sanctions on other countries; currently, the United States alone is able to so effectively pressure global ports and freighting companies, for example, to deny insurance cover to Iranian vessels transporting oil and other goods. The United States is also the only actor able to threaten the Belgium-based Society for Worldwide Interbank Financial Communications (SWIFT) financial messaging service, to keep Iranian banks out of their global financial network. With US hegemony now more contested, however, the UK, France, Germany, Russia, China and Iran launched INSTEX (Instrument in Support of Trade Exchanges) to bypass unilateral US trade sanctions on Iran.[36] In 2016 China established a train service to Iran, increasing the prospect of an alternative supply chain completely independent of US-controlled sea lines of communication (SLOCs).

Chinese naval and commercial fleets are not the only instruments by which China is increasingly disrupting the US-led maritime order. Washington's ability to underwrite global shipping and the pre-eminence of its navy to protect sea trade is under stress from Chinese investments in alternative land-based trade routes which bypass US naval protection and its insurance industry. Land-based transportation networks across Eurasia will not deliver an era of shipless oceans, but in the coming decades high speed land networks are likely to draw a significant proportion of international cargo away from the oceans. The impact of competitive land routes on the future of the oceanic order, as well as US maritime hegemony, is being overlooked by much of the American strategic community.

It should be noted that before its departure from office in 2017, the Obama administration sensed this erosion of maritime American power but was unable to see that the troubles were emerging primarily from land. To tackle Chinese challenges to US command of the oceans, Obama and then Trump both identified the Indo-Pacific as the primary strategic theatre, relying almost exclusively on the navy. Mahanian sea power theories, which focus exclusively on commanding the maritime domain and controlling global commerce, have served America well in the past. Yet Halford Mackinder saw Europe and Asia as an amalgam, and believed that the key to global power was ultimately located in the Eurasian landmass rather than in major SLOCs. Mackinder advocated controlling this "World Island", but not necessarily through military means or by engineering strategic splits within the continental landmass. He believed this vast landmass could either be controlled from Eastern Europe or from maritime "marginals" – seas which border the continents such as the Baltic Sea or the Arabian Sea.[37]

In early 2019, it is clearer than ever that Washington cannot continue to shy away from positively engaging with the "heartland" of Eurasia, to establish an improved maritime–continental equilibrium. The mobility advantage that sea power enjoyed over land power is unlikely to hold for much longer, as drones, hyper-links and bullet trains become the new carriers of global online commerce. Moreover, the three major regional continental powers of Germany, Russia and China are unlikely to waste this opportunity which now sits on the horizon after centuries, and certainly not to help keep the United States' maritime order intact. Retaining hundreds of overseas military bases and carrier-borne fighter jets, which can penetrate deep inside a land-locked country with precision guided munitions, cannot guarantee the United States a continental edge; the United States spent around US$6 trillion on the war on terror between 2001 and 2019,[38] but struggles to save its empire. In contrast, China, which has spent less than US$50 billion so far on enhancing transcontinental connectivity, is bringing economies including those of Sri Lanka, Pakistan, Kazakhstan, Myanmar and many others into the global supply chain. It is also maintaining a judicious balance between its maritime ambitions and continental concerns.

The United States built a good rapport with central Asian states after the fall of Berlin Wall, before losing its advantage with its disastrous post-9/11 wars in Afghanistan and Iraq. The result has been that China (as well as Russia) has been able to advance its Eurasian interests. Obama's departure from the foreign policies of the Bush era was only partial; he lacked the vision to discard the relevance of the foreign wars he inherited and walked the beaten tracks by making the navy the fulcrum of US external engagements. Obama could not imagine new ways to interact with the world, and ultimately failed to devise a strategy to effectively engage with Eurasia.

Despite the "America First" rhetoric and his tirades against the so-called liberal international order, Donald Trump has so far been unable to overcome Washington's war-syndrome which has afflicted almost all post-war presidents. Trump's primary disagreement with the order is that Washington's partners and allies of which it is constituted are not contributing enough to support it and, in the end, to fight America's wars. Across his first two years, Trump also chose not to deviate from Obama's concern with keeping the navy at the centre of US Indo-Pacific policy. The reassertion of sea power fits well with Trump's unilateral and populist ideology; America's maritime moorings are an emotive issue, and a useful political tool to whip up cultural nationalism. Yet Trump has so far proven devoid of ideas about how to make the world a more secure environment, and how to sustain US authority in a rapidly changing geopolitical climate.

Conclusion

This chapter has argued that in the transition between the presidencies of Barack Obama and Donald Trump, little continuity was evident in their US re-involvement strategies in the Indo-Pacific. Some elements of the current policy of penetrating China's Exclusive Economic Zones, and the territorial claims it makes in the South China Sea and elsewhere, were visible in President George W. Bush's Asia Pacific strategy too. Efforts by Washington to build wider alliances in the region, with key partners like India, also started before the announcement in 2011 of Obama's Pivot to Asia. The question now is over the extent to which the Trump administration in its remaining time in office, as well as Trump's presidential successor, can sustain the United States' regional naval involvement and retain the confidence of its Indo-Pacific allies.

Both Obama and Trump have pinned their hopes on the US Navy to save the US empire. Neither, to early 2019, has offered much in the way of new and innovative policy to rescue US strategy from the Mahanian trap which prevents it from exploring continental connectivity options that are more benevolent than retaining naval bases and maritime control. Their strategy has been aimed at ensuring that Washington uses its core competences to contain power shifts in the global political economy, which broadly speaking sees the centre of economic gravity shifting from West to East. However, this strategy is heavily skewed in favour of the maritime domain. Beyond actual war-fighting, Washington has few big ideas in its policy toolkit and, particularly since the election of Donald Trump as president in 2017, even fewer which find widespread acceptance among Washington's international partners.

China's naval build-up may be good for the revival of the US Navy, and for the profits of Washington's arms industry, but the efficacy of the strategy in preserving US hegemony is less clear. Investments in the navy alone will not deliver strategic dividends to America. Engaging in hostile situations far from home will only continue to increase the financial burden on America and cause the Indo-Pacific region to become more prone to war. The continental powers cannot suck the oceans dry, but they are already diverting trade away from the primary SLOCs. The possibility of managing this fundamental shift in the international political economy without resorting to war is risked by blind faith at home in the United States' maritime destiny. Mahanian bondage keeps Washington from recognising that a successful empire is unbound and unshackled from geographic confinements – maritime or continental.[39]

Notes

1   T. Kane, 'Global US Troop Deployment, 1950–2005', The Heritage Foundation (24 May 2006), p. 7, www.heritage.org/defense/report/global-us-troop-deployment-1950-2005, accessed 6 March 2019.

2   J. F. Kennedy Presidential Library, 'Remarks Intended for Delivery to the Texas Democratic State Committee in the Municipal Auditorium in Austin, November 22, 1963 [Undelivered]' (21 November, 2013), www.post-gazette.com/news/nation/2013/11/22/Full-text-JFK-s-never-delivered-speech-from-Dallas/stories/201311210356, accessed 5 April 2019.

3   A. Bhardwaj, 'Cold War 2.0 – Sino-US strife and India', *Economic and Political Weekly*, 1:34 (2015), pp. 10–11.

4   See B. Bender, 'Navy's Numbers Far from the Whole Story', *Boston Globe* (24 October 2012), www.bostonglobe.com/news/nation/2012/10/23/size-navy-thrust-forefront-campaign/Lm0WxYRAYTggln0VG58qgN/story.html, accessed 5 April 2019.

5   N. Monteiro, 'Unrest assured: Why unipolarity is not peaceful', *International Security*, 36:3 (2012), p. 11.

6   M. J. Green, 'The legacy of Obama's "Pivot" to Asia', *Foreign Policy* (3 September 2016), https://foreignpolicy.com/2016/09/03/the-legacy-of-obamas-pivot-to-asia/, accessed 14 April 2019.

7   W. Kyle, 'Strategic logic of the American "Pivot to the Pacific"', *International Journal of Naval History* (1 July 2014), www.ijnhonline.org/2014/07/01/strategic-logic-american-pivot-the-pacific/, accessed 12 April, 2019.

8   Government Publishing Office, Congressional Record – Senate (19 February 1959), www.govinfo.gov/content/pkg/GPO-CRECB-1959-pt2/pdf/GPO-CRECB-1959-pt2-12-1.pdf, p. 2745, accessed 20 April 2019.

9   H. Clinton, 'America's Pacific Century', *Foreign Policy* (11 October 2011), https://foreignpolicy.com/2011/10/11/americas-pacific-century/, accessed 12 April 2019.

10 US State Department, 'America's Pacific Century' (10 November 2011), https://2009-2017.state.gov/secretary/20092013clinton/rm/2011/11/176999.htm, accessed 14 April 2019.

11 J. Greenert, 'The Sea Change: The Navy Pivots to Asia', *Foreign Policy* (14 November 2012), https://foreignpolicy.com/2012/11/14/sea-change/, accessed 1 April 2019.

12 US Department of the Navy, 'A Cooperative Strategy for 21st Century Seapower' (October 2007); US Department of the Navy, 'A Cooperative Strategy for 21st Century Seapower' (March 2015).

13 P. Swartz, W. Rosenau and H. Kates, 'The Origins and Development of a Cooperative Strategy for 21st Century Seapower', *CNA: Analysis and Solutions* (September 2017), p. 10, www.cna.org/cna_files/pdf/DRM-2015-U-012011-2Rev.pdf, accessed 17 April 2019.

14 Z. Lu, 'US and China's Underwater Rivalry Fuels Calls for Submarine Code of Conduct to Cut Risk of Accidents', *South China Morning Post* (21 March 2019), www.scmp.com/news/china/military/article/3002736/us-and-chinas-underwater-rivalry-fuels-calls-submarine-code, accessed 10 April 2019.

15 M. Chan, 'Submarines Arms Race Heating up in Indo-Pacific Amid "Great Threat" from China', *South China Morning Post* (16 February 2019), www.scmp.com/news/china/military/article/2186376/submarine-arms-race-seen-heating-indo-pacific-amid-great-threat, accessed 18 April 2019.

16 US Department of State, 'America's Engagement in the Asia-Pacific' (28 October 2010), https://2009-2017.state.gov/secretary/20092013clinton/rm/2010/10/150141.htm, accessed 3 April 2019.

17 Australian Department of Defence, 'Defence White Paper 2013' (2013), www.defence.gov.au/whitepaper/2013/docs/WP_2013_web.pdf, accessed 10 April 2019.

18 D. Scott, 'The "Indo-Pacific": New regional formulations and new maritime frameworks for US-India strategic convergence', *Asia Pacific Review*, 19:2 (2012), pp. 85–109.

19 H. B. Harris, 'Statement of Admiral Harry B. Harris Jr., U.S. Navy Commander, US Pacific Command Before the House Armed Services Committee on US Pacific Command Posture' (14 February 2018), https://docs.house.gov/meetings/AS/AS00/20180214/106847/HHRG-115-AS00-Wstate-HarrisJrH-20180214.pdf, accessed 12 April 2019.

20 N. Rolland, 'Eurasian Integration "a la Chinese": Deciphering Beijing's Vision for the Region as a "Community of Common Destiny"', *The Asian Forum* (5 June 2017), www.theasanforum.org/eurasian-integration-a-la-chinese-deciphering-beijings-vision-for-the-region-as-a-community-of-common-destiny/, accessed 12 April 2019.

21 *Guardian*, 'Chinese Warship Sails Within Yards of US Destroyer in "Unsafe" Encounter' (2 October 2018), www.theguardian.com/world/2018/oct/01/chinese-warship-american-destroyer-uss-decatur-unsafe-encounter, accessed 12 April 2019.

22 See N. Hong, 'Understanding the Freedom of Navigation Doctrine and the China-US Relations in the South China Sea: Legal Concepts, Practice, and Policy Implication', Institute for China-America Studies (May 2017).

23 I. Rehman, 'India, China, and Differing Conceptions of the Maritime Order', The Brookings Institution (June 2017), www.brookings.edu/wp-content/uploads/2017/06/rehman-india_china_and_differing_conceptions_of_the_maritime_order.pdf, accessed 4 September 2018.

24 D. Cahn, 'Fitzgerald, McCain Collisions: Are the Right People Being Held to Account?', *Stars and Stripes* (15 July 2018), www.stripes.com/news/special-reports/featured/fitzgerald-mccain-collisions-are-the-right-people-being-held-to-account-1.537879, accessed 18 April 2019.

25 S. Cropsey, 'Has the Navy Reached its Breaking Point?', Hudson Institute (23 August 2017), www.hudson.org/research/13851-has-the-navy-reached-its-breaking-point, accessed 13 April 2019.

26 N. Kassam, 'What the Pessimists Get Wrong about Trump in Asia', *The Interpreter* (8 March 2019), www.lowyinstitute.org/the-interpreter/what-pessimists-get-wrong-about-trump-asia, accessed 15 March 2019.

27 R. Joe, 'Predicting the Chinese Navy of 2030', *The Diplomat* (15 February 2019), https://thediplomat.com/2019/02/predicting-the-chinese-navy-of-2030/, accessed 10 March 2019.

28 *Ibid.*

29 A. J. Tellis, 'Primacy in the Indo-Pacific', The Carnegie Endowment for Peace (25 April 2017), https://carnegieendowment.org/2017/04/25/protecting-american-primacy-in-indo-pacific-pub-68754, accessed 23 June 2017.

30 M. Ryan and D. Lamothe, 'Pentagon: Chinese Naval Ship Seized an Unmanned US Underwater Vehicle in South China Sea', *The Washington Post* (17 December 2016), www.washingtonpost.com/news/checkpoint/wp/2016/12/16/defense-official-chinese-naval-ship-seized-an-unmanned-u-s-ocean-glider/, accessed 13 April 2019.

31 A. Bhardwaj, 'China is not alone in adding to the Indian Ocean woes', *Economic and Political Weekly*, 53:17 (2018), pp. 10–11.

32 *The Economist*, 'Maritime Power – Your Rules or Mine?' (15 November 2014), https://www.economist.com/special-report/2014/11/13/your-rules-or-mine, accessed 13 April 2019.

33 *Ibid.*

34 *The Lloyd's List*, 'One Hundred Ports 2017' (2017), https://lloydslist. maritimeintelligence.informa.com/one-hundred-container-ports-2017, accessed 5 March 2019.

35 L. Qiu, 'China's Growth Fuels Boom in World Shipping Traffic', *National Geographic* (27 November 2014), https://news.nationalgeographic.com/news/2014/11/141126-shipping-traffic-oceans-china-trade-environment/, accessed 13 April 2019.

36 Aljazeera, 'EU and Iran Agree on New Payment System to Skirt US Sanctions' (25 September 2018), www.aljazeera.com/news/2018/09/eu-iran-agree-payment-system-skirt-sanctions-180925050920569.html, accessed 25 April 2019.

37 A. W. McCoy, *In the Shadows of the American Century: The Rise and Decline of US Global Power* (London: Oneworld Publications, 2017), p. 571.

38 N. Crawford, 'United States Budgetary Costs of the Post-9/11 Wars Through FY2019: $5.9 Trillion Spent and Obligated', Watson Institute (16 November 2018), https://watson.brown.edu/research/2018/59-trillion-spent-and-obligated-post-911-wars, accessed 4 April 2019.

39 I am grateful to Professor Inderjeet Parmar and Dr Oliver Turner for editing and refining the chapter, as well as helping to make the arguments presented more coherent and cogent.

Conclusion: Legacies and transitions in the twenty-first-century Indo-Pacific

Inderjeet Parmar and Oliver Turner

The world changes quickly, and a challenge for this volume was always to avoid being left behind by unfolding events. It is perhaps clichéd to argue that the world is in flux, but it is difficult to deny that today's political-economic-security landscapes are rapidly evolving, and arguably nowhere more so than across the twenty-first-century Indo-Pacific. All of the "big questions", then, remain difficult to answer. Is the "rise" of the Asia, or broader Indo-, Pacific, sustainable? Are we witnessing, or have we already witnessed, the birth of an Asian Century? Are China, India, Indonesia, Vietnam and others central pillars of a new "world order"? Are they prepared to lead as rule makers? If so, what exactly would this mean?

The principal focus of this volume has been the legacies former US President Barack Obama and his administration leave in Asia and the Pacific after two terms in office between 2009 and 2017. His successor, President Donald Trump, was from the outset unusually vocal in his stated dissatisfaction with the intentions and achievements of his predecessor and the Washington "Establishment" he is said to have represented. From the outset, this left Obama's presidential legacy unusually vulnerable; very likely more so than if Hillary Clinton, as a primary architect of the "Rebalance" or "Pivot" strategy, had been elected as president in late 2016.

Contributors to the volume, focusing on US engagement with Indo-Pacific states and institutions and on key policy realms, wrote up until early 2019, to around the halfway point of Donald Trump's 2017–21 term in office. The purpose of this final chapter is to form some concluding thoughts on what we see as the "big picture" issues and developments in the Indo-Pacific today, with close attention to what they mean for the United States as the region's traditionally dominant actor. Moreover, it is to revisit the central, interconnected questions of the volume outlined in the Introduction: of the legacy former President Barack Obama leaves behind in the Asia and Indo-Pacifics, and of the nature of the transition taking place in regional US engagement from Obama to Trump.

We begin with the relationship between the United States and China which, while explored by a number of our authors in varying contexts, can be afforded further attention here because of the unparalleled degree to which its nature and contours are set to steer the course of wider regional (and global) affairs. We broadly frame this discussion around a question increasingly posed by observers and commentators of US–China dynamics: of whether or not the relationship they share, which so heavily weighs upon the constituent actors of the Asia and Indo-Pacifics, is planting the seeds of a new Cold War. We then discuss the development and apparent future trajectory of the wider multilateral frameworks of Asia and the Pacific, and the United States' present and future place within them. We conclude by drawing together some of the key arguments and conclusions of the individual chapters of this volume, to speak directly to the themes of "legacy" and "transition", about which this volume is so centrally concerned.

The United States and China: A new Cold War?

When the Obama administration formulated its Pivot to Asia, the increasing economic and military capabilities of China were a primary driving factor,[1] though combined with its identity as an Other which is understood to fundamentally contradict core American values.[2] As Peter Gries explains in Chapter 2 of this volume, in many important respects the relationship the United States shares with China – its most significant and consequential both regionally and globally – deteriorated during Obama's time in office. Indeed, one short- to medium-term legacy Obama seems to have left is a noticeable decline in favourable views of China among the American public. Favourable views of China increased during the first few years of the Obama presidency, but reduced in frequency from around 2011, after the formal announcement of the Pivot.[3] (It should be noted, however, that the American public is yet to become as concerned about a "China threat" as are their nation's political and military elites.[4])

Rana Foroohar argues that the so-called US–China tariff war, which began in early 2018, may represent more than mere posturing by an unpredictable president, and the possible beginnings of a new Cold War. This is not a policy emanating from the President alone, but 'something much more dangerous and lasting: a true reset of economic and political relations between the US and China, and the beginning of something that looks more like a cold war than a trade war'. The "reset" is supported by wider sections of the political establishment, including the Democrats, the Pentagon, and what Foroohar refers to as the 'labour faction of the progressive left' which 'coalesce around the idea that the US and China are in a long-term strategic rivalry, and that ... US trade policy and national security policy should no longer be separated'.[5] While this idea has broad support within the political, military and American elite think tank establishment, under Trump we have nevertheless seen a significant intensification of strategic competition aimed at subordinating China via comprehensive pressure, some of which has the support of American allies and partners in Asia.[6]

It is important to be cautious with predictions of a new Cold War. The Cold War period of the 1950s to 1980s was defined by open ideological conflict between the United States and Soviet Union; diplomatic dislocation, hostility and silences; the isolation of peoples and societies; and the forging of spheres of influence physically divided from one another. China's economic model remains heavily state-driven, but has a strong and growing private sector. It is a "socialist market economy" with large numbers of state-owned corporations, but ones still driven by market incentives and profit-maximisation goals which have created China's new "billionaire class", now the world's second largest. Today's US–China relationship is so fundamentally interdependent as to be referred to as "Chimerica".[7]

As Gries explains in Chapter 2 of this volume, it is the 'narcissism' of Donald Trump, over structural international forces, which largely explains the downturn in Washington's ties with Beijing which has characterised the relationship's transition from Obama since 2017. Obama before him may have failed to "reset" the relationship onto a more productive, long-term footing, Gries argues, but he still handed Trump a robust network of regional alliances grounded in a collective sense that China's regional ambitions were becoming destabilising. Trump's "America First" foreign policy strategy, then, has weakened many of these alliances, but one does not need to look very far into wider administration and congressional reports to see how systematically China is seen as a threat to American power and hegemony.

A 2019 report by US Senator Marco Rubio's Committee on Small Business and Entrepreneurship, for example, entitled 'Made in China 2025 and the Future of American Industry', indicates that the threat from China is not primarily one of trade deficits. Rather, it is from the very model of China's statist strategy which, it is claimed, provides unfair subsidies to Chinese businesses which enable them to outcompete high end US companies. China is no longer content to be the manufacturer of low end industrial products, the report concludes. Chinese corporations with close ties to the ruling Communist Party are said to be outmuscling Apple, Microsoft and others in 5G and other modern technologies, to make China 'the global leader in innovation and manufacturing'.[8]

The Eurasia Group argued that in 2019 the Sino-US rivalry is the second biggest geopolitical risk in world affairs. Dangers highlighted by the Group include the perpetuation of trade disputes and clashes over territorial claims in the South China Sea, as well as the increasingly critical realm of cyber security.[9] Indeed, the Trump administration's National Cyber Strategy, published in 2018, labels China, alongside Russia, Iran and North Korea, an aggressor through cyber espionage and other forms of technological interference. Among other things, these states are accused of conducting cyber-attacks against the United States, targeting its economy, its democracy, and stealing intellectual property. The Cyber Strategy is a preparation for punishing adversaries who, it is claimed, 'will conduct cyber attacks against the United States during a crisis short of war'.[10] In a section entitled 'Preserve Peace through Strength', it also states the objective to 'identify, counter, disrupt, degrade, and deter behaviour in cyberspace ... while preserving United States overmatch ...'[11]

Finally, a September 2018 Interagency Task Force report to the President claimed that the United States is unready in broad terms to 'fight tonight' and should therefore 'retool for great power competition'. To 'win the future fight', it argues, the United States must prepare to 'combat Chinese industrial policies targeting American intellectual property'; establish a more skilled technical work-force; diversify its sources of supply away from competitor and politically unstable states; stockpile key resources; and create 'an industrial policy in support of national security efforts'. Ultimately, the United States must possess greater 'surge capabil-ities' to ensure imminent war readiness.[12] This type of rhetoric complements the words of FBI Director Christopher Wray who, in February 2018, argued in terms highly reminiscent of the Cold War era that Chinese spies now represent 'a whole of society threat' to the United States.[13]

Today's US–China relationship, so interdependent as to be referred to as "Chimerica",[14] seemingly already precludes a repeat of Cold War history. As such, Sino-US tensions are often not over fundamental ideology but the reach of the Chinese state into its economic strategy and capabilities, which the United States claims places it at a disadvantage. In addition, of course, the United States itself plays a key role in China's development, beginning with the Washington–Beijing economic and political rapprochement of the 1970s and 1980s, to its support for China's entry into the World Trade Organization in 2001, to its importation of more than US$500 billion worth of Chinese goods each year. The concept of "Sino-capitalism", as a symbiosis of state-led, bottom-up and globally networked entrepreneurship, points to the hybrid character of Chinese power and its compe-tition as well as complementarities with Anglo-American capitalism. Indeed, the gap between the world's traditionally dominant ("liberal") economic models and Sino-capitalism has diminished since the 2008 financial crisis, not least from the rise of economic nationalism in the United States and Europe further increasing Western intervention in the economy.[15]

As Michael Mastanduno observes in Chapter 11 of this volume, across its first two years in office the Trump administration largely abandoned both the rhetoric and policies of American hegemony, the type of which was so firmly entrenched during the Cold War era. Instead it favoured an "America First" nationalism and a determination to counter perceived threats. Others including Dian (Chapter 4) and Kelton and Rogers (Chapter 6) point to Trump's will-ingness from the beginning to undermine key regional relationships which Obama – like his predecessors before him – worked to draw closer into the US security umbrella.

What we perhaps increasingly see, then, are signals that the United States and China, particularly through the nationalisms of Trump as well as President Xi Jinping, are willing to draw on their respective nation's strengths to repel what they see as threatening or subversive influences from "the other side", but in the name of individual security rather than a global ideological project. Thus while observations of a new Cold War between the United States and China can be premature and even historically myopic, intensifying rhetoric of competition and rivalry – audible under Obama but more forceful under Trump – along with a deeper narrative throughout the policy machinery of Washington, DC of a China which poses an "all of society" threat, points to a fundamental trend of American anxiety and suspicion. This trend is in many respects a hangover of the Cold War against communism and indeed reflective of the underlying US discourse of the "China threat" which has evolved for generations.[16] As such, the froth at the surface of the water can be soothed, but powerful undercurrents are less easily controlled.

US Indo-Pacific authority and contested multilateralisms

The tone of the reports of the Eurasia Group, the Interagency Task Force, and the Committee on Small Business and Entrepreneurship, among others, lent further texture and detail to the principal concerns of the Trump administration's 2017 National Security Strategy (NSS) and the Pentagon's 2018 National Defence Strategy (NDS), both of which construct the image of a more dangerous, zero-sum and ultimately more Hobbesian world than that perceived by the Obama administration. The NSS and the NDS clearly articulate Trump's highly nationalistic "America First" foreign policy programme.[17] Not only do they explicitly portray China and Russia as "revisionist", but they treat close allies like the EU, Canada, Japan and South Korea as threats to US (economic) authority, to legitimise punitive measures against them.[18]

Nevertheless, there have also been concerted efforts by the Trump administration to realign relations with regional powers through renewed bilateral agreements and multilateral and minilateral organisations and institutions. The Quadrilateral Security Dialogue, for example, aka the Quad, formalises the four-way links between the United States, Australia, India and Japan with closer security relations. The Quad was formally established in 2007, with Japan the driving force, as an intended "Asian Arc of Democracy" with perceived challenges of China's non-democratic system firmly in mind.[19] The Quad quickly stalled when Australia withdrew the following year, principally over concerns that it would antagonise China, but Canberra re-joined in 2017.

The role of the Quad, to a large extent, is interpreted to be in restricting China's regional and global ambitions.[20] Indeed, it is China's vast Belt and Road Initiative (BRI), officially intended to enhance Asia's physical connectivity and promote both intra-regional and inter-regional economic growth, which is increasingly viewed in Washington and elsewhere in geopolitical and security terms, as a potentially enormous expansion of China's influence across the Eurasian landmass. It is expected that China's ability to transport goods, people, and other resources overland to the Middle East, Africa and Europe, avoiding the regional sea power of the US Navy and its allies, will correspondingly increase.

The BRI, although promoted as peaceful economic development by Beijing, is open to military adaptation. For example, a cooling of US–Pakistan relations after President Trump openly criticised Islamabad in early 2018 for persistently "lying" to Washington about the locations of terrorists in Afghanistan, before withdrawing millions of dollars of military aid, created space for enhanced military cooperation including weapons development between Islamabad and Beijing.[21] The China–Pakistan Economic Corridor represents a multi-billion dollar flagship project of the BRI, but in late 2018 a senior Chinese official stated that military ties were the 'backbone' of the bilateral relationship.[22] The reach of China's BRI into the Middle East brings expectations that its security interests there may also correspondingly increase.[23] Ultimately, both the (land) Belt and (maritime) Road networks are designed to grant China more ownership of the markets and transport routes of Eurasia, which have long been dominated both physically and ideationally by the United States and its allies.

Italy's commitment to join the BRI in early 2019, which represented a notable diversion both from US policy prescriptions as well as the European Union's declaration just weeks before that China constitutes a 'systemic rival',[24] was significant. That move by the Eurozone's third largest economy, no matter how embedded within the BRI Italy eventually becomes, was an indicator of further erosion of what many call the prevailing US or Western-led world order. Indeed, since 2012 China's 16+1 Initiative has enticed Eastern European nations into deals their governments find difficult to turn down, exacerbating existing political-economic cracks within the EU by laying bare the willingness of its relatively poorer nations (where democratic systems are less well established) to welcome the overtures of an authoritarian outsider, despite stated concerns from their richer neighbours and Brussels.[25] In the past, Washington would have had comparably more resources to draw these countries back into its sphere of orbit. Today, China's vast wealth reserves – along with the post-2007/8 economic struggles of the European Union – mean that, for now at least, Beijing's economic influence in Europe (and elsewhere) continues to expand despite emerging resistance.[26]

A 2019 trilateral report by US, Russian and Chinese think tank and university scholars of the Carnegie-Tsinghua Center for Global Policy, the Carnegie Moscow Center, and the Center for Russia and Central Asia Studies at Fudan University respectively outlines some of the key opportunities and challenges presented by China's BRI programme.[27] Given the links of these institutions to national policy makers, such interactions constitute semi-official diplomacy that has long been used to manage great power relations, including hegemonic transition.[28] Certain US corporations are involved in BRI projects,[29] but embedded within the debate between American sceptics on the one hand and China's promoters of the Initiative on the other is disappointment nonetheless over the relative lack of success by

Western firms in securing BRI contracts. This, it is argued, fuels suspicion that the BRI fundamentally constitutes a 'Trojan horse' for Chinese global power, or an attempted 'return to nineteenth century style imperialism'.[30] A particular concern is that the *Made in China* initiative operates as a *Made for China* initiative, with Western firms excluded by a lack of transparency and opaque governance processes. The report presents a scenario neither of liberal hegemonic accommodation/"assimilation" of China, nor near-inevitable military conflict, as liberal internationalists and realists, respectively, typically contend. Rather, it points to two interdependent powers jostling for position and primacy while cooperating on numerous fronts.

It is worth noting at this point that, beyond IR realism and liberal internationalism, and Sino-capitalism, a Kautksyian approach based on the concept of "ultra-imperialism" may provide a more powerful explanation of recent and indeed future trajectories of Sino-American relations. For Kautsky, ruling classes form international class-based alliances to exploit and dominate the world's resources and peoples, including their own citizens.[31] Acknowledging the emergence of a transnational historic bloc encompassing US and Chinese ruling classes, political elites, civil societies, and firms (or at least major elements of them), can aid explanations of China's integration into a traditionally US-led global system and of why laws of uneven capitalist development and geopolitical interests combine to create turbulence and competition,[32] including possible military confrontation. As Michael Swaine argues, however, managing the Sino-US relationship requires delicate diplomacy at all levels from their presidents down, not to mention track II (semi-official/unofficial) diplomacy.[33] This kind of work, funded by corporate foundations interlocked with US and Chinese power elites, has been undertaken by think tank networks over several decades.[34]

Under Obama, and before the announcement of the BRI in 2013, Washington had pinned its own hopes of regional economic authority on the vast Trans-Pacific Partnership (TPP). Comprising twelve economies of the Asia Pacific which collectively accounted for around 40 per cent of global trade, the TPP was envisioned to help reignite US and international economic growth after the financial crash of 2007/8. So too was it designed to ensure that the United States remained a principal architect of the blueprints for international trade and serve to pressure China's statist economic model. Trump's withdrawal of the United States from the TPP in January 2017 is covered by authors in this volume, including Michael Mastanduno (Chapter 11). As Sutter (Chapter 9) explains, the Trump administration's formal exit from the TPP, as well its broad rejection of the central tenets of Obama's Rebalance to Asia which was rhetorically framed around regional cooperation and multilateralism, generated anxiety and dismay among some of Washington's closest partners and allies over US commitment to the region.

As Parameswaran argues in Chapter 7, however, Obama's legacy in Southeast Asia in particular – a key hub of wider Asia (and Indo-) Pacific multilateralism – is mixed; his administration achieved successes including further committing Washington to Asia's multilateral diplomatic frameworks such as the Association of South East Asian Nations (ASEAN). Despite this, however, key issues such as how to formulate effective, joined-up responses to China's territorial advances in the South China Sea, or engage the region in a manner which accommodated the diversity of its economies, were left relatively unaddressed for his successor. Since then President Trump has for the most part favoured a more crudely utilitarian approach to foreign policy in the form of bilateral transactionalism.

The Trump administration's aim, moreover, is to build utilitarian measures into trade deals which reveal more than purely bilateral concerns. Under a clause of the US–Mexico–Canada Free Trade Agreement (USMCA) which replaced NAFTA in late 2018, for example, Washington can withdraw with six months' notice in protest at another signatory's efforts to strike a free trade deal with "non-market economies", such as China. This confirms the tandem operations under Trump of international trade and national security. The tools and methods may differ, then, but the aims of both the TPP under Obama and of US trade agreements under Trump are designed in part to isolate China and bring pressure upon it to reform its economic model by restricting trade with American allies.

The future operations of the Comprehensive and Progressive Trans-Pacific Partnership (CPTPP), which brought together the eleven remaining signatories to the TPP, and the Regional Comprehensive Economic Partnership of ASEAN plus six states (including China), will be monitored closely by Washington in the years to come. At the centre of the CPTPP is Japan and at the centre of RCEP is ASEAN, with China the largest trade partner of each; suddenly, it is the United States which risks being frozen out of the rule-making machinery of some of the world's largest, long-term economic projects, by both allies and "rivals" alike. Importantly, the overlapping memberships of both agreements also bring the potential for cross-breeding in rules and norms. For as long as it endures, Washington's self-imposed absence from the CPTPP therefore leaves it even more distanced from the workings and future direction of RCEP, and by extension the wider landscape of modern international trade.

The US in the Indo-Pacific: Legacy and transition

As noted in the introductory chapter to this volume, alongside the core theme of "legacy", the importance of "transition" has been a central concern of the book. The transition from the presidency of Barack Obama to that of Donald Trump did not begin and end during the formal handover of power on 20 January 2017. In most important respects, it was a process which unravelled gradually over the weeks and months of Trump's first two years in office to early 2019 – at which point the scope of this book ends – and indeed beyond.

Contributors to this volume argue that, through the Pivot, or Rebalance, to Asia, President Obama helped reassure regional allies like Japan (Dian, Chapter 4) that the United States was "returning", and remained committed, to the Asia Pacific after its lengthy and expensive war on terror in the Middle East and Afghanistan under the Bush administration (Bisley, Chapter 10). Obama's rhetorical concern with multilateral regional structures was welcomed and helped to reinforce Washington's bonds with Southeast Asian actors in particular, including their peoples and societies (Parameswaran, Chapter 7). The Obama administration's engagements with regional institutions was comparatively exceptional in the level of attention he afforded them, though not sufficiently transformational to ensure this high-water mark would continue to be met (Cook, Chapter 8). Indeed, in the context of the most serious challenges such as that posed by North Korea, Obama successfully diffused bilateral tensions before proving powerless to prevent Pyongyang from accelerating the advancement of its missile and nuclear capabilities (Cumings, Chapter 5).

Several authors (for example, Colley and Ganguly, Chapter 3; Mastanduno, Chapter 11; and Kelton and Rogers, Chapter 6) point to "constraints" and "restrictions" on Obama, notably within domestic American politics, which served to make the achievement of a clear legacy in the Asia (and wider Indo-) Pacific difficult. Others explain that Obama's regional legacy in particular relationships and arenas of the Asia Pacific is subtle and not always materially visible, for example in closer people-to-people relations (Parameswaran, Chapter 7); or that it is "complex" by generating moments of both of solidarity and frictions with close partners (Dian, Chapter 4); or even that it is "paradoxical" (Bisley, Chapter 10). In the end, then, we must speak of "legacies", as the influences and impacts Obama had on Asia and Pacific between 2008 and 2017 are various and uneven.

So too is the transition from Obama's presidency to that of Trump proving complicated and unpredictable. Obama's somewhat "paradoxical" legacy in Asia and the Pacific emerged from a strong, strategic emphasis on the region but one combined with a vision for reduced capacity and leadership, causing Washington to act as if nothing there was changing. This long-standing inertia by the United States continued into the presidency of Donald Trump (Bisley, Chapter 10). This transition has no doubt been marked by a clear hardening of rhetoric towards perceived threats and allies alike, causing long-standing US partners to once again question Washington's commitment and leadership qualities in the region (Sutter, Chapter 9). In the case of China, a far more confrontational approach leaves the United States under Trump in 'painful search for a credible China policy', but much in the same way as it was under Obama (Ljunggren, Chapter 12). Across its first two years in office the Trump administration also made few policy decisions to demonstrate that it was intent on withdrawing firmly embedded American resources from Asia and the Pacific (Mastanduno, Chapter 11; Kelton and Rogers, Chapter 6). In many important respects, then, historically familiar, long-term patterns of US engagement in the Asia, and now Indo-, Pacifics endure.

To return full circle to Chapter 1 of this volume by Turner, the United States today is in many respects haunted by continuous expansions into Asia and the Pacific which, for more than 150 years, have passed down the responsibility to sustain US authority throughout an ever-inflating imaginative geography which is now reconstructed as a vast and unwieldy Indo-Pacific. Trump's legacy in that region is yet to be written. What we know now, however, is that the myriad actors of the Indo-Pacific – individual, state, non-state, institutional, and so on – are becoming increasingly influential authors of a region which appears set to dominate twenty-first-century global affairs. As Turner observes, a key question today is how the current and future US administrations will respond to this rapidly evolving and highly unfamiliar set of global circumstances.

Notes

1   K. J. Lieberthal, 'The American Pivot to Asia', The Brookings Institution (21 December 2011), www.brookings.edu/articles/the-american-pivot-to-asia/, accessed 5 April 2019.

2   O. Turner, '"Threatening" China and US security: The international politics of identity', *Review of International Studies*, 39:4 (2013), pp. 914–18.

3   R. Wike and K. Devlin, 'As Trade Tensions Rise, Fewer Americans See China Favorably', Pew Research Center (28 August 2018), www.pewglobal.org/2018/08/28/as-trade-tensions-rise-fewer-americans-see-china-favorably/, accessed 2 April 2019.

4   See K. Friedhoff and C. Kafura, 'China Not Yet Seen as a Threat by the American Public', Chicago Council on Global Affairs (19 October 2018), www.thechicagocouncil.org/publication/china-not-yet-seen-threat-american-public, accessed 28 March 2019.

5   R. Foroohar, 'US Trade Hawks Seize Their Chance to Reset China Relations', *Financial Times* (23 September 2018), www.ft.com/content/a42e0402-bd7a-11e8-94b2-17176fbf93f5, accessed 28 March 2019. The possibility of a new Cold War in US–China relations has been debated in the academic literature for some time. See for example D. Shambaugh, 'The United States and China: A new cold war?', *Current History*, 94:593 (1995), pp. 241–7; V. Cha, 'The New Cold War in Asia', Center for Strategic and International Studies (14 June 2011), www.csis.org/analysis/new-cold-war-asia, accessed 2 April 2019; J. Woodward, *The US vs China: Asia's New Cold War?* (Manchester: Manchester University Press, 2017).

6   H. Brands and Z. Cooper, 'After the Responsible Stakeholder, What? Debating America's China Strategy', *Texas National Security Review* 2:2 (2019), https://tnsr.org/2019/02/after-the-responsible-stakeholder-what-debating-americas-china-strategy-2/, accessed 28 March 2019. See also J. Oertel, A. Small and A. Studdart, *The Liberal Order in the Indo-Pacific*, German Marshall Fund of the United States (GMFUS) Asia Program, No. 13, 2018, http://www.gmfus.org/publications/liberal-order-indo-pacific, accessed 12 April 2019. According to this report, the West and

China are now virtually locked into a new Cold War in which China deploys "sharp power" to sow discord and chaos in the West. Despite some scepticism regarding President Trump's unpredictability and unreliability, the report supports US tariffs and broader pressure on China.

7   See P. Nolan, 'Who are we? Who are they? The real facts of a globalised Chimerica', *New Perspectives Quarterly*, 28:3 (2011), pp. 51–60.

8   US Senate Committee on Small Business and Entrepreneurship, 'Made in China 2025 and the Future of American Industry' (February 2019), p. 4.

9   Eurasia Group, 'Top Risks 2019' (7 January 2019), www.eurasiagroup.net/files/upload/Top_Risks_2019_Report.pdf, accessed 28 March 2019.

10 White House, 'National Cyber Strategy of the United States of America' (September 2018), p. 3, www.whitehouse.gov/wp-content/uploads/2018/09/National-Cyber-Strategy.pdf, accessed 28 March 2019.

11 *Ibid.*, p. 20.

12 Interagency Task Force, 'Assessing and Strengthening the Manufacturing and Defense Industrial Base and Supply Chain Resiliency of the United States', US Department of Defense (September 2018).

13 J. Gehrke, 'FBI Director: Chinese Spies "a whole of society" Threat to US', *Washington Examiner* (13 February 2018), www.washingtonexaminer.com/fbi-director-chinese-spies-a-whole-of-society-threat-to-us, accessed 20 March 2019.

14 See Nolan, 'Who are we? Who are they?'

15 See Christopher A. McNally, 'Sino-capitalism: China's re-emergence and the international political economy', *World Politics*, 64:4 (October 2012), pp. 741–66.

16 Turner, '"Threatening" China and US security'.

17 White House, 'National Security Strategy of the United States of America' (December 2017), www.whitehouse.gov/wp-content/uploads/2017/12/NSS-Final-12-18-2017-0905.pdf, accessed 14 March 2019; US Department of Defense, 'Summary of the National Defense Strategy of the United States' (January 2018), www.defense.gov/Portals/1/Documents/pubs/2018-National-Defense-Strategy-Summary.pdf, accessed 12 March 2019.

18 See H. Long, 'Trump Has Officially Put More Tariffs on US Allies Than on China', *Washington Post* (31 May 2018), www.washingtonpost.com/news/wonk/wp/2018/05/31/trump-has-officially-put-more-tariffs-on-u-s-allies-than-on-china/?utm_term=.44e269369e23, accessed 28 March 2019.

19 A. Mulgan, 'Breaking the mould: Japan's subtle shift from exclusive bilateralism to modest minilateralism', *Contemporary Southeast Asia*, 30:1 (2008), pp. 52–72.

20 See R. Roy-Chaudhury and K. Sullivan de Estrada, 'India, the Indo-Pacific and the Quad', *Survival: Global Politics and Strategy*, 60:3 (2018), pp. 181–94.

21 M. Abi-Habid, 'China's "Belt and Road" Plan in Pakistan Takes a Military Turn', *New York Times* (19 December 2018), www.nytimes.com/2018/12/19/world/asia/pakistan-china-belt-road-military.html, accessed 17 April 2019.

22 Reuters, 'China Says Military Ties "Backbone" to Relations with Pakistan' (19 September 2018), www.reuters.com/article/us-china-pakistan-defence/china-says-military-ties-backbone-to-relations-with-pakistan-idUSKCN1LZ03P, accessed 17 April 2019.

23 H. Yang, 'Time to up the game? Middle Eastern security and Chinese strategic involvement', *Asia Europe Journal*, 16, pp. 283–96.

24 V. Zeneli, 'Italy Signs onto Belt and Road Initiative: EU-China Relations at Crossroads?', *The Diplomat* (3 April 2019), https://thediplomat.com/2019/04/italy-signs-on-to-belt-and-road-initiative-eu-china-relations-at-crossroads/, accessed 5 April 2019.

25 See R. Turcsanyi, 'Growing Tensions Between China and the EU Over 16+1 Platform', *The Diplomat* (29 November 2017), https://thediplomat.com/2017/11/growing-tensions-between-china-and-the-eu-over-161-platform/, accessed 6 April 2019.

26 See for example LSE Ideas and CIMB ASEAN Research Institute, 'China Belt and Road Initiative (BRI) and Southeast Asia' (October 2018), www.lse.ac.uk/ideas/Assets/Documents/reports/LSE-IDEAS-China-SEA-BRI.pdf, accessed 10 April 2019.

27 F. Yujun, A. Gabuev, P. Haenle, M. Bin and D. Trenin, 'The Belt and Road Initiative: Views from Washington, Moscow, and Beijing', Carnegie-Tsinghua Center for Global Policy (8 April 2019), https://carnegietsinghua.org/2019/04/08/belt-and-road-initiative-views-from-washington-moscow-and-beijing-pub-78774, accessed 12 April 2019.

28 I. Parmar, *Think Tanks and Power in Foreign Policy* (Basingstoke: Palgrave Macmillan, 2004); I. Parmar, *Foundations of the American Century* (New York: Columbia University Press, 2012).

29 See for example GE Report Staff, 'Five Years On – Belt and Road Breaks New Ground, Forges New Partnerships', *General Electric* (14 November 2018), www.ge.com/reports/five-years-belt-road-breaks-new-ground-forges-new-partnerships/, accessed 12 April 2019.

30 Yujun *et al.*, 'The Belt and Road Initiative', p. 3.

31 K. Kautsky, 'Ultra-imperialism', *Die Neue Zeit*, Marxists' Internet Archive (14 September 1914), www.marxists.org/archive/kautsky/1914/09/ultra-imp.htm, accessed 12 April 2019.

32 I. Parmar, 'The US-led liberal order: Imperialism by another name?' *International Affairs*, 94:1 (2018), pp. 151–72.

33 M. Swaine, 'The Deepening US-China Crisis: Origins and Solutions', Carnegie Endowment for International Peace (21 February 2019), https://carnegieendowment.org/2019/02/21/deepening-u.s.-china-crisis-origins-and-solutions-pub-78429, accessed 28 March 2019.

34 Yujun *et al.*, 'The Belt and Road Initiative'. For a detailed analysis of elite networks, see Parmar, *Foundations of the American Century*.

Index

Note: Page numbers in *italic* refer to figures.

CPSIA information can be obtained
at www.ICGtesting.com
Printed in the USA
JSHW010453180820
7324JS00004B/137

9 781526 135032